Adult Comics

In a society where a comic equates with knockabout amusement for children, the sudden pre-eminence of adult comics, on everything from political satire to erotic fantasy, has predictably attracted an enormous amount of attention.

Adult comics are part of the cultural landscape in a way that would have been unimaginable a decade ago. In this first survey of its kind, Roger Sabin traces the history of comics for older readers from the end of the nineteenth century to the present. He takes in the pioneering titles pre-First World War, the underground 'comix' of the 1960s and 1970s, 'fandom' in the 1970s and 1980s, and the boom of the 1980s and 1990s (including 'graphic novels' and *Viz*). Covering comics from the United States, Europe and Japan, *Adult Comics* addresses such issues as the graphic novel in context, cultural overspill and the role of women.

By taking a broad sweep, Sabin demonstrates that the widely-held notion that comics 'grew up' in the late 1980s is a mistaken one, largely invented by the media. *Adult Comics: An Introduction* is intended primarily for student use, but is written with the comic enthusiast very much in mind.

Roger Sabin is a freelance arts journalist, living and working in London. He has written about comics for several national newspapers and magazines, including *The Guardian*, *The Independent* and *New Statesman and Society*.

New Accents

General Editor: Terence Hawkes

Adult Comics

AN INTRODUCTION

Roger Sabin

LONDON and NEW YORK

First published 1993
by Routledge
11 New Fetter Lane, London EC4P 4EE

Simultaneously published in the USA and Canada
by Routledge
29 West 35th Street, New York, NY 10001

Typeset in Sabon 9/13 point Compugraphic by
Mathematical Composition Setters Ltd, Salisbury, UK

Printed in Great Britain by Butler & Tanner Ltd, Frome and London

∞ printed on paper manufactured in accordance with the proposed
ANSI/NISO Z 39.48-199X and ANSI Z 39.48-1984

British Library Cataloguing in Publication Data
Sabin, Roger
Adult Comics: An Introduction. –
(New Accents Series)
I. Title   II. Series
741.5

Library of Congress Cataloging in Publication Data
Sabin, Roger
Adult Comics: An Introduction/Roger Sabin.
p.   cm. – (New accents)
Includes bibliographical references and index.
I. Comic books, strips, etc. – History and criticism.   I. Title.
II. Series: New accents (Routledge (Firm))
PN6710.S23 1993
741.5'09 – dc20   92–6670

ISBN 0–415–04418–9   ISBN 0–415–04419–7 (pbk)

Contents

Figures

General editor's preface

How can we recognise or deal with the new? Any equipment we bring to the task will have been designed to engage with the old: it will look for and identify extensions and developments of what we already know. To some degree the unprecedented will always be unthinkable.

The *New Accents* series has made its own wary negotiation around that paradox, turning it, over the years, into the central concern of a continuing project. We are obliged, of course, to be bold. Change is our proclaimed business, innovation our announced quarry, the accents of the future the language in which we deal. So we have sought, and still seek, to confront and respond to those developments in literary studies that seem crucial aspects of the tidal waves of transformation that continue to sweep across our culture. Areas such as structuralism, post-structuralism, feminism, marxism, semiotics, subculture, deconstruction, dialogism, postmodernism, and the new attention to the nature and modes of language, politics and way of life that these bring, have already been the primary concern of a large number of our volumes. Their 'nuts and bolts' exposition of the issues at stake in new ways of writing texts and new ways of reading them has proved an effective stratagem against perplexity.

But the question of what 'texts' are or may be has also become more and more complex. It is not just the impact of electronic modes of communication, such as computer networks and data banks, that has forced us to revise our sense of the sort of material to which the process called 'reading' may apply. Satellite television and supersonic travel have eroded the traditional capacities of time and space to confirm prejudice, reinforce ignorance, and conceal significant difference. Ways of life and cultural practices of which we had barely heard can now be set compellingly beside – can even confront – our own. The effect is to make us ponder the culture we have inherited; to see it, perhaps for the first time, as an intricate, continuing construction. And that means that we can also begin to see, and to question, those arrangements of foregrounding and backgrounding, of stressing and repressing, of placing at the centre and of restricting to the periphery, that give our own way of life its distinctive character.

Small wonder if, nowadays, we frequently find ourselves at the boundaries of the precedented and at the limit of the thinkable: peering into an abyss out of which there begin to lurch awkwardly-formed monsters with unaccountable – yet unavoidable – demands on our attention. These may involve unnerving styles of narrative, unsettling notions of 'history', unphilosophical ideas about 'philosophy', even un-childish views of 'comics', to say nothing of a host of barely respectable activities for which we have no reassuring names.

In this situation, straightforward elucidation, careful unpicking, informative bibliographies, can offer positive help, and each *New Accents* volume will continue to include these. But if the project of closely scrutinising the new remains nonetheless a disconcerting one, there are still overwhelming reasons for giving it all the consideration we can muster. The unthinkable, after all, is that which covertly shapes our thoughts.

TERENCE HAWKES

 ADULT COMICS

Acknowledgements

I have a great many people to thank. Because secondary sources are few, I have had to make extensive use of interviews. The following very kindly gave their time for questions – sometimes minutes, sometimes hours – either for articles I have written for the press, which I was later able to make use of, or specifically for the book: (in no particular order) Paul Gravett, Lee Harris, Alan Moore, Gilbert Shelton, Dave Gibbons, Hunt Emerson, Bryan Talbot, Mick Farren, Melinda Gebbie, Angus McKie, Neil Gaiman, Julie Hollings, Myra Hancock, Ed Pinsent, Dave Huxley, Igor Goldkind, Steve MacManus, Grant Morrison, Ray Lowry, Carol Bennett, Tony Bennett, Martin Skidmore, Nick Landau, Jean 'Moebius' Giraud, Dez Skinn, Stuart Green, Thierry Groensteen, Enki Bilal, François Vié, Catherine Yronwode, Gary Groth, Denis Gifford, Will Eisner, Paul Hudson, Art Spiegelman, Peter Milligan, Archie Goodwin, Don Melia, Mark Nevelow, Bob Burden, Dick Hansom, Pat Mills, Angie Mills, Pepe Moreno, Phil Clarke, Dominic Wells, John Brown, Frank Wynne, Michael Bennent, Eve Stickler, Duncan McAlpine, Charles Shaar Murray, Frank Plowright, Ravi Mirchandani, Graham Keen, David Lloyd, Carol Swain, Guy Lawley, Seiji Horibuchi, Leo Baxendale, Dave Thorpe, Chris Donald, Thomas Harrington, Dave Sim, Michael O'Donaghue, Heidi MacDonald, Trina Robbins, Jean-Marc Lofficier, Alan Grant, Trevor Hughes, Lionel Lambourne, Don Donahue, Denis Kitchen and Suzy Varty.

Above all, for assistance, advice and encouragement: Martin Barker, Paul Dawson, and Steve Edgell.

Finally, thanks also to Janice Price and Terence Hawkes for their patience, Sally Townsend for those early commissions at *MT* and *NSS*, the staff at Senate House Library, and my flatmates Sue and Chris, the dynamic duo. Apologies for any omissions.

Comics are reproduced as historical illustrations to the text, and grateful acknowledgement is made to the publishers and creators. Copyright is credited according to the original copyright date as printed in the comics. Any omission or incorrect information should be notified to the author and publisher, who will be pleased to amend any future edition of the book.

Introduction

The traditional image of a comic in most people's minds is of a cheap, throw-away periodical for children – if you're British, that invariably conjures up memories of knockabout characters inflicting unspeakable violence on each other; if you're American, of brightly-costumed superheroes dispensing two-fisted justice. The Oxford English Dictionary definition until recently was 'A children's paper . . . having as its express aim to excite mirth.' Comics are not seen as the most sophisticated of media, but then they don't have to be, orientated as they are towards the juvenile and uncritical.

But in recent years, that image has been challenged as a 'new breed' of adult comics has come to the fore. Their aims are much more ambitious: today it is common to come across examples that are expensively produced (often in book form), and which deal with subject-matter ranging from political satire, to erotic fantasy, to eyewitness accounts of the Nazi holocaust. Such publications are reviewed in the quality press, and are available from newsagents, bookshops, specialist comics shops and even local libraries. The latest dictionary definition has been modified to: 'a children's periodical [or] . . . similar publication intended for adults'.

The media has called it a 'revolution'. The press, and to a lesser extent radio and TV, have all made much of the story that comics 'grew up' in the mid-to-late 1980s and are no longer 'kids' stuff'. From being the preserve of 8- to 15-year-olds, we are told that suddenly comics are respectable reading matter for post-adolescents. It was, and is, a seductive interpretation of events, and has become one of the recurring clichés of arts journalism.

But what the media did not do (could not do) was to provide any sort of context for events, any kind of informed background to the current boom. Which is why *Adult Comics* exists. The intention here is to show that the history of comics for older readers stretches back a long way before the mid-1980s, to the nineteenth century in fact, and to show that the 'adult revolution' is actually just one stage in the long and complicated evolution of the form. The method will be to survey the main titles from the past, and thereby to map the contours of an adult comics history. The book is intended above all to be an introduction to the subject, and assumes no prior knowledge.

It is also intended to plug a gap. In the 1990s, with the new sophisticated titles, comics are beginning to be taken seriously, and can find themselves co-opted as a subject for study on to courses in literature and cultural studies at every level (a similar kind of assimilation happened to pulp novels in the 1960s, and to science fiction in the 1970s and 1980s – comics were bound to be next). Although this process is still in its early stages, there is nevertheless a need for a primer-textbook that treats adult comics as an identifiable area for discussion.

Having said that, it is necessary to define our boundaries. First, this is a history of comics periodicals – not strips or cartoons in newspapers and magazines. These areas are linked very closely, of course, as each uses a combination of words and pictures to communicate (additionally it could be said that the newspaper is the principal place where adults come into contact with such a form). Yet, cartoons and strips ultimately conform to very different aesthetics – in the case of the former, this might involve the need to be topical or to make some kind of political point; for the latter, to get to a punch-line in three or four panels; and so on. As such, distinct traditions are involved, which are not the concern here.

Nor is the book about all comics. It is about 'adult' comics – a particular, and historically minor, sector of the industry. Children's comics have constituted the vast majority of titles published since the beginning of the form, and although a chapter has been included on them in order to provide background information, they are not the focus here. Readers wishing to find out more about them are advised to consult one or other of the general histories listed in the bibliography.

But even narrowing down the compass of the book in this way, the subject-matter remains very broad. As we shall see, the history of comics for older readers is a surprisingly rich one, and it has been impossible to give anything but a very selective account. Indeed, whole genres have had to be ignored – educational, propagandist and religious comics to name three. Moreover, in respect of those titles that have been mentioned, comment has had to be kept to a minimum, space being dictated more-or-less by historical importance, and by the extent to which they have been covered in sources elsewhere. Therefore it is only fair to warn any reader expecting a detailed analysis of fifteen years of *Cerebus*, for example, that they are likely to be disappointed.

Where an 'adult' comic begins, and any other kind ends, however, is much harder to say. The fact is that comics, like any other medium, can be read on a number of levels. It would be silly to deny, for instance, that a number of children read adult comics, or that some adults read the *Beano*. For this reason, many comics fans find the 'adult' distinction patronising ('the last time I said I was "adult"', as one fan said to me, 'I was 6 years old'). More usefully, they claim, the split should be made between children's comics and comics for a general readership: after all, we don't have 'adult TV' or 'adult libraries'. This argument undoubtedly has some validity.

And yet, 'adult comics' is the terminology the industry itself prefers. It is in widespread use in advertising, marketing and wherever else comics are discussed, and has been taken up wholesale by the press. It is an easy shorthand, and in general terms describes a comic with a mature bent, in contra-distinction to titles in the traditional pre-adolescent and adolescent categories.

To be more specific than that, however, raises the issue of precise age-groups – and here even the industry itself is not so definite. The biggest publishers of adult material for the British market, for instance, DC Comics, Marvel, Titan Books and Fleetway, target the over-16s, and generally include a 'Mature Readers' label on their comics; but the label 'Adults Only' that appears on many other American and British titles is an indication to retailers not to sell to anybody under 18. To confuse things further, there are a variety of other labels, such as 'Not For Sale To Children', which are also not age-specific. The whole question is set against a background of ambiguity in British society as to where adulthood begins; the school-leaving age is 16, but the voting age is 18. Such confusion suits some publishers of course. So long as boundaries remain blurred, they can seek to maximise the age-range that will buy their comics. Indeed, a few have openly admitted that they use labels such as 'For Mature Readers' specifically to generate curiosity among a younger audience.

Thus, for the purposes of our discussion, we are forced to take a somewhat arbitrary stance, and to consider an 'adult comic' to be any title orientated primarily towards an over-16 readership, and a 'children's comic' to be for any age younger than this. It should be noted that within these categories the historically predominant target age-range for an adult comic is 16 to 24, and for a children's comic 8 to 12 (comics falling between the two camps, i.e., 13 to 15, are sometimes, though rarely, referred to as 'adolescent comics', and below 8 years as 'nursery comics'). Any instances of titles targeting a 'general' readership or of the occurrence of 'crossover' readerships – for example, where a children's comic picks up an adult following or vice versa – will be noted as we go along.

Finally, the book has two underlying idiosyncrasies. First, it is written from a British perspective, which may be an obvious statement since the author is British, and bound to bring a British sensibility to his subject. But it is necessary to bear in mind the overwhelming impact American comics have made in Britain in the last two-and-a-half decades (the 'adult revolution' itself, as we shall see, was built almost entirely on American-originated titles). For this reason, comics history is too often seen as 'American comics history' – a distortion reinforced by the fact that almost all the secondary sources on the market are themselves American and largely ignore comics originating in other parts of the world.

Second, an effort has been made to get away from the predominant treatment of comics as collectable commodities. Most books about the subject tend to treat it from a 'fan' perspective – that is, informed by a combination of artwork appreciation, nostalgia, 'trash aestheticism' and, increasingly, investment potential. There is nothing wrong with this on its own terms, of course. But in order to explore comics' wider role, and their place in modern society generally, it is necessary to approach them from another angle, one which stresses historical and cultural imperatives. Indeed, some historians are beginning to reverse the equation, and to ask what comics can offer as an historical source. Significantly, then, *Adult Comics* is not written by someone with a fan background, and is not intended primarily for fans. Indeed, at a time when fan culture is becoming more and more business-orientated, perhaps it is more appropriate than ever to stress that comics have a value beyond that which a dealer might put on them.

Methodology

Adult Comics is divided into three parts. The first two attempt to put the 'adult revolution' in historical context by giving a general chronological account of adult comics in Britain and the USA. The third endeavours to give a wider contextual picture by looking at adult comics in other parts of the world – particularly Europe and Japan – as well as at the relationship of adult comics to other media, the role of women and the significance of the 'graphic novel'. Suggestions for further reading are given at the end of each chapter, and a select bibliography appears at the end of the book, broken down into categories including sources in English, foreign language sources, fanzines and videos.

Names and dates

Where a comic is a collaborative effort, the name of the writer will be given first, followed by that of the artist (space forbids the listing of inkers, letterers and editors where involved). Dates given are of the first date a comic appears; this is simply due to the sometimes erratic nature of comics publishing – titles have been known to cease, restart, cease, merge with another title and restart. Full dates for key comics are given in Appendix 2.

What is a comic?

It seems a simple enough question – after all, we've all read comics, so we all know pretty much what they are. But actually to define one is a little more difficult. Terms tend to mean 'what they have come to mean', and putting a neat definition on a 'common-sense' idea can often lead to descriptive contortionism. All we can do is work backwards, in a sense, trying to fix certain essentials that hold true for most examples of the form – old and new, adult and juvenile.

The fundamental ingredient of a comic is the 'comic strip'. This is a narrative in the form of a sequence of pictures – usually, but not always, with text. In length it can be anything from a single image upwards, with some strips containing thousands. A 'comic' *per se* is a publication in booklet, tabloid, magazine or book form that includes as a major feature the presence of one or more strips.[1] Comics are usually published regularly (weekly, monthly, occasionally quarterly), and are generally cheap in order to be accessible to the widest possible audience.

Strips usually share certain conventions. In terms of graphics, the most obvious are bordered panels, which serve to break down the action into readily-understandable segments. These are like windows, through which events are seen, and are occasionally expanded or enlarged to emphasise a dramatic moment. Other visual conventions include speed-lines, speech-balloons, think-balloons and various forms of graphic symbolism such as bulging eyeballs to suggest surprise.

The text too has conventions. There are three basic types of language in comics – narrative, dialogue and sound effects. Narrative often appears in a box at the top of the panel, usually to introduce a situation depicted therein. Dialogue is typically presented in speech-balloons, which issue from characters' mouths (it has been argued that this device originates from the appearance of 'steam clouds' when a person speaks on a cold day). Finally, sound effects are often onomatopoeic – 'pow!', 'ker-splat!' and so on. The size of the lettering in each case is sometimes varied to suggest loudness.

Taken together, these conventions constitute an abbreviated

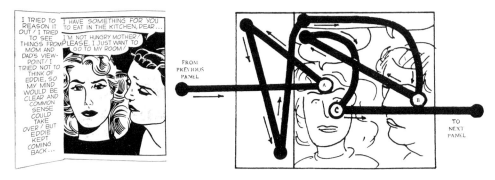

Figure 0.1 A schematic illustration to show the passage of the reader's eye over a panel from a romance comic. Reproduced from research published in the *Journal of Popular Culture*, no. 19, 1986. © 1986 Lawrence Abbott

style or shorthand that allows the reader to fill in the gaps using his or her imagination. Like anything else, reading a comic is an acquired skill. It takes an amazing number of eye-movements to understand a panel – flicking from picture to text and back again – though the strip itself is invariably read traditionally, left to right, like a book (see Figure 0.1). Since comics require this high level of reader-participation, newcomers sometimes find them tiring to read for any length of time.

In terms of content, strips basically tell stories. Most are fictional, and most conform to a formula – working through a series of typical phases and ending in foreseeable fashion. They characteristically star a number of regular characters, who appear in every issue of the comic and who act within relatively predictable ranges of behaviour. Historically most, though by no means all, have been humorous (hence the origins of the word 'comic').

In telling these stories, strips predominantly utilise a 'cinematic' approach (the analogy with cinema is a useful one, although it should be noted that the two forms developed independently).[2] Compositionally, they often make use of 'establishing shots', 'close-ups', 'panoramas' and so on; different 'camera-angles' can add greatly to the drama of a strip. Editing techniques also associated with film are similarly used: for example, 'segueing' – the device of echoing the image in the final panel of one page in the first panel of the next; and 'jumpcutting' – flashing abruptly from one scene to another. (The advantage of a comic over film, of course, is that entire universes can be created with the stroke of a pen – with just the price of the ink to consider.)

Finally, because comics involve text and pictures, most are produced not by one person, but by a team – a writer and an artist, with sometimes an inker, colourist and letterer. These team members are known as 'creators'. In addition, there may be another member, the editor, whose job, among other things, is to be in overall control of the strip and to cut out superfluous material.

Many of these points may seem obvious, but we should pause here for a moment to consider some qualifications. Above all, any definition is an 'evolving' concept, and characteristics will accrue or disappear over time. Hence, fixing an archetype has its limitations: all we can really say is that a clearer idea of 'what a comic is' at any particular time will emerge as the book progresses chronologically.

Similarly, there are exceptions to the rules, and even the most seemingly self-evident characteristics are open to question. The key word in the definition thus far has been 'most' – what most strips and comics are like. Yet, it is worth bearing in mind that there are strips in existence that are not 'sequential', and have 'jump-cuts' every panel; there are strips that are not narratives, and feature a series of unrelated abstract images; there are strips that do not use conventions, and do not star a recurring cast; there are comics that are not cheap (£20 is not unheard of), and that do not come out regularly. The list could continue.

Nevertheless, flawed as it may be, this definition is a starting-point. It allows us to go a stage further and to look briefly at some of the storytelling possibilities a comic can suggest.

To begin with, a strip can compress or extend time. For example, in the detail from the horror comic *Reaper of Love* (Figure · 0.2) the assailant mutters '. . . and disable . . .', while in the process of slamming down a large club on to his victim, who simultaneously screams 'Gar!! . . . My Leg . . .' Clearly this is not 'real time'. A com-pression has taken place to create the maximum dramatic effect.

Figure 0.2 Panel from the horror comic *Reaper of Love* (1991). Art/script: Berni Wrightson. © 1991 The creator

By the same token, strips can compress information in a clear and understandable fashion. Recent research into the production of military training manuals by the US Defense Department concluded that, out of all of the options – plain text, illustrated text, text with photos and comic strips – comic strips proved the most effective in getting the requisite information across.[3] The research showed it is possible in comics to convey enormous amounts of information in a very limited space.

Finally, strips are capable of innumerable narrative 'tricks'. Words and pictures do not have to refer to the same thing, and creators

Figure 0.3 The first page of *Watchmen* (1987), demonstrating several comics techniques and characteristics: narrative, dialogue, 'camera positioning' (in this case going from close-up to long-shot), and an expanded final panel for dramatic effect. Art: Dave Gibbons. Script: Alan Moore. © 1987 DC Comics Inc.

can play with juxtaposition to create a variety of dramatic moods (for example, a nursery rhyme in caption-form over an image of a vicious murder would produce a disturbing and chilling effect). Strips are a great form for metaphor, and ironic or dramatic counterpoint is a frequently used technique.

All of these devices highlight the fact that a strip does not 'happen' in the words, or the pictures, but somewhere in-between, in what is sometimes known as 'the marriage of text and image'. The strips may be just a mix of words and pictures, but the permutations of the two are almost endless – limited only by the imaginations of the creators. In short, strips have their own aesthetic: they are a language, with their own grammar, syntax and punctuation. They are not some hybrid form halfway between 'literature' and 'art' (whatever those words might mean), but a medium in their own right.

Having come to this simple but crucial conclusion, it follows that, technically speaking, there is no good reason why comics should be confined to any particular age-group. They are capable of the same range of subject-matter as novels, films or any other media – as well as the same degree of depth in artistic and literary expression. Theoretically at least, comics have the same potential as a means of communication for adults as for children. How theory and practice have matched up historically is one of the key themes of this book.

Further reading

Will Eisner's *Comics and Sequential Art* (Tamacac, Florida: Poorhouse Press 1985) is an excellent 'how-to' guide to storytelling from a creator's point of view, a masterpiece of instructional simplicity. Alan Moore's essay 'On Writing for Comics', *FA*, 92–5 (August 1985–February 1986), reprinted in *Comics Journal*, 119–21 (January–April 1988), contains useful insights into the thought-processes of one of today's top *auteurs*. The best study in English of the semiotics of comics is Lawrence Abbott's article 'Comic Art: Characteristics and Potentialities of a Narrative Medium', *Journal of Popular Culture*, 19 (spring 1986), pp. 155–73.

part I

BRITAIN

The first adult comics

For the Benefit of Old Boys, Young Boys, Odd Boys
Generally and Even Girls
(Subheading, *Ally Sloper's Half Holiday*, 1884)

The first comics in the world to fit our basic definition are generally acknowledged to have appeared in Britain towards the end of the nineteenth century. Born out of economic opportunism, they were designed as cheap and cheerful entertainment for the working classes. At the time, Britain was one of the chief industrial nations of the world, and not only did the economic capacity exist for mass-produced leisure publications, but the level of literacy among the population was relatively high. To maximise the audience, the comics were orientated not solely towards children, but had a mixed market in mind, with white-collar, male adults as their main target readership.

The distant historical origins of comics are disputed. Certainly they did not just appear out of a vacuum, fully-formed, but evolved out of previous forms of visual narrative communication. It is a common starting-point for histories of comics, for example, to trace them to ancient beginnings, such as the Bayeux Tapestry or Egyptian hieroglyphics – sometimes even to paleolithic cave paintings. However, this kind of historical extrapolation is dubious in its logic, and often used to 'justify' comics by association with more culturally-respected forms.

More usefully, some historians have looked to illustrated literature in the eighteenth and nineteenth centuries for roots. One popular theory traces comics to the growth of children's book illustration; another sees comics as an outgrowth of (or reaction to) the 'penny dreadfuls' – sensationalist, illustrated, bit-part novels – that flourished in Victorian Britain. But although both forms have tangential links, they constitute historical tributaries rather than the mainstream.[1]

For the first comics were above all intended to be funny. It is, therefore, necessary to place them in the context of the developing humorous publications of this era, a genre that can be said to begin with the emergence of prints, broadsheets and illustrated magazines dealing with satire. Here were to be found not only the origins of modern satirical joke-telling, but also the widespread use of techniques such as captions, speech-balloons and drawn-in panel borders.[2]

Technology played a major part in the satire boom. The

dominant eighteenth-century method of printing involved etching a design on to a copper plate by means of a special tool: prints and broadsheets produced by this method were occasionally advertised as 'comic cuts' (a 'cut' being the traditional name for an engraving). This process gave way in the 1820s to 'lithography', based on the chemical reaction between ink and grease, which made multiple reproductions possible without any deterioration in quality. As humorous lithographs became common, so the term 'the comicals' became the established colloquialism, sometimes abbreviated to just 'the comics'. Thus the word 'comics' itself was in frequent use long before the category as such had been invented.

In terms of the content of these early publications, the tone was set by four outstanding talents. William Hogarth (1697–1764) is today recognised as the founding father of modern satire, and refined the use

Figure 1.1 '"The Friend of the People" and his Petty New Tax Gatherer Paying John Bull a Visit' (1806) by James Gillray, the first political cartoonist in the modern sense (the 'friend of the people' caricatures the statesman Charles James Fox, and the 'Petty Tax Gatherer' the Chancellor of the Exchequer, John Petty)

of sequential images for his scathing didactic images of poverty and affluence. Thomas Rowlandson (1757–1827) belonged to the next generation of social commentators, and took the art of caricature to new levels, creating outrageous likenesses of public figures – among them royal dukes, actresses and auctioneers. James Gillray (1757–1815) is today acknowledged as the first political cartoonist in the modern sense: his acidic attacks on the social injustices of the reign of George III still have the power to shock. Finally, George Cruickshank (1792–1878) was arguably the finest draughtsman of the four, and produced many penetrating party-political satires in a meticulously-rendered style.

Audiences were of two basic types. Traditional prints and broadsheets had small print-runs and were.well-produced and expensive (by 1820, this usually meant 1 shilling a time, rising to as much as 6 shillings for a colour version). They tended to be highly political in orientation: a print might depict a single caricature or cartoon of a public figure or politician, while a broadsheet typically consisted of a page of a variety of such images. The readership was thus intended to be monied, educated and middle class; and moreover to have a better than average knowledge of politics. Similarly, the few magazines that utilised such illustrations were expensive and select.

But there were also lower-class prints and broadsheets aimed at a much wider audience. Usually these were more slapstick than satirical, and much cheaper (prints usually retailing for 1 penny), with bigger print-runs. Big names like Gillray, Rowlandson and Cruickshank still featured fairly regularly, though usually in pirated form. The Seven Dials region of Holborn in London was the centre of this kind of publishing in the early nineteenth century, and sometimes the circulation of a particularly popular sheet from here could top 100,000.

Thus we can speak of a satire 'industry' by the second decade of the nineteenth century, catering to a wide spectrum of the population. Taking the middle-class and working-class markets together, it employed many hundreds of cartoonists and caricaturists, most of whom toiled for little money, and less esteem. Many indeed remained anonymous for the whole of their careers, and assumed a cultural status somewhere on a par with sign-painters. According to one historian:

> As a mere draftsman, illustrator or engraver, [the cartoonist] was not admitted to full membership of academies; nor was his work exhibited, except in a peripheral and subordinate way, for his engravings and comic sketches were not considered art like painting.[3]

As printing technology became ever-more sophisticated, so certain humour magazines began to concentrate on pictorial content. One in particular set new standards in production – *Punch*, a monthly founded in 1841. Named after the popular puppet, *Punch* belonged to the middle-class tradition, and apart from a brief period at its inception was not 'radical' in the recognised sense, but gently satirical – a humorous vein the magazine tapped until its demise in 1992. It featured a mix of funny prose stories, cartoons (the forerunners of today's newspaper editorial cartoons) and occasional strips (usually with the text running underneath). A number of brilliant cartoonists and caricaturists were showcased, among them John Leech, Richard Doyle and John Tenniel, but although their work was often outstanding, their craft was still not held in great respect: as Leech commented '[I] would rather be the painter of one really good picture than the producer of any number of "the kind of things" [I do]'.[4]

Punch was a huge commercial success, however, and pioneered a formula that others would soon follow. By the 1860s some publishers had come to the conclusion that a readership for similar humour magazines might exist among the working and lower middle classes. (Even before the famous 1870 Education Act, which introduced the principle of elementary education for all, the level of literacy among these classes was reasonably high.) Hence, more 'popular' versions of *Punch* began to appear. These included *Fun* (1861), *Judy* (1867) and *Funny Folks* (1874). Like their working-class broadsheet predecessors, they tended to be cheaper than their middle-class counterparts (usually 1 penny), less politically sophisticated and more inclined towards slapstick. They also featured a greater number of strips.

There were other, less obvious differences. In order to keep costs down to within the range of working men and women, corners were often cut. In particular, cheap paper was used, and cartoons and strips were sometimes 'borrowed' from foreign publications. This latter exigency caused much resentment among the regular staff (being openly compared on occasion to the hiring of scab labour), and led to even more depressed rates of pay. This trend towards cost-trimming and exploitation was one that would intensify over the next few years, leaving an unfortunate legacy for the comics industry.

In the 1870s, however, the British working class itself began to change. Historians have shown that complex economic and social forces converged to 'remake' the class, especially in the south, with the result that a new culture was born, based on pubs and music halls. It has also been persuasively argued that this culture was politically conservative; that after the collapse of Chartism, working-class radicalism was stifled, and that thereafter the tendency was to accept class divisions and the distribution of wealth as the natural order of things. From the point of view of popular publishing, a publication that could tap into this new mood of political fatalism, but make a joke of it, was bound to have an enormous impact.

That publication was *Ally Sloper's Half Holiday* – the first modern comic – published by Gilbert Dalziel in 1884. Like the working-class humour magazines, it had strips, cartoons and funny stories. Like them it was cheap (1 d), and aimed at a primarily adult readership. What made it different, however, and gives it its claim to being the first of a kind, was that it was based on a recurring character – the eponymous Alexander Sloper.[5]

Ally Sloper was a conman-cum-tramp with a bulbous nose and spindly legs who was always scheming, always getting into trouble, but always coming out on top. He appeared first as a character in *Judy*, created by comic novelist Charles Ross, and was probably influenced by a number of sources: almost certainly by Dickens's Mr Micawber, to whom he had a strong physical resemblance, and possibly by various of the contemporary musical hall acts about tramps and misfits. At the

Figure 1.2 Cover to *Ally Sloper's Half Holiday*, no. 1 (1884), the first ever comic and the first adult comic. Art/script: various. © 1884 Gilbert Dalziel

start of his existence, Sloper was nothing more, and nothing less, than a feckless layabout from working-class origins.

When the character was given his own magazine, however, Ross was replaced by a number of other artists (the most famous being W. Baxter), who went on to modify the character in certain respects. Sloper now became a 'man of the people', a social commentator who took on a 'mock gentrified' appearance (he was still identifiably working class and kept many elements of his previous persona, but it was a significant shift in emphasis).[6] In this way, two further precedents were set: it was the first occasion a creator had lost control of a character; and the first time a character had undergone a revision.

But there were certain constants to Sloper's behaviour that were crucial to his satirical appeal. Drink was an undisguised feature of his life, and he was often depicted with a bottle sticking out of a back pocket or in close proximity (his nose was undoubtedly meant to be swollen by gin, his favourite tipple). This may not seem terribly daring now, but the temperance movement was still at its height in the 1880s. Moreover, his name was a pun on the Victorian practice of sloping up alleyways to avoid the rent-collector. Again, this has to be seen against a background where the penalty for rent evasion was a spell in one of Her Majesty's less-than-humane jails. In short, Sloper was the ultimate Victorian anti-hero, and articulated a side of working-class life rarely touched upon in other publications. Today he seems charming rather than trenchant, but to a contemporary audience he was a sensation.

This is not to say that the comic was 'radical' in the same sense as some of its broadsheet ancestors. On the contrary, as an expression of the new working-class culture, it was ultimately quite conservative. There was no suggestion of class struggle, and the depiction of the rich was comic rather than hostile, with no reference to the source of their income. Similarly, the contemporaneous rise of socialism was seen as something to scoff at, and the comic was proudly monarchist. On the occasion of the Queen's Golden Jubilee in 1887, for example, a

AT IT AGAIN.

Figure 1.3 'At It Again', Ally Sloper's Half Holiday (1884). Art/script: Charles Ross. © 1884 Gilbert Dalziel

celebratory song-sheet was given away free.[7] Thus, the character of Sloper, for all his cheekiness, was like that of many popular music hall acts (notably Dan Leno and, later, Charlie Chaplin) – namely, the 'little man' who 'knows his place'.

But it was because *Half Holiday* articulated people's feelings that it became such a success. The readership was mainly male, in their teens and 20s and white-collar (clerks and office juniors), though there was a vast variation outside this. From the start the publishers were careful to point out that the comic could be read by everybody: it also had a large blue-collar readership and was a cult among the intellectual middle class (William Morris and Edward Burne-Jones were known to be avid fans).[8] With such a broad constituency, it soon became, in its own words, 'the largest-selling penny-paper in the world', with estimated sales at the height of its popularity of 350,000 per week. Sloper, for his part, became a veritable institution – spawning Sloper mugs, watches, pipes and all manner of other paraphernalia (disproving the widely-held belief that comics merchandising began in the 1950s). Ally Sloper was truly Britain's first comics star, and *Half Holiday* lasted, with minor interruptions, until 1923.

However, it wasn't until 1890 that the success of this pioneering comic was capitalised upon. Alfred Harmsworth, the 25-year-old proprietor of the magazine and story-paper publishers Amalgamated Press, had some spare space on his presses, so decided to exploit the new craze. He felt the only way to make a real impact was to keep the price of his comics down to ½d, in order to undercut rivals (*Half Holiday* and the humour magazines) by half. This was an enormous risk, and went against the wishes of many newsagents, who couldn't envisage making any profit with prices so low.

Harmsworth's flagship comics were *Comic Cuts* ('One Hundred Laughs for One Halfpenny!') and *Illustrated Chips*, both launched in 1890. They followed the basic style laid down by *Half Holiday*, and starred their own working-class anti-heroes (this was blatant plagiarism, and in its first editorial, *Comic Cuts* paid specific homage to its predecessor). Hence a new range of tramps, bungling thieves and misfits was foisted on the British public – all of whom were in the same basically 'cheekily conservative' mould as Sloper. These comics, too, were aimed primarily at adults but, like *Half Holiday*, had one eye on a younger readership.

To keep to the all-important ½d price, further corners were cut. For the first few issues Harmsworth 'borrowed' material from other British magazines and American Sunday paper strips, without permission or recompense. The editorials claimed he was using good quality paper, but that was manifestly not the case. As for the conditions of his staff, we can presume that they were routinely exploited, as was now customary for this kind of work.

It is paradoxical, in the light of the above comments, that *Cuts* and *Chips* were also notable for refining comics art. In particular, *Chips* had an outstanding artist in the person of Tom Browne, who created two picaroons in the established fashion, 'Weary Willie and Tired Tim', who were to become almost as well-known as Sloper. What was unique about them was that Browne eschewed the conventional Victorian drawing style, with its heavy shading, in favour of a much more up-beat, uncluttered technique. He had grasped that strips flowed better when unembellished, and thus set an example that a whole generation of future comics artists was to follow. Browne can therefore be seen as Britain's first major comics creator.[9]

Despite the fears of the newsagents, Harmsworth's gamble paid

Figure 1.4 Cover to *Illustrated Chips* (1902), featuring Tom Browne's ground-breaking 'Weary Willie and Tired Tim'. © 1902 Alfred Harmsworth

off. *Cuts* and *Chips* proved to be extremely successful, and were soon selling over half a million a week between them. Harmsworth had shown that, even with unprecedentedly low prices, if the circulation was big enough sizeable profits could be made. It is usually agreed that their spectacular sales mark the point historically where comics became a 'mass' medium.

They were followed by a number of emulators, of varying quality, some more 'adult' than others. Most attempted to keep to the ½d line set by Harmsworth and thus were under the same pressure to economise and exploit staff. Most were satirical – *Comic Life* was particularly notable for its jokes about 'new women' and socialism – while others appealed to adults in different ways – *The Joker*, for example, included pin-up cartoons of female music hall stars. However, all kept to the broadly conservative consensus of the day.

Though other publishers joined the fray in this period, Amalgamated Press retained its primacy, and by 1892 Harmsworth was boasting of overall sales of 2.5 million. He went on to launch the *Daily Mirror* and *Daily Mail* on his comics' proceeds, and in the process became 'Lord Northcliffe', one of the biggest tycoons on Fleet Street. It would not be the last fortune to be made out of the comics medium.

Thus, within a decade, a whole new kind of publication had emerged on the British cultural scene. Gradually two sides to the definition of a comic took shape. On the one hand, comics were seen as 'what they said they were' – jolly, lightweight, gag-orientated entertainment. Although the term 'comic' had been in use for about seventy years, it was only now that it came to mean a specific kind of amusing publication with strips about recurring characters (*Comic Cuts* had been the first to use the word in its title).

On the other hand, comics were not 'respectable', and in the pantheon of Victorian and Edwardian literature, they came at or near the bottom. Previously this dubious distinction had belonged to the penny dreadfuls, but with their decline in the 1880s, comics became the next worst thing. The reasons for this were many and complex, but were rooted in prevailing middle-class prejudices. At worst, comics were considered to be base ephemera: working-class, mass-produced, often shoddy-looking and essentially flippant. At best, they were 'railway literature', mildly diverting lowbrow entertainment to read between stops on a train. [10]

But more than this, being heavily visual, comics were considered by some to be detrimental to reading, a 'threat to literacy'. The 'threat', of course, was to the working class, since the middle-class audience was relatively small. Middle-class paternalists thus decreed that working-class literacy and educational standards were at stake, and that British working men and women should be encouraged instead to read 'improving literature', which is to say texts without illustrations.[11] Consequently, anything with words and pictures was deemed by nature to be inferior to a proper book.[12]

It is thus evident that although comics were tolerated in Britain – after all, there was nothing politically subversive about them – they were not respectable. The word 'comic' came to mean jolly fun, but it also had underlying derogatory associations, and this is the definition that has persisted until the present.

Respectable or not, by 1905 the comics themselves were showing signs of change. As we have seen, many publishers had from the beginning calculated on having children among their readers: many comics, indeed, created 'children's corners' specifically for them. However, it was becoming increasingly apparent that the more juvenile sections were the most popular, and, by extension, that if a publisher could keep the price within pocket-money range (meaning the traditional 'Saturday penny') it should be possible to make even bigger profits by producing comics specifically for this market.

Thus, the 'children's corners' were gradually expanded, and comics editors added more slapstick and extra strips, while reducing the satire and amount of text. Some titles even experimented with colour to appeal to youngsters (*Puck* did so in 1904, and immediately alienated its adult readership, who associated it with children's book illustrations). This strategy of lowering the target age-range was one which was to herald a complete transition from adult comics to children's comics.[13]

By 1914 the vast majority of comics were aimed at a juvenile readership. Vestiges of their adult beginnings remained (there were odd incongruously satirical strips and cartoons in some titles), but now the favoured age-range was 8 to 12 years – the standard audience for the industry ever since. Clearly, by leaving the way open to this market in the first place, the adult titles had almost by accident uncovered the roots of their own demise.

Further reading

David Kunzle's *History of the Comic Strip, Volume 1: The Early Comic Strip*, and *Volume 2: The Nineteenth Century* (Berkeley, Calif.: University of California Press, 1973, 1989) provide an excellent broad background. For a narrower focus on British comics, see Denis Gifford's still useful (and at the time pioneering) article 'The Evolution of the British Comic', *Historical Journal* (1971), pp. 349–58; and on Ally Sloper see Peter Bailey, 'Ally Sloper's Half Holiday: Comic Art in the 1880s', *History Workshop*, 16 (1983), pp. 4–31. On the transformation of working-class life in the late Victorian era see Gareth Stedman Jones's article, 'Working Class Culture and Working Class Politics in London, 1870–1900: Notes on the Remaking of a Working Class', *Journal of Social History*, 7 (1973–4).

Kids' stuff

Comics and children were made for each other
(Denis Gifford, comics historian and collector)[1]

From roughly 1914 until the late 1960s, comics were produced almost exclusively for children, and took on the characteristics that most people associate with them today – innocuousness, naivety and juvenility. Although the period saw the medium stretching into subject-matter other than humour, comics were nevertheless perceived as an integral part of 'British childhood', a romanticised and fiercely-guarded state of innocence, and therefore became ever-more rigidly stereotyped as a 'children's medium'. Although children's comics are not strictly part of our story, it is necessary to look at them briefly for background purposes and also because some of the later adult comics would refer back to them directly.

The sheer number and variety of titles would take a book in itself to explore: therefore the following will concentrate on the period that is generally agreed to be the heyday of children's comics, the mid-1930s to the mid-1960s, and will highlight by genre the most influential and important titles.[2]

As we have seen, the mainstay of the industry pre-1914 was, and was to remain, humorous comics. Amalgamated Press had set the tone with *Illustrated Chips* and *Comic Cuts* in the 1890s, both of which became progressively 'younger' with time, and built on their success with further funny titles aimed more specifically at children – notably *Funny Wonder*, *Larks* and *Playbox*. By adapting to the new juvenile market, the publisher consolidated its lead as the biggest in Britain.

However, by the late-1930s, Amalgamated Press's virtual monopoly was challenged by a new company based in Dundee: DC Thomson. In 1937 and 1938 they launched two new humour titles *Beano* and *Dandy* – which were to redefine the genre altogether. These comics introduced a new type of sharper, more knockabout japery, and a range of bizarre but lovable characters that made the old AP stable look decidedly dated – the best-known being 'Desperate Dan' (by Dudley Watkins), a stubble-chinned cowboy who ate whole cow pies, and 'Korky the Cat' (by James Crichton), a prank-playing feline.

Beano and *Dandy* went from strength to strength during the 1940s, and in the 1950s added more crazy characters to their existing roster – including 'Dennis the Menace' (by David Law), an unruly shock-haired urchin with a dog called Gnasher, 'Minnie the Minx', a sort of female Dennis, and 'The Bash Street Kids', a school class of hyperactive misfits. The latter two strips were created by a young northerner, Leo Baxendale, who specialised in quick-moving, anarchic stories about children outwitting figures of authority (teachers, the police, dads). He would later be cited by certain important creators of adult comics as a major influence.[3]

Thus *Beano* and *Dandy* were the titles which, more than any others, set the definition of a 'comic' in the postwar period: slapstick, childish fun. At their height in the 1950s they were selling an estimated 2 million copies a week – to both boys and girls. Although they spawned a host of rivals – *Topper, Beezer* and *Wham* to name three – they always managed to keep ahead of the pack, and both are still being published in the 1990s.

However, humour was not the only genre in this period, and in the 1950s British adventure comics made their first appearance. It had taken a long time for the idea that comics could be used for other kinds of storytelling to take root: before the 1950s, adventure was generally confined to the boys' 'story papers' that had emerged in the interwar years – *Hotspur, Rover, Wizard* and others. These were illustrated text narratives (not comics), and had their roots in Harmsworth's boys' papers of the 1890s, and before them the penny dreadfuls.[4]

Actual adventure strips in comics began to become popular in the 1930s, but were very much a secondary feature to the funny stories. They were generally inserted somewhere at the back of the publication, and although there were some great creators working in the field (notably Reg Perrott), they were not usually allowed the space or the presentation to shine.[5]

The comic that changed all that, and made a success of having adventure as its selling-point, was *Eagle* (1950). The cover strip, and focus for the comic, was 'Dan Dare – Pilot of the Future' by Frank Hampson. It told of the adventures of a square-jawed British spaceman and his intergalactic battles with the Mekon, an evil green alien with a huge head (this was in the days when a British space programme seemed a feasible prospect). Beautifully produced in photogravure colour, *Eagle* was intended as wholesome boys' entertainment, and had a highly moral tone (with an overt Christian religious bent): it was also very 'British', and imperialist/coldwar undertones were never far from the surface.[6] Although expensive at 3d, it was an immediate hit, and was soon selling over a million a week, with Dan Dare becoming

Figure 2.2 Cover to the *Eagle* (1954), featuring the fearless Dan Dare. Art/script: Frank Hampson. © 1954 Hutton Press

a cult figure in a way not seen since the days of Slopermania – with spin-offs like watches, water pistols and even Dan Dare lemon squash.

Eagle put adventure firmly on the map, and inspired a plethora of imitators – *Valiant, Lion, Tiger* and a re-vamped *Hotspur* (previously a story paper) to name a few. All stuck to the high-minded 'decent' feel of the original, featuring 'goodies' that were really good and 'baddies' that were unspeakably evil (a formula not really bucked until the coming of *Action* in 1976 (see pp. 52–4). But no sooner had the trend begun than the adventure genre itself began to fragment, with new titles concentrating on particular themes – notably war, football and TV programmes.

The war comics were undoubtedly the biggest subgenre, re-fighting the Second World War every issue with an unprecedented blood-lust and lurid xenophobic language (the Germans were 'krauts', 'jerries', even 'sausage-eaters'; the Japanese, 'nips', 'slant-eyes', 'yellow-skins'; and so on). Particularly popular in the 1960s were the pocket-sized *Battle-* and *War Picture-Library* titles, published by IPC (previously Amalgamated Press), and *Commando*, published by DC Thomson, which consisted of lengthy and well-drawn self-contained stories.

The soccer comics were dominated by the figure of Roy Race, otherwise known as 'Roy of the Rovers', the dashing centre-forward for Melchester Rovers, who became the cover-star of *Tiger* in 1954 and stayed there for twenty-two years. Although other soccer heroes followed during the 1950s and 1960s none eclipsed the popularity of Roy, who was eventually given his own title in 1976.

Finally the TV comics were especially notable for their quality artwork – particularly the offbeat *TV Century 21* (later, *TV21*), which 'brought to life' the Gerry Anderson puppet-shows – for example, *Captain Scarlet, Thunderbirds*, and *Stingray*. It featured some of the most talented artists of the era, including Frank Bellamy and Ron Embleton, and was the best selling comic of 1965.

But as well as these essentially male comics, there was a growing industry aimed at girls (albeit staffed almost entirely by men). The genre also had its roots in story comics of the 1930s – text-based publications like *Schoolgirl, The Crystal* – and, like adventure, was a relatively 'late starter'. But when it did take off, in the 1950s, the results were equally dramatic: *The School Friend* staked out the territory in 1950, with stories on what were perceived as 'girlish' subjects – typically involving boarding-school pranks, mysteries and horses – and was soon selling a million copies a week. *Girl* followed in a similar middle-class vein in 1951, a companion comic to *Eagle*.

Girls' comics in the 1960s continued this tradition with titles like *Bunty, Judy* and *Tammy*. However, these were joined by a more worldly-wise set of titles aimed at the 10 to 14 age-bracket that

Figure 2.3 Cover to *Girl* (1956). Art/Script: Ray Bailey. © 1956 Hulton Press

concentrated on romance. *Jackie* (1964) dominated this latter group, and became the best-selling comic of the genre, with sales approaching half a million copies an issue by the end of the decade, and over a million by 1973–4.

Finally, there were American comics. Although America undoubtedly had the biggest comics industry in the world in this period, not much was seen of them in Britain before the 1960s because there was no official distribution. This can partly be explained by the general prejudice that existed against American culture – especially in the immediate postwar years. In short, it was considered gauche, crass and commercial: the writings of Evelyn Waugh, George Orwell and Richard Hoggart were full of sneering references, while BBC Radio was famously unwelcoming to American rock 'n' roll. With hindsight we can see that underlying these attitudes was the fact that the infiltration of American culture was symbolic of the relative decline and rise of Britain and America as world powers.

Nevertheless, some comics did get through, either imported by small companies (often transported by ships as ballast) or via American airbases here. It was a highly erratic arrangement, however, and the American comics that did find their way into British newsagents (or, more commonly, on to market stalls) were generally returns from American newsagents: hence, if they sold well in America, they were rare in Britain.

For youngsters able to get hold of them, though, they were a window on to another world. Designed as monthlies rather than week-lies, they were smaller in format than British comics, with more pages, four-colour artwork and eye-catching covers. As such, and because of the element of naughtiness involved in reading them, they possessed a glamour that the indigenous product patently lacked. According to one source, in playground currency certain American comics could be traded for 'almost anything'.[7]

There were also an increasing number of British reprints of American comics, especially in the early 1950s when the Government banned dollar imports. Less prized than the originals, these were usually in black and white and sometimes re-edited to Anglicise American words.

In the 1940s, the main genres of American titles were the superhero and 'funny animal' comics. The superheroes were massively popular in the States, and fell into two main categories: those who pos-sesed supernatural powers, and super-athletes. Epitomising the former group was the mighty Superman, who could 'leap tall buildings in a single bound!' and 'fly faster than a speeding bullet!', and who was 'sworn to devote his existence to helping those in need!' His opposite number in the latter category was Batman, a much darker personality who dressed like a bat to wreak vengeance on a criminal underworld he deemed responsible for the murder of his parents. Both these characters eventually became the property of Detective Comics, or DC for short.

However, although the superheroes had their appeal, there was no tradition of costumed characters in Britain, and they did not estab-lish themselves to anything like the same extent. It is even true that DC experimented with official distribution of *Batman* to Britain in 1940, but gave up due to lack of interest.[8]

The 'funny animal' genre had no such reservations to overcome, and by the 1940s was dominated by the Disney characters (Donald Duck, Mickey Mouse and so on) already familiar to British audiences from the animated movies. (The work of one artist in particular was especially distinctive, that of Carl Barks – though only the name of Disney appeared on the comics at the time.) The Disney strips were fre-quently reprinted in Britain, as they were all over the world. Later, further funny animals appeared, including those other cartoon favourites Bugs Bunny and Daffy Duck.

The late 1940s and early 1950s saw another type of American comic gaining popularity, one which brought latent British prejudices bubbling to the surface – crime and horror comics. The most famous of these were the horror titles produced by Entertaining Comics (EC) – *Tales From the Crypt, The Haunt of Fear* and *The Vault of Horror* (reprinted in Britain by the Arnold Book Company). They certainly were 'entertaining', with cleverly constructed stories, often with a twist at the end, and beautiful artwork by artists like Johnny Craig, Will Elder, Jack Davis and Graham Ingels. However, they also contained a large amount of gore (dismembered limbs, rotting corpses and so on) which, although always integral to the plot and often tongue-in-cheek, was typically presented in a fairly explicit manner.[9]

Figure 2.4   Cover to *The Haunt of Fear*, no. 1 (1954). The 'ABC' (Arnold Book Company) logo appears instead of the original 'EC' logo. Art: Jack Davis. © 1954 Arnold Book Co/EC Comics

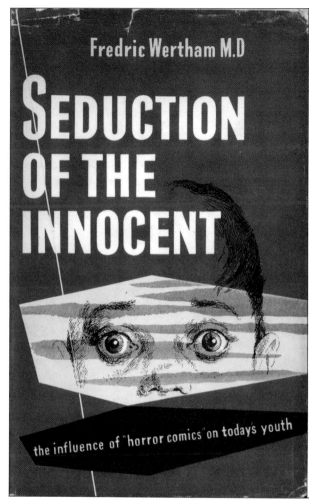

Fredric Wertham M.D

SEDUCTION OF THE INNOCENT

the influence of "horror comics" on today's youth

Figure 2.5 Dust-jacket to Fredric Wertham's *Seduction of the Innocent* (1955). Who better to personify the struggle against 'American vulgarity' than Randolph Churchill, son of Winston. © 1955 Museum Press

It was inevitable that, in a country where a comic was associated with 'jolly, naive fun', they would be deemed to be totally unaccept-able. Branded as the ultimate in American tastelessness, a campaign was started to have them banned. This involved pressure groups representing all shades of the political spectrum (the British Commu-nist Party, indeed, was especially active, seeing all American comics as encouraging a pro-American, pro-capitalist ideology to form in British children's minds). [10]

The campaign was fuelled by reports of research by an American psychiatrist, Fredric Wertham, eventually published in a book, *The Seduction of the Innocent* (1955), which claimed that such comics could actually lead to juvenile delinquency. [11] Although there was no firm evidence to support this assertion, and subsequent research has shown it to be without foundation, it was widely believed at the time.[12] As we shall see in chapters 12 and 15, on the back of Wertham's work, there were similar campaigns against the ECs and their like in many other parts of the world, and most seriously in America itself.

Under enormous pressure, the British government eventually banned the importation and publication of crime and horror comics under The Children and Young Person's Harmful Publications Act (1955). In America, a 'Comics Code' was instituted, proscribing violence, sex and, significantly, anti-establishment messages in comics, and forbidding the distribution of any title not bearing a Code seal of approval. These measures effectively ensured that only material conforming to the traditional, 'innocuous' formula was allowed.[13]

Once the panic over the horror comics had died down, official distribution of American comics in Britain was eventually instituted in 1959. This was predicated on three factors: (a) the belief that the Code was doing an efficient job; (b) the fact that anti-Americanism was no longer as rife as it once had been; and (c) because fears about the maligning influence of the media were being directed elsewhere – notably to the rapid rise of television.

In the years that followed, a new range of superheroes began to appear, published by Marvel to compete with the older-established DC line. The stars of comics like the *Fantastic 4, Spider-Man, Thor* and

Figure 2.6   Cover to *The Hulk*, no. 1 (1962), one of the best-loved Lee-Kirby superheroes. Art: Jack Kirby. © 1962 Marvel Comics

The Hulk were more complex than their predecessors, and incorporated a psychological dimension ('superheroes with super-problems', as they were touted). It was a tribute to the skill of Marvel's chief creators, writer Stan Lee and artist Jack Kirby, that they could make them interesting within the limits of the American Code.

The Marvel comics were very successful, and DC were temporarily left struggling. There followed a general renaissance for American comics in Britain, and as the 1960s progressed they took up an increasing proportion of the market compared to indigenous product. Other successes included a revamped *Batman* which made a comeback as a result of the hugely popular TV series in 1966, and the war comic *Sgt Fury and his Howling Commandos*, which was no less ideologically unsound than its British counterparts. Even horror comics made a comeback in the mid-1960s with titles like *Eerie, Creepy* and *Vampirella*, published by Warren Publications. [14] Later, in the 1970s and 1980s, this trend for increasing American market-penetration was consolidated with the establishment of a network of specialist shops dealing solely in American comics – a story we take up in chapter 5.

However, the rise of the American comic was only relative because, from the mid-1960s on, the sales of juvenile comics in general in Britain declined. This has been blamed on everything from demographic change to the widespread introduction of TV (and later, home-computers and video). There have been some successes – for example, the British SF comic *2000AD* (1977) which we look at in chapter 4 – but individual high-points have not stopped the overall downward trend. The market for children's comics in the 1990s is probably less than half the size it was in the mid-1960s, though despite the advent of adult comics it still forms the mainstay of the industry.

In summary, the main categories of children's comics in the peak period of the 1930s to the 1960s were humour, adventure, girls' and American comics. By the mid-1960s, two companies dominated the British industry – IPC, the descendant of Amalgamated Press, and DC Thomson, the Scottish giant. In the USA, there were also two dominant companies – DC Comics (which had no connection with DC Thomson) and Marvel. These, combined with the many smaller publishers that existed, constituted a thriving industry, putting out hundreds of thousands of comics per week for British youngsters to spend their pocket-money on.

But the survey is not complete without some consideration of the economics of the industry, and of the place of comics within British culture generally. In some ways, very little had changed since the earliest days of the form – except, of course, that comics were for youngsters rather than any other age-group. Yet this reorientation of the target age-range was in itself the major cause of a fundamental change in perceptions of what 'a comic' constituted.

To begin with, comics were, as ever, produced for profit. Surveys have a tendency to focus on the very best examples in the field, but it is important to recognise that most comics produced in this period were not anywhere near the quality of the *Beano, Eagle* or *Fantastic Four*, and were produced with the aim of making as much money as possible for as little effort. Hence, most humour comics were made up of hackneyed, repetitive gags; most adventure comics were contrived and dull; most girls' comics were trite and 'wet'; and most superhero comics were constructed around endless fight-scenes.

By the same token, the exploitation of staff continued. In Britain, a system developed (rooted firmly in the experience of the nineteenth century) whereby writers and artists were paid a flat per-page fee, without royalties or any rights over their creations. Pay was usually very low, and deadlines punishing (there was pressure on most comics to come up with pot-boiler stories week after week to string the readership along). Creators were not even allowed to sign their work – ostensibly because children could then see it was a drawing rather than 'real', but in fact because anonymity was in the interests of the publishers and pre-empted any notion of bargaining power.

There were other negative aspects to working conditions. DC Thomson, for instance, strictly forbade unions,[15] and it was not unusual for the big companies to keep page-rates down by using cheap foreign labour. IPC used Spanish and South American artists, for example (which is why one occasionally finds illustrations of cars with the steering wheel drawn on the wrong side, or with other tell-tale mistakes).[16]

In America, the situation was roughly analogous. Here, the pay and royalties set-up was repeated, and anonymity was further assured by the splitting of work among artists, writers, inkers, letterers and colourists (in Britain, artists generally tended to ink and colour their own work). Only EC in the 1950s, and Marvel from the 1960s, credited creators.

In both countries, it was a work-for-hire system, and staff were essentially considered factory hands, working an 'assembly-line' to produce a consumable product. The overall quality of comics in this period can thus partly be explained by the fact that staff were paid for quantity rather than quality. This is not to say that there weren't publishers that 'cared' (EC, for example, took particular pride in what they put out), but they were very much the exceptions.

Such treatment of creators not unnaturally built up a wall of resentment. In Britain, for example, Frank Hampson assumed that because he had created Dan Dare he owned the copyright, and became embittered when he realised the truth: he left comics for good, and never received royalties for any Dare reprints in the years that followed. Similarly, Leo Baxendale, the *Beano*'s top artist, eventually felt compelled to take DC Thomson to court for recompense over the use of his characters, and only settled with them in 1984 after a seven-year legal battle. In America, the creators of Superman, Jerry Siegel and Joe Shuster did not receive any royalties for their work, and again, were only compensated in the late 1970s. More recently still, in 1988, Jack Kirby, artist on *Fantastic Four, Thor* and others, went through an acrimonious dispute with Marvel to get his original artwork returned. There have been many more such dispiriting stories on both sides of the Atlantic.

As for the place of comics in British culture, it is not surprising that they were still not respectable. Even though comics were now being produced for children rather than adults, there was still a feeling that they were a 'threat to literacy', and that a child's time might be better spent reading something without any pictures. This prejudice was reinforced in time as critics began to deconstruct comics for their 'deeper meanings': war comics were criticised for their racism and xenophobia, the *Beano* and its ilk for 'encouraging laughter at society's unfortunates', the girls' comics for reinforcing sexual stereotypes and so on.[17] The American comics, as we have seen, were a special case – British comics might be frowned upon, but some American titles could allegedly 'seduce the innocent' into delinquency.

But now there was a new element in the equation. The fact that comics were being produced exclusively for a younger age-range meant that increasingly they were perceived as being incapable of appealing to any other constituency. This was because, despite all their shortcomings, comics were progressively seen as an integral part of 'childhood', a word which in Britain by the 1950s had come to mean a romanticised state of innocence – according to historian Martin Barker, 'a special world inhabited by children, whose special natures not only need social action to protect them, but also act as moral measures of the rest of us'.[18]

Comics, like hopscotch and grazed knees, were symbolic of a distinct and protected stage of life, a never-never world epitomised by the literature of Enid Blyton, where 'chums' had wholesome adventures, and the equally anodyne 'Children's Television' of the BBC, which ceased abruptly at a 6 p.m. watershed. Here the creed was studiously to eschew any notion of adult reality: social realism, sexuality and, to a lesser degree, violence were to be avoided at all costs.

Nowhere in the world was this mythology of childhood stronger than in Britain. Unlike the years before the First World War, children were no longer sent out to work, and had more freedom as consumers to make choices in the market-place. Yet, it was a limited freedom, and a child's spare time was policed more heavily than ever by adults.[19] In terms of comics, the mythology reinforced previous notions of them as harmless entertainment, and made any deviation from the norm seem an attack on a much wider range of values (explaining in part why the anti-horror comics campaign was pursued with such vigour).

For comics more than any other medium, the form was now seen to dictate the content. A comic was what was produced 'under the definition of a comic' – which is not a tautology, but a recognition of the very strict parameters postwar society put around the idea. Comics were for children, and woe betide anybody who attempted to prove differently.

Further reading

For a concise history of British children's comics, see Lew Stringer's article, 'A History of British Comics', *Comics Journal*, 122 (June 1988). Denis Gifford's *The International Book of Comics* (London: W. H. Smith 1984) contains a wealth of information, but is confusingly organised. For a history of the horror comics campaign, see Martin Barker's superb *A Haunt of Fears* (London: Pluto Press 1984), while Barker's follow-up book *Comics: Ideology, Power and the Critics* (Manchester: Manchester University Press 1989) looks in detail at the various criticisms of children's comics down the years. References for he history of American comics are given in part II.

Underground comix

Suddenly anything was possible! . . . But we still had to go all the way to the Old Bailey to prove that such a thing as an adult comic existed.

(Mick Farren, ex-editor *Nasty Tales*)[1]

The so-called 'underground' comics that emerged at the end of the 1960s marked a revolutionary break with the past. For the first time in the post-First World War era, it was shown that comics did not have to be exclusively for children: instead, the new breed of counter-culture inspired titles concentrated on specifically adult themes – notably sex, drugs and radical politics. It was a controversial new direction and, though confined to a particular kind of audience, one which redefined irrevocably concepts of what the comics medium could encompass.

The underground is best understood as a product of the profound social divisions that racked the west in the 1960s and 1970s. These years are remembered for widespread protest at America's involvement in Vietnam, the emergence of the civil rights and women's movements, and the 'May Events' in Paris. At the centre of these developments was a generation that viewed society as essentially reactionary and bellicose, and which instead interested itself in pacifism, sexual freedom, minority rights and, perhaps most notoriously, the benefits (spiritual or otherwise) of drugs.

This – in very basic terms – was the counter-culture, which at its most extreme aimed not just to protest society's abuses, but actually to replace the dominant culture with one based on egalitarian ideals. As a 'movement' (for that is what it was), it touched every aspect of the arts and creative endeavour – literature, music, theatre, film and, transfiguratively, comics.

The underground comics both reflected and transmitted the counter-cultural message: unlike the first adult comics of the nineteenth century, they were satirical *and* revolutionary. Produced outside the commercial mainstream, they were often called 'comix' (sometimes 'komix') both in contra-distinction to their straight counterpart and to denote their 'x-rated' content. However, they were not 'underground' in the sense that they were produced clandestinely under conditions of totalitarianism, and always included the name and address of the publisher on the inside cover.

In Britain, the comix were very much an imported idea. The

British counter-culture quickly generated a thriving alternative press, with newspapers and magazines like *IT (International Times)* and *Oz* deliberately using graphics to a much greater extent than the mainstream press. There were also a number of illustrated radical poetry pamphlets, notably by Jeff Nuttall. But because comics were so rigidly associated with children's entertainment, there was no attempt initially to produce them for adults. Instead, the first comix came from America, and it is to there that we must briefly turn.

In America, the first undergrounds can be traced to the mid-1960s – self-published, small-scale affairs, that were often not intended for wider distribution. Often they originated in the universities, where the tradition of college humour magazines that had existed since the 1930s was now revitalised by the influence of *Mad* magazine and its imitators. At the same time, individual 'alternative' strips found a home in the American counter-culture newspapers – notably the *Berkeley Barb*, *LA Free Press* and *East Village Other*.

The first widely available underground comic appeared in 1967, originating from the so-called 'hippie capital' San Francisco, and was entitled *Zap*.[2] The brainchild of Robert Crumb, the most popular contributor of strips to the alternative press, it featured characters that were to become counter-cultural icons. They included 'Whiteman', an uptight, racist, pillar of the establishment, 'Angelfood McSpade', a grotesque racist caricature, and above all 'Mr Natural', a misanthropic, capitalistic guru – perhaps Crumb's greatest creation, a satire on the gullability of the love generation, and a cipher for the intellectual conundrum 'how do you "teach" wisdom?'

The comic's hallmarks were an attractive 'Disneyesque' drawing style, contrasted with subject-matter involving explicit sex, sophisticated politics and drugs (including one ground-breaking wordless strip depicting an LSD trip). *Zap* had started life in the usual way – Crumb had self-published it with a friend, Don Donahue, and the two of them stapled the original copies and sold them on street corners – but was soon being reprinted and selling in thousands.

As *Zap*'s reputation spread, with new distribution deals that took it all over America, it became clear that it was a catalyst for a publishing revolution that had been waiting to happen. Fuelled by the new accessibility of offset litho printing,[3] copyists began to sprout like (psychedelic-) mushrooms. As one historian has written: '*Zap* was *the* book that inspired so many other artists to do their own comix, and in so doing, started the entire comix field rolling.'[4]

In the process, Crumb became the figurehead for the boom (the 'pope of the underground', as he was dubbed). In titles like *Despair*, *Head Comix*, *Big Ass Funnies* and further issues of *Zap* he expanded his repertoire and edged into ever-more challenging areas. He developed other characters, most famously an old favourite from the

Figure 3.1 A selection of covers of solo comix by the great Robert Crumb, including the seminal *Zap*, no. 1

Zap, no. 1 (1967), © 1967 The creator

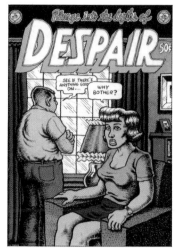

Despair (1969), © 1969 The creator

Mr Natural, no. 2 (1971), © 1971 The creator

Fritz the Cat (1969), © 1969 The creator

alternative press, 'Fritz the Cat', who was originally a rambunctious 'hep cat' (literally) with a voracious sexual appetite, but who evolved into a burnt-out media star.[5] He also increasingly featured himself as a subject for strips, using them as confessionals, never disguising his self-loathing or hostility towards women. He later explained the evolution of his work in terms of catharsis:

> You had to break every taboo first and get that over with ...
> y'know, doing racist images, any sexual perversion that came
> into your mind, making fun of authority figures ... and get past
> all that, and then really get down to business.[6]

It was this ability to keep progressing that confirmed Crumb's position as not only the pivotal figure in the underground, but in the history of adult comics as a whole.

But there were other creators who made a significant impact, often clustered around regional publications. In San Francisco, for example, *Zap* became an anthology after the second edition, and provided a platform for other local talents who were simultaneously producing solo comix. Foremost among them was Gilbert Shelton, perhaps the wittiest of all underground creators (and another favourite from the alternative papers), who was best-known for his characters 'WonderWarthog', a superhero parody, and the 'Fabulous Furry

Figure 3.2 Panels from
'The Freaks Pull a Heist!',
*The Collected Adventures of
The Fabulous Furry Freak
Brothers*, no. 1 (1971).
Art/script: Gilbert Shelton.
© 1971 The creator

Freak Brothers', three permanently-stoned hippies who live by the motto 'grass will see you through times of no money better than money will see you through times of no grass'. Shelton has become self-deprecating about his work ('the humour was simply based on updating alcohol jokes and changing them to marijuana'),[7] though at the time – as now – the idea that drugs were fun was itself subversive.

The humour of Manuel 'Spain' Rodriguez was much harsher. Considered the 'hard man' of the underground, his most famous creation was 'Trashman – Agent of the 6th International', a sort of anarchist superhero who thinks nothing of gunning down a few braying members of the bourgeoisie. 'I tried to make him as plausibly working class as possible', his creator explained at the time, 'A lot of the radical scene is dominated by middle-class people who have funny ideas about politics. Trashman isn't a vegetarian.'[8]

Meanwhile, the more 'experimental' contributors to *Zap* included the hypnotic S. Clay Wilson, best-known for his fetishistic and still-shocking depictions of sado-masochistic sex (often involving images of demons and pirates), and the threesome of Victor Moscoso, Rick Griffin and Robert Williams, all of whom were closely linked with the psychedelic poster-art scene, and who commonly produced wild, non-linear work, inspired by LSD.[9]

Figure 3.3 Panels from 'Trashman', *The Collected Trashman*, no. 1 (1970). Art/script: Spain Rodriguez. © 1970 The creator

In Chicago, the 'second city of the underground', *Bijou Funnies* (1968) became a forum for creators who couldn't make it into *Zap*. These included Justin Green, master of tortured 'catholic guilt' humour, Skip Williamson, creator of the hapless *ingénue* 'Snappy Sammy Smoot', Art Spiegelman, whose '*noir*' abstract parables were as entertaining as they were impenetrable, Kim Deitch, who matched woodblock-style art with occult obsessions, and Jay Lynch, creator of the very popular 'Nard n' Pat', which pitted a conservative suburbanite against a bohemian cat.

Key creators having established themselves, this 'first wave' of the American underground was then followed by a period in which the subject-matter began to diversify and include more specific areas of political struggle. In 1970, the first comic devoted to women's liberation appeared – *It Ain't Me, Babe*, which was followed by the better-known *Wimmins Comix* line in 1972. Both were a direct feminist response to what was seen as the profound sexism present in many of the existing undergrounds (particularly the work of Crumb, Wilson and Spain), and provided a valuable platform for new female talent (see also, pp. 224–7). Other 'cause comix' included *All Atomic Comics*, about nuclear politics, *Slow Death Funnies*, which developed a green bent, and, later, *Gay Comix*, closely linked to the gay liberation movement and featuring the very amusing work of Howard Cruse.

By the early 1970s, there was thus a whole new, alternative, comics culture in America. Publishers like Last Gasp, Kitchen Sink and Rip Off were putting out entire lines of comix, while at the grass-roots level, self-publishing was more widespread than ever. At the underground's height – roughly 1968–74 – it has been estimated that the six major comix publishers were between them selling 100,000 comix per month. [10] This was a remarkable figure, though it should be said that very few were of the standard of those mentioned above.

The comix publishers were not in any way competing with Marvel or DC because they were going for an entirely different readership. This is also why they were able to so easily ignore the Code. By the same token, underground art found its way on to T-shirts, posters, record-covers and anywhere else hippie culture might find expression. (Fritz the Cat was even made into two movies, much to Robert Crumb's displeasure.) In late-1960s and 1970s America, comics were definitely hip. There would eventually be a price to pay for success in terms of a backlash from the 'establishment'; yet for several years the industry thrived and, in the process, its influence spread beyond the shores of America.

When the comix first arrived in Britain, the effect was galvanising. Individual strips were first seen in the alternative newspapers (especially *IT* and *Oz*), while the comix themselves first began to appear in numbers in 1968–9, either as reprints or imports. They soon found a sizeable audience among Britain's own hippie population, with the readership among students being particularly significant ('red brick' tertiary education having been recently expanded). Again, the work of Robert Crumb proved especially popular.

However, a British version of the underground took a while to get going, and the first comic did not appear until 1970.[11] This was *Cyclops*, a tabloid published by a group of comix enthusiasts from *IT*, headed by Graham Keen. It reprinted American strips by Spain and Gilbert Shelton alongside new British work by, for example, Edward Barker (a popular *IT* contributor), Ray Lowry (later a cartoonist for *New Musical Express* and *Private Eye*) and Martin Sharp (already famous for his psychedelic posters). The comic was considered somewhat avant-garde at the time, and was very expensive at 3 shillings: with unimpressive sales, it lasted only four issues.

Nasty Tales followed in 1971. This was an 'official' sister-publication to *IT* (intended in part to subsidise the paper), and was this time closer to the American format comic book and much more in the *Zap* mould. Again, American and British work was mixed, but with a more slapstick sensibility and an emphasis on outrage (as the title suggested). American contributors included Crumb, Spain, Shelton and Williamson, while the British names were headed by Edward Barker,

Figure 3.4 Cover to *Cyclops* (1970), the first British underground. Art: Ed Barker. © 1970 The creators/Innocence and Experience

Malcolm Livingstone and Chris Welch. It was still pricey at 20 pence, but notched up respectable sales over its seven issues, eventually being cancelled amid controversy in 1973.

This in turn was succeeded by *Cozmic Comics* (1972), which were initiated partly to make money for the ailing *Oz* magazine (hence the name). These were arguably the best-known of all the British underground comix, and the longest running, with over twenty titles published under the Cozmic imprint. Yet again, American work featured (especially that of Crumb and Shelton), though an increasing number of British creators were used, including Dave Gibbons and Brian Bolland (both later to make names for themselves in mainstream comics like *2000AD* and American adult comics) and Angus McKie (who went on to work for the pioneering French comic *Métal Hurlant* and to become a well-known book-cover illustrator). The line included solo comix by British creators Mike Weller (*The Firm*), Edward Barker (*Edward's Heave*) and Joe Petagno (*It's Only Rock 'n' Roll Comix*).

There followed a hiatus around 1974–5, which was broken by the emergence of *Brainstorm Comix* (1975) in which American work was eschewed altogether (issue one of the comic bore the proud legend 'Made in Britain'). It was produced to showcase the work of one creator in particular, Bryan Talbot, whose character 'Chester Hackenbush, the Psychedelic Alchemist' was a beautifully-drawn paean to illegal chemicals. 'The strip was pure Alice in Wonderland', Talbot later recalled, 'at the beginning of a story [Hackenbush] would go on a trip, and at the end he'd come down'. [12] Undoubtedly the most drug-orientated of all the Brit-comix, *Brainstorm* also became the best selling, with peak figures of around 12,000 copies an issue. The line was cancelled in 1977 however, after six issues.

Finally, *Street Comix* (1976) was again an all-British line, emanating from the Birmingham Arts Lab – a sort of counter-cultural arts workshop. [13] These took an altogether different tack to *Brainstorm* and dropped drug references in favour of more experimental and autobiographical work, including contributions from Steve Bell (later to produce the daily strip 'IF' for the *Guardian*), Kevin O'Neill (who went on to work for *2000AD*) and Suzy Varty (the most prominent female British underground creator). The comics' chief asset, however, was Hunt Emerson, the most respected (and most prolific) creator of the British scene, who doubled as the line's co-editor. His strips were characterised by a spontaneous, flowing drawing style and 100 m.p.h. humour, which could often veer into delightfully surreal tangents: 'When I started out, I'd begin in the top corner and just see what happened', he later explained, 'only later did I tie the strips down to actual stories.' [14] There were five *Street Comix* in all, the last one appearing in 1978.

These were the best-known British examples of the form,

Figure 3.5 Cover to *Street Comix*, no. 5 (1978). Art: Hunt Emerson. © 1978 The creators

though there were many more, often produced on a Do-It-Yourself basis. In terms of subject-matter, all were derivative of the American scene to a greater or lesser degree (*Cyclops* and the *Street Comix* were unquestionably the most adventurous), and as well as reprinting American strips, the British contributions themselves were invariably in the American style.[15]

However, this pervasive American influence did not mean the Brit-comix were devoid of personality, as has been suggested by some commentators. As well as producing their own 'star' creators (especially Emerson and Talbot), the comix had their own preoccupations, and among the more generalised subject-matter it is possible to find reference to, for example, British labour relations, Edward Heath's government, the rise of the National Front and British punk. One minor title, *Ally Sloper*, even referred in its name to a specifically

British satirical past.[16] Finally, as if to reinforce the identity of the British scene, there were two 'Konventions of Alternative Komix' in Birmingham in 1976 and 1977.

The British underground was thus a vibrant complement to its American counterpart. Together they represented both an alternative to the comics establishment and a ribald satirical challenge to the political and cultural status quo. Yet it was not just the content of the comix that made them unique. The principles of the counter-culture extended to their means of production and distribution as well, innovations which again set important precedents for the future.

In terms of production, the underground set-up was totally different to IPC/DC Thomson or Marvel/DC. Most significantly, in contrast to the work-for-hire arrangements that existed in the mainstream, the comix were generally co-operatively owned and edited, and creators not only received royalties (when there were any), but owned the copyright over their creations.[17] Print-runs were frequently small (sometimes only a few hundred), and so profits were often slim, but the system did at least secure an equal distribution of poverty.

Moreover, there was rarely any deadline pressure in the same sense as in commercial comics, nor pressure to come up with constant pot-boiler stories, as the comix tended to be published 'when they were ready', and with the maximum artistic freedom (which often meant breaks of many months between issues). If there was a guiding creed for the underground, it could be summed up as 'anything goes!', but with the caveat 'all in good time ...'.

Similarly, distribution and sales were on an entirely different basis. It was unthinkable, for the most part, that the undergrounds could be sold in the traditional fashion by newsagents, so an alternative network had to be developed.[18] As Mick Farren, ex-editor of *Nasty Tales*, later explained 'W. H. Smith had a stranglehold on the market just as they do today. They didn't even take *Private Eye*, so it was pretty obvious what they'd make of Robert Crumb's pictures of anthropomorphic dogs fucking.'[19] Thus, following the lead of America, a retail network was created based on alternative record shops, bookshops and, above all, headshops – hippie shops that sold fashionable clothing, joss-sticks, drug paraphernalia (pipes, reefers) and so on. Although it's difficult to imagine today, these headshops were a familiar feature of most big towns in the late 1960s and 1970s – the ones in the King's Road and Portobello Road in London perhaps being the most well known.

Thus the economics of the underground were by necessity of an entirely different character to the mainstream comics industry, and this had a value above the purely practical. Though it is easy to romanticise, it gave creators a pride in what they were doing, and inspired original, self-motivated work. 'It was the absolute freedom that was

BEN-ETHEUS

THE MOROCCAN SHOP

A gallery of splendid clothes, leather goods, pottery, jewellery, carpets, perfume, etc. from Morocco and the Far East. All at reasonable prices.

134 ALCESTER RD. MOSELEY. BIRMINGHAM 13.

involved', Crumb later explained, 'We didn't have anybody standing over us saying "you can't draw this".'[20] Of course, there was shoddy work, and it would be naive to think that the counter-culture did not have its own exploiters and exploited. Moreover, the totally un-businesslike attitude of many publishers was responsible for the early demise of countless titles. Yet for all that, this alternative infrastructure survived for most of the 1970s, and produced some of the most remarkable comics in the history of the medium.

Why the underground declined is essentially the story of why the counter-culture declined. There were three main reasons that applied in both Britain and America: the backlash from 'straight' society, the fracturing and co-option of alternative society and the rise of new kinds of adult comic. Although there is some disagreement among ex-underground contributors today, it would appear that a deterioration was evident in Britain from around 1975.

In retrospect, the comix were bound to provoke a hostile reaction for two reasons: because they were an integral part of the counter-culture and thus a conduit for anti-establishment ideas; and because they subverted what was considered 'by nature' a childish form. In a country where 'a comic' equalled the *Beano* and 'innocent fun', it was obvious that the comix would not be tolerated – though it was equally obvious that objections to sexual and violent content were excuses for much wider political aims. As with the horror comics campaign of the 1950s, the backlash cannot be taken at face value.

The mainstream press was the first to go on the offensive. The underground was a story begging to be sensationalised, and duly shock articles began to appear about 'the American sex-comics'. They were characterised as pornographic, perverted and generally beyond the pale, though usually very little attempt was made to explain why. This was followed by police confiscations and a number of court cases. In addition, customs played a role in keeping American comix out of Britain. Finally, in 1972, the creators of *Nasty Tales* were arrested for obscenity and sent to the Old Bailey for trial. It was to be the most important court action in the history of British adult comics.

The trial was preceded by the more famous *Oz* trial of the previous year, which had been billed by the media as 'the counter-culture versus the establishment'. This again had been brought for obscenity, and *Oz*'s comic strips had been a major focus for the case (especially an example derived from Robert Crumb, showing the children's character Rupert the Bear in various sexual acts, and an instalment of the Fabulous Furry Freak Brothers). The trial resulted in the conviction of the editors, who were sent to prison, only to be released when their sentences were quashed on appeal.[21]

The *Nasty Tales* trial went over much of the same ground. The case went to court ostensibly because an 8-year-old had managed to buy a copy of the comic (though it transpired she had been put up to it by her mother). However, the trial proceedings ranged over a much

Figure 3.7 Panels from *The Trials of Nasty Tales* (1973). Art: Dave Gibbons. Script: Trial transcript. © 1973 The creators/H. Bunch/Bloom Publications

broader terrain than the Obscene Publications Act, and nobody was left in any doubt that once again it was really the counter-culture that was in the dock. In a much-publicised move, the defence called upon the testimony of George Perry of the *Sunday Times* and Germaine Greer, feminist writer–philosopher and 'queen of the alternative society', to present a case for adult comics satire. In the end, *Nasty Tales* was let off with a caution, but not before the judge had summed up by saying that the pendulum of permissiveness in modern society had swung too far. The outcome was then promptly celebrated by the underground in a comic, *The Trials of Nasty Tales* (Figure 3.7).

But it was a pyrrhic victory in many ways. Whatever the

Figure 3.8 'Komix Comics', *Street Quomix* (1977), Bryan Talbot's melancholy comment on a dying underground. © 1977 The creator

outcome of the trial, it was damaging for the image of the comix in general. This and the various other police raids and confiscations were also very harmful financially in the long run for the publishers (despite the short-term benefits of a rise in sales provoked by notoriety). In the words of Mick Farren, 'money was tight enough as it was without having to worry about lawyer's fees'.[22]

But already by this time there were even more ominous signs for the underground. Just as the comix had grown out of the counter-culture at large, so their fate was intimately linked to it. On one level, the counter-culture was being anaesthetised and co-opted into main-stream culture (put simply, the alternative press was disappearing and

being co-opted by a hipper rock press, alternative theatre by fringe theatre, protest rock by heavy rock and so on). On another, its anger was finding new expressions: this was the period of the rise of the 'New Left', on one hand, and terrorist groups like the Weathermen, Baader-Meinhof and Angry Brigade, on the other ('Trashman' could be said to have been prophetic in this respect). When, in 1973, America withdrew from the Vietnam War, the chief unifying element for the old hippie consensus was ended.

Flower power was going to seed, and its demise meant that comix began to lose their natural audience. It became a question of adapt or die, but breaking out of self-imposed limitations was an increasingly difficult problem. Some comix did explore new avenues – notably historical narrative and genre fiction – but most were stuck in a satirical, iconoclastic rut. The sort of humour they depended on was bound to become repetitive and out of date, and it is fair to say that, generally, their overall quality declined steadily towards the end of the decade.

Similarly, the retail and distribution system had a natural tendency to ghettoise things – orientated towards the already converted, there were very few possibilities of expanding the readership. Thus, eventually, even the headshops began to disappear – to close down or turn into 'legitimate' boutiques.

But the final indication that the underground was becoming an anachronism was the emergence of a new type of adult comic, closely linked with the growth in specialist comics shops. These boasted more colour and better production standards and, as a consequence, often much flashier art-styles. In terms of content, they built on the achievements of the comix, but dealt with different subject-matter, often jettisoning the counter-cultural message altogether. They were thus fundamentally different in quality to the underground, and can be considered the next stage in the evolution of adult comics. They will be discussed in more detail in chapter 5.

The underground has never died out completely. Despite a sharp contraction in the late 1970s, it is still around in the 1990s. Crumb, Shelton, Emerson and many others are still working, and continue to produce some fine comix (and sell many more now than they ever did twenty years ago). Moreover, many publishers survived, and continue to conduct their business on the basis of the same principles – and are still subject to periodic police raids. Survivors in America include Rip Off, Last Gasp and Kitchen Sink, while in Britain the torch has been taken up by Knockabout Comics. The underground may no longer be 'talking to a generation', but it is still talking, and saying some still relevant things.

Further reading

On the American underground, Mark Estren's *A History of Underground Comics* (San Francisco, Calif.: Straight Arrow 1974) is an invaluable guide: its profuse illustrations give a good idea of the sheer variety of comix produced. On individual American creators, see the interviews in Gary Groth and Robert Fiore (eds), *The New Comics* (New York: Berkley, 1988). (Astonishingly, Robert Crumb awaits a proper biography, although Don Fiene's *R. Crumb Checklist* (Cambridge, Mass.: Boatner Norton Press 1981) includes details of press criticism.) There are, sadly, no histories *per se* of the British underground, though Mal Burns's *Comix Index* (Brighton: John Noyce 1978) is a useful place to begin. On the background to the counter-culture in general: for America, see Abe Peck's *Uncovering the Sixties: The Life and Times of the Underground Press* (New York: Pantheon 1985); for Britain, Elizabeth Nelson's *The British Counter-Culture 1966–73* (London: Macmillan 1989) is a good, if dry, introduction, while a more immediate sense of the era can be gleaned from Jonathon Green's *Days in the Life* (London: Heinemann 1988).

2000AD: 'The comic of tomorrow!'

Seeing an issue of *2000AD* for the first time and reading these aware and funny stories, I realised there were adults at work here who were doing stuff that they enjoyed, and that other adults could enjoy.

(Alan Moore, ex-contributor *2000AD*)[1]

All through the period of the underground, the British mainstream comics industry had shown no interest in producing comics for adults. However, ironically, towards the end of the 1970s, a children's science fiction weekly called *2000AD* managed to garner a large adult following – and in the process bucked the trend of declining sales in commercial comics. In branching out to this new audience, it formed a bridge with the underground, and introduced a number of comix creators to a much wider readership. Along with a willingness to experiment with American comics styles, this revolutionised the mainstream, and showed the possibilities for future commercial material aimed specifically at an older age-group.

The *2000AD* story begins with a precursor called *Action*. *Action* was an IPC comic, launched in 1976, which offered thirty pages of stops-out boys' adventure. However, it was not like other adventure comics available at the time. Under the editorship of Pat Mills, it was deliberately orientated towards a new kind of juvenile reader – street-smart pre-adolescents. To this end, the comic included material directly influenced by contemporary trends in the cinema – strips about giant *Jaws*-influenced killer sharks ('Hookjaw'), tough Dirty Harry-style cops ('Dredger') and *Rollerball*-type science fiction ('Death Game 1999') – almost all 'X' or 'AA' films the target readership were too young to be allowed into.

It also featured unorthodox, politically-resonant, heroes: for instance, a German infantryman of the Second World War, a black boxer and a working-class secret agent. Later, it would include stories about hitherto unexplored areas of urban youth culture (in particular 'Look out for Lefty', which dealt with football hooliganism).

Action was cynical, anti-authoritarian and very violent – and an instant success. It became the biggest seller IPC had had for years, with figures settling at a steady 150,000 copies per week. Moreover, the loyalty it provoked among readers was unprecedented, and the quantity of *Action*'s fan-mail was legendary in the industry.

But it also broke the traditional unwritten rule that children's comics be 'innocuous fun'. Before long, and with a dreary inevitability, *Action* became the subject of a major controversy and censorship campaign, in much the same way as had the American horror comics before it (if not on the same scale). The *Sun* featured a double-page centre spread denouncing the 'The Sevenpenny Nightmare',[2] and there were several hostile radio and TV reports. W.H. Smith, Britain's most powerful newsagent, threatened not to handle any more issues until it cleaned up its act – which it eventually had to do.

Ostensibly, it was the violence that was the cause of the outrage. But as with the horror comics, there were other less explicit reasons. Historian Martin Barker has shown that when the time came for the comic to be censored, it was not the violence that was cut so much as the episodes that featured a challenge to authority.[3] After a severe toning down, *Action* became just another run-of-the-mill adventure comic: reader support waned, and it was eventually merged with another title.

2000AD was intended as a science fiction version of *Action*, and was launched in 1977. Pat Mills once again created the comic, but the editor was to be Kelvin Gosnell. Their brief was to try to recapture the *Action* readership, but also to try to avoid a similar controversy. So, like *Action*, *2000AD* featured film and TV-influenced material, most notably a *6 Million Dollar Man*-type story entitled 'MACH 1' and a strip based loosely on *The Omega Man*, starring a character who would later become synonymous with the comic, 'Judge Dredd'. The anchor strip, intended to sell the comic, was a revamped version of 'Dan Dare' – a more hard-bitten Dare this time, taking his fight against the Mekon into the 1970s. The early comic's line-up was completed by 'Future Shocks', throwaway stories with EC-type twist endings, which

Figure 4.2 Cover to *2000AD* (1980), depicting future lawman Judge Dredd. Art: Brian Bolland. © 1980 IPC

appeared occasionally as fillers, and a letters page edited by the egotistical Tharg, a green alien who boasted about imposing 'his' comic on the human populace.

The stories still had a cynical edge, but they were set exclusively in the future and so, it was hoped, were not as vulnerable to criticism as *Action*'s more contemporary material. They were also more tongue-in-cheek than *Action*, and writers John Wagner, Alan Grant and Mills himself set a more humorous tone.

2000AD was also more adventurous artistically, and used devices that had proved popular in American comics. There was an awareness that American titles were doing increasingly well commercially, in contrast to their struggling British counterparts, and so there was a willingness to allow artists to experiment with large American-style splash-panels, more eye-catching covers and so on. From the start, *2000AD* was 'flashier' than other British comics, and made the traditional 'chessboard' comic layout look decidedly dated.

However, despite all the distinctive traits, the new comic was not initially a big commercial success. Issue one did sell out, but after that sales declined, with 'Dan Dare', in particular, proving unpopular with readers. After a year, some of the managers at IPC were seriously considering halting production.[4]

But *2000AD* had an 'attitude' that was unmistakable, and it was this that attracted the notice of writers and artists outside mainstream British comics. Specifically, creators from the underground saw in *2000AD* a comic they could relate to. Although in its terms of employment *2000AD* was still tied to the work-for-hire system, it nevertheless seemed that under the guidance of Pat Mills (who by this time had acquired a reputation as something of a 'maverick') it would allow room for at least some measure of self-expression.

Thus, as the underground declined in the late 1970s an increasing number of ex-comix creators found a home at *2000AD* – among them Dave Gibbons, Brian Bolland, Kevin O'Neill and Bryan Talbot. Similar feelings towards the comic also prompted another young writer to join the team: Alan Moore, who had previously produced underground-style strips for the music papers.[5] It should be noted that these creators, as well as having an underground pedigree, were also often involved with American comics 'fandom' – an area of comics' history we shall be looking at in chapter 5. Suffice to say that this meant they tended to be admirers of certain American mainstream comics (those published by Marvel especially), and were highly versed in American comics art and writing styles.

It is easy to exaggerate the aesthetic attractions of *2000AD* for these new creators. For many, it represented quite simply a way to make a living, and a few had already worked for commercial comics at the same time as contributing to the comix.[6] It should also be noted that Gibbons, O'Neill and Bolland had been contributing to *2000AD* from its earliest days. But whatever the individual circumstances, it is fair to say that they brought with them a more sophisticated and adult comics sensibility – an element that would prove crucial in turning the comic's fortunes around. With their input, *2000AD* now entered what is generally agreed to have been its 'golden era', dating roughly from the end of 1978 to 1985.

New kinds of adventure strips began to flourish, typically involving hell-for-leather, hard-boiled violence. They included 'Rogue Trooper' (by Gerry Finley Day and Dave Gibbons) about a genetically-engineered infantryman who could breathe the atmosphere on a poisoned planet; 'Strontium Dog' (by Alan Grant and Carlos Ezquerra), concerning a team of mutant bounty-hunters in a post-holocaust future; and 'Nemesis the Warlock' (by Pat Mills and Kevin O'Neill/Bryan Talbot), a darkly humorous tale that featured aliens as heroes, and humans as the scourge of the galaxy, and which made points about racism and imperialism.

Complementing these blood-and-thunder epics was the subtler work of Alan Moore. He wrote a number of strips which created a

Figure 4.3 Panels from 'Nemesis the Warlock', *2000AD* (1983). Art: Kevin O'Neill. Script: Pat Mills. © 1983 IPC

template that would be imitated by countless creators in the years which followed. 'Halo Jones' (with art by Ian Gibson) was a sympathetic portrayal of a frightened woman caught up in a bloody future war, and featured some clever feminist twists, 'Skizz' (with art by Jim Baikie) concerned a Birmingham schoolgirl who finds and befriends an alien living in the garden shed (the story was conceived pre-*ET*). In a much lighter vein, 'DR and Quinch' (art by Alan Davis) was a humour strip about a pair of teenage alien hucksters – 'the Bash Street Kids with a nuclear capacity', as Moore later described them.[7] Finally, 'Future Shocks' was revamped by Moore in a much more satirical fashion, and duly became one of the most popular features of the comic.

But dominating them all was a more mature, more highly-evolved Judge Dredd. No longer a second-rate Omega Man, he had developed a personality all his own, and was now the indisputable star of the comic (having out-lived Dan Dare and all the other early strips). Dredd was judge, jury and executioner in a future metropolis called Mega City One (a thinly disguised New York) – essentially a fascist character whose catchphrase was 'I am the Law!'. Yet the stories always carried a sense of irony, and sometimes raised quite searching questions about the nature of Dredd's power. Written by Alan Grant and John Wagner, he was drawn by a number of artists, the most popular being Mike McMahon and Brian Bolland. Alan Grant later recalled: 'We always tried to make Dredd as amusing as possible. Although there was a time when we experimented to see how far we could push things in terms of the violence, the point was to entertain.'[8]

This mix of American pizzaz and underground irreverence made for an exciting and uniquely stylish comic. The confidence of its producers was summed up by the tag-line 'The Comic of Tomorrow – Today!' Dave Gibbons later recalled the working atmosphere on the comic thus: 'We were all very enthusiastic about each other's work, and I think that sense of pride in what you were doing was passed on to the readers. This was a friendly rivalry, but we also sparked off each other. There was definitely a positive attitude.'[9]

By 1982, sales were steady at around 120,000 a week, representing a spectacular resurrection. The readership fell, more or less, into three categories. First, there was the comic's primary target group, children, who liked it for the action, the punch-ups, shoot-outs and so on. (Tharg was also very popular among the youngsters, and his mailbag was always full.) Then there were American comics fans, generally teenagers, who tended to like *2000AD* for its artistic style, which was not dissimilar to American productions. Finally, there was a general adult readership, who enjoyed the black humour, the sophistication of the strips and the overall playfully subversive attitude. What the percentage was of each group is not known exactly: the 8–12-year-olds were always in a majority at this stage, but it is clear that the adult readership was substantial, as indicated, for instance, by the large number of student unions that subscribed to the comic.

What undoubtedly reinforced this older following was the patronage of the music papers. The mainstream press still managed to find fault with *2000AD*, and there were a number of articles criticising its violence. However, the music press – *New Musical Express, Record Mirror, Sounds* and *Melody Maker* – were hugely enthusiastic, and made a point of recommending it to readers. (The music papers themselves had been greatly influenced by the alternative press of the 1960s and early 1970s, and in a sense continued the close connection with comics that had existed then between them and the undergrounds.)[10] Features on *2000AD* were common, and rock stars when interviewed often made a special point of saying they read it (mentions for *2000AD* characters in records themselves were not infrequent). *2000AD* was, in short, the first mainstream rock 'n' roll comic.[11]

Naturally, with this sort of coverage, and in the knowledge that a sizeable percentage of the readership was adult, the writers and artists tended to play up the sophisticated aspects of the comic. This was reinforced by the fact that the younger audience was getting older all the time. As Pat Mills later recalled:

> In the very early days, what you might call the more perceptive readers did not come through in large numbers, so we had to cater to the bulk audience. But in time, as they got older, so their tastes changed, and we as creators were able to introduce less simple-minded content.[12]

Thus as the 1980s progressed, *2000AD* managed to blur the differentiation between an 'adult' comic and a children's comic as it became ever-more 'knowing'. It had always been closer to the underground than to the old *Eagle*, but now that orientation seemed doubly pronounced.

But even 'The Galaxy's Greatest Comic' could not sustain this level of success indefinitely, and from the mid-1980s on a decline was evident. There were many reasons for this. On the one hand, there was increasing competition, both from Britain and America, and, on the other there were internal problems linked to the work-for-hire system.

The British competition from children's comics did not constitute a major threat. Titles like *Starblazer* (DC Thomson), *Tornado* and *Starlord* (themselves IPC comics) featured science fiction stories and borrowed some of *2000AD*'s artistic and storytelling ideas, but were aimed at a more traditional children's market. (Indeed, the latter two titles ended up being merged with *2000AD*.)

Figure 4.4 Cover to *Warrior*, no. 7 (1992). Art: Mick Austin. © 1982 The creator/Quality Communications

A potentially more serious threat was *Warrior*, an independent monthly founded in 1982 by publisher Derek 'Dez' Skinn specifically to concentrate on older readers. It utilised the talents of several *2000AD* contributors – among them Alan Moore and Brian Bolland – and featured some outstanding SF strips. Indeed, Moore was the writer for three of the most popular stories – 'Laser Eraser and Pressbutton', about two futuristic assassins (a variant on a strip Moore had created for *Sounds*); 'Miracleman', a revamping of the British 1950s superhero Marvelman which situated him in 'real' settings (a forerunner of Moore's acclaimed *Watchmen*, which will be discussed in chapter 6); and above all 'V for Vendetta', a taut thriller set in a fascist Britain of the future, and outstandingly illustrated by David Lloyd. However, *Warrior*, for all its merits, did not dent *2000AD*'s sales, and though successful for several years folded in 1983 due to distribution problems and internal wrangles.

A much greater danger in reality were the American comics. Certainly, *2000AD* had borrowed from them in the past, but now, with the advent of specialist shops devoted almost entirely to American product and a whole new range of superhero titles, *New Teen Titans* and the revamped *X-Men* in particular, *2000AD* was beginning to look a little dated. American comics were once more the 'glamour comics', and Marvel and DC began increasingly to eat into *2000AD*'s readership as the 1980s progressed.

Moreover, the American companies were increasingly offering better employment opportunities for creators – something which led some of *2000AD*'s brightest talents to quit and work for them. Put briefly, creators at *2000AD* could expect the traditional working arrangements – a flat page fee, with no royalties or rights over creations.[13] In America, however, it was now possible to get a royalty of anything up to 4 per cent, even if copyright arrangements were little better.

IPC refused to adapt to the new economic conditions, and eventually paid the penalty. Despite the fact that *2000AD* had introduced one important advance for creators by allowing full credits to appear, there was no escaping the fact that there was more money in America, and more kudos. *2000AD* simply could not keep up, and in time there were mass defections to the enemy: Alan Moore, Dave Gibbons, Pat Mills, Kevin O'Neill, Alan Grant and John Wagner, among others, all went to American companies. Many members of this so-called 'Britpack' would be of central importance in the adult comics boom a few years later.

The departure of the old guard marked a watershed in many senses. It brought an era to an end at *2000AD*, and the comic never really regained the spirit or charm of its early 1980s incarnation. The task of filling the gaps was left to editors Steve MacManus and, later, Richard Burton. To their credit they managed to unearth a new generation of British talent to keep the comic going. New creators such as Grant Morrison, Brendan McCarthy, Peter Milligan, Steve Yeowell, Glenn Fabry and Simon Bisley had themselves been avid readers of the early comic, and therefore slipped smoothly into its established style. Moreover, many had also been involved in the American comics fan scene – something which was given expression in 1986 with the introduction of *2000AD*'s first ever superhero story, the popular 'Zenith' by Grant Morrison and Steve Yeowell. It was perhaps an obvious step, but emblematic of a new willingness at the comic to follow trends rather than to set them.

They were also responsible for continuing the trend towards adult material. There was now more sex and violence, more cerebral plots, and more rock-'n'-roll references (some of the later strips were self-consciously hip to the point of being incomprehensible). This was matched by a dramatic hike in production standards as glossy magazine-paper was adopted, and every strip appeared in full colour. In taking this direction, the comic dropped any pretence at aiming for a juvenile audience: a survey undertaken in 1991 put the average age of readers at 17, with over 30 per cent over 25. But by growing with its readership, *2000AD* was able to maintain relatively high sales, holding steady at around 100,000 until the late 1980s – a remarkable achievement. 'The readership was, and is, incredibly loyal', MacManus later explained. 'If there is a lean patch, they wait for the next wave to come along.'[14]

But the comic's problems were not over. The management were still not offering royalties right up until the late 1980s. Thus, like their predecessors, most of the new creators found the lure of the dollar too much to resist in the long run, and *2000AD* remained a cheap training ground for its American rivals. This naturally had a knock-on effect for the quality of stories. Despite the best efforts of successive editors, how could any creative chemistry be generated if people kept leaving? The artwork started to get patchy, and the plotting weaker. It was inevitable that fans began to complain that they'd rather have good stories on poor paper than poor stories on good paper. Thus, despite the vogue for adult comics, *2000AD* was not able to stand its ground, and by 1992 the total circulation had slipped to around 78,000.

Management's response has been to diversify, In 1990, the *Judge Dredd Megazine* was launched, a spin-off monthly focusing entirely on *2000AD*'s (still-) most popular character. To date it has sold reasonably well (settling at around 40,000 copies), and there are reports that a Hollywood Dredd movie may be in the offing. More interestingly, a new SF title has been conceived for publication in 1993, in a clear attempt to recapture the juvenile audience that *2000AD* lost sometime in the mid 1980s. This policy is perhaps the final recognition of the original comic's schizophrenic nature. Less symbolically, it represents a diversion of money and energy into other areas, which is always an ominous sign. We should be wary of writing off *2000AD* prematurely: it has an unequalled record for bouncing back. Yet few commentators seriously believe it will still be here in the year 2000.

Further reading

No written history of *2000AD* exists, but the video *Ten Years of 2000AD – A Video Celebration* (London: Acme Video/CA Productions 1987) includes perceptive interviews with all the major creators. On *Action*, see Martin Barker's excellent *Action: The Story of a Violent Comic* (London: Titan 1990), and also chapters 2 and 3 in his *Comics: Ideology, Power and the Critics* (Manchester: Manchester University Press, 1989).

Fandom and direct sales

You just weren't supposed to read comics after puberty in this country . . . but then the industry caught on that if they added more sophisticated elements to the comics and added a bit more sex and violence, they could hang on to readers for a *lot* longer.

(Dez Skinn, publisher and veteran fan)[1]

The growth of an organised comics 'fandom' and of a network of specialist comic shops in the 1970s and 1980s marked the genesis of a new comics culture, separate from the mainstream and separate from the underground. The adult comics it spawned built on the achievements of the comix, and were to be the direct precursors of the majority of those available in the 1990s.

The first part of this chapter will attempt to explain the origins of organised fandom, the growth of the specialist shops and the emergence of the 'direct sales' method of distribution and retailing. The second part will look more closely at the adult comics that were either co-opted by the new culture, or grew directly from it. The story spans roughly the period from the mid-1960s, when fandom first began to get organised, to the mid-1980s and the media's discovery that comics had 'grown up'.

Fandom

Comics fandom grew out of comics collecting (or 'panelology' to give it its technical name). Adults had collected comics since the beginning of the form, mainly for nostalgic reasons. But although British comics had always had their fans, it was their American counterparts that gradually came to be more prized. As we have seen, they were generally glossier than British comics, with four-colour production, and exciting, attention-grabbing covers. Also, some were more sophisticated in content, and aimed at a slightly older (adolescent) readership which, again, had its attractions. To most collectors, it was the difference between Hollywood and the Ealing comedies.

Because American comics were first distributed on a regular basis in Britain in 1959, collecting only really took off as a hobby in the 1960s. Gradually, a small fraction of the overall readership began to take them more seriously, and instead of throwing issues away, kept them to file away in a collection. A selection process developed that privileged certain aspects of a comic – and certain creators – over others. Artwork, for instance, became much more appreciated than story content, with specifics like anatomical correctness and attention to detail being a sure sign of collectability. It was the beginning of a kind of 'connoisseur readership', and prices for collectable comics would eventually be calculated accordingly.

Most esteemed of all were the new Marvel comics, especially those drawn by Jack Kirby. Titles like *Fantastic Four* and *The Incredible Hulk* were much-admired for Kirby's explosive, imaginative style, and also for their relatively more complex story-lines (usually by Stan Lee). There were other favourite creators – Steve Ditko for his work on *Spider-Man*, for example – but generally Kirby was considered 'king', an epithet that would stay with him in fan circles for the rest of his career.[2]

Getting a series in sequence was a priority for collectors since the comics were sold in newsagents on a sale-or-return basis, which meant that once an issue became out of date it was sent back to the distributor (and therefore virtually impossible to obtain). This was especially a problem with the Marvel comics, which were designed to have tight continuities, with plots and situations closely interlaced from one issue to the next. (Indeed Marvel actively encouraged collecting as company policy.)[3] Thus, in order to obtain collectable titles, and to fill gaps in runs, fans had to develop a network of communication.

Mail-order was the obvious answer, and by the mid-1960s *Exchange and Mart* had become the focus of collectors' attention. It was here that individuals from different parts of the country advertised their lists of American comics to swop or sell: early traders included Dez Skinn in Yorkshire, Frank Dobson in London and Phillip Clarke in Birmingham.[4] It was a short step for proper mail-order businesses to develop from these beginnings. Mail-order grew very rapidly in the latter half of the 1960s, and as it boomed, it became increasingly obvious that a more organised approach to collecting would be required. Just as the British underground looked to America for inspiration, so too did British collectors.

In the US, panelology had already made the transition to organised 'fandom': by now, American fans had their own conventions, fan publications and so on. However, even American fandom wasn't entirely 'original' and had itself borrowed a good deal from science fiction fandom, which had a history of some thirty years behind it. Indeed, most of the earliest US comics 'fanzines' (a conflation meaning 'fan-magazine') covered SF as well.

A specialised fan press was the first aspect of organised fandom to emerge in Britain. The early fanzines tended to be primitive affairs, growing out of the mail-order lists and ideas borrowed from America. They were primarily concerned with giving the latest prices for collectable comics, and like their American counterparts often took in SF.

The earliest indigenous example was *Fantasy Advertiser* (1965) later to be joined by many others, notably *Comic Media News*, *BEM* (*Bug-Eyed-Magazine*) *Arken Sword* (*Ark*) and *Speakeasy*. American fanzines, meanwhile, could be obtained by post. Only gradually did these publications evolve to include proper articles, interviews, artwork illustrations and so on – the trappings, in other words, of today's comics press.

The first British fan convention took place in Birmingham in 1968. It was organised by Phillip Clarke and three others (who had met by coincidence at the 1964 World Science Fiction Convention in London), and was intended as an event where collectors could simply meet and trade. As such, it was not particularly sophisticated (a few stalls in a hall), and the total number of attendees was around seventy: 'That doesn't sound like a great number by today's standards', Clarke later recalled, 'but at the time we had no idea so many people were interested!'[5] Deemed an unqualified success, subsequent 'cons' were planned for succeeding years. Again, it was only gradually that they became more formalised to include discussion panels, auctions of artwork, special guest appearances, prize-giving ceremonies and the like.

Finally, actual specialist comics shops began to emerge. This was a natural progression, as the success of the various mail-order businesses and the growing popularity of the cons had shown the financial viability of such a step, and there had already been an historical precedent for an alternative comics retail system in the underground head-shop network. Meanwhile, in America, a number of specialist shops had already opened and were doing good business. Once again, it was the long-term fans themselves who put their money and effort into them, as opposed to entrepreneurs from outside.

The first shop in Britain was Dark They Were and Golden Eyed, which opened in London in 1969. It was followed by a clutch of others, the most well-known being Forever People in Bristol (1973), Nostalgia and Comics in Birmingham (1977) and Forbidden Planet in London (1978). Although many of the early shops were science fiction bookshops as well, later examples sold only comics. Almost all also ran a mail-order service.

The shops became the focus for the new culture. Although they sold a core of collectable comics, and this was their original reason for coming into existence, this was not enough to sustain them financially. Therefore, from the start they also sold general hot-off-the-press American imports – which meant predominantly Marvels and DCs.[6] Thus the clientele for the new shops tended to be a mixture of older collectors and a larger number of younger (adolescent) American comics fans. The big sellers in the 1970s tended to be titles like *The Hulk*, *Fantastic Four*, *Spider-Man* and old favourites *Superman* and *Batman*.

Figure 5.1 Advertisement for the Dark They Were shop. The figure depicted is a Lee/Kirby superhero, 'The Silver Surfer' (Published in *Cyclops*, no. 1 (1970))

Inevitably the shops had a particular atmosphere – by nature specialist and rather insular. They were also extremely 'male', dealing in a particular kind of macho power-fantasy: women were not made welcome. To outsiders therefore, the shops appeared as slightly sinister places – bizarre, gaudy and obsessive – and they had difficulty understanding how people could get so excited about something that had so little cultural worth in the first place.

But to fans the shops were often an alternative home. The service was informed and friendly, and it was possible to obtain comics and fanzines it was impossible to get hold of anywhere else. They thus had a certain magic, and fans would often travel many miles on a regular basis to visit them. By the end of the 1970s there were nine shops in all – not a large number by any means, but enough to sustain a 'scene' – and they were getting more numerous all the time. As one fanzine concluded in 1979: 'Comic shops are springing up faster than McDonalds!'[7]

If the founding of the shops was phase one in the development of organised fandom, by the end of the 1970s phase two was about to begin: the era of 'direct sales'. This initiated a new method of distributing and selling comics, and in the process sparked an unprecedented boom in American titles. Once again, events in Britain followed very much in the wake of those across the Atlantic.

By now in the USA, there were already approximately 400 shops, and it had been recognised by distributors and publishers that a specialised market meant a specialised demand. In other words, here was a captive audience for whom it was possible to calculate with some accuracy the number of a specific title that would sell.

A system developed whereby instead of publishers selling bundles of a mixture of comics to outlets in the expectation of a large number of returns (the traditional method for the news-stand market), they could now print exactly the number required by the specialist shops, and sell directly to them by means of specialised distribution. (Indeed, the system was devised by a distributor.) In addition, the arrangement enabled surplus stock to be sold as back-issues.

This 'direct sales' method of retailing thus cut out the need to over-print , and hence reduced overheads at a stroke. It also opened up the possibility of an entirely new market, as it became feasible to publish comics solely for the specialist shops – which is to say, not necessarily for sale in the newsagents (a technique the underground had earlier perfected in the headshops).

For Marvel and DC, this was a godsend. Newsagent sales had been declining quite drastically in America throughout the 1970s, but in the specialist market, direct sales represented the opportunity to cut costs and halt the decline. Marvel tested the water with a title called *Dazzler*, and was amazed to find it sold 400,000. From now on, this sector would be given much greater attention, and marketing strategies restructured around it.

But, it was't just the corporate giants who benefited. Soon new American publishers were springing up to take advantage. These were the so-called 'independents', generally set up by long-time fans specifically to compete with the duopoly in direct sales (it was generally futile to try to challenge their power-base on the news-stands, but here there were distinct opportunities). The new companies included Pacific, Eclipse, First and Fantagraphics, later to be joined by many more. Some, it should be said, were less independent than others, being tied to Marvel/DC through complex licensing arrangements.

With new players in the field, and a whole new market to exploit, the entire basis of the American comics industry began to change. To begin with, and perhaps most obviously, there was more variety in the kinds of comics for sale. Most independents were content to compete with Marvel and DC on the level of superhero titles and adolescent fantasy; this made sense, as it was what the already-available market desired. Some, however, did experiment with different subject-matter in an effort to carve their own niche, which in turn prompted Marvel and DC to compete and to be more ambitious. This widening of the agenda could also encompass adult material – as we shall see below.

By a similar logic, comics design and presentation now became important considerations – arguably for the first time in their history – as the various companies competed for customers' attentions. The 1980s is sometimes referred to as the 'designer decade', and it is true that ideas from graphic design were now incorporated into comics in an unprecedented fashion (as well as vice versa). It marked the beginning of a drive towards smarter comics, with different formats, at more expensive prices.

But, less obviously, direct sales led to two changed relationships: those between the industry and creators, and between the industry and fans. To look at the industry first: as we have seen, artists and writers had previously worked for a flat-page fee and with no control over royalties or copyright. But now the independents, in order to attract creators to work for them rather than Marvel or DC, began to offer major incentives in these areas. Pacific were the first to break the mould by offering both royalties and a measure of copyright control. This forced others to follow suit, including eventually Marvel and DC, thus finally achieving, within the mainstream, the conditions that had pertained in the underground over a decade earlier.[8]

Connected with this was the genesis of a 'star system'. Because the shops ordered specific numbers of comics it was possible for a publisher to see immediately which creators were 'selling' and which were not (in other words, to track with some accuracy a creator's progress). Thus, it made commercial sense to feature top creators' names more prominently on comics covers: the fans had already signalled their devotion to the creators by buying the comics in the first place, and this was a kind of official recognition – going totally against the tradition of keeping creators as anonymous as possible. In time, this would lead to a situation where the creators were actually more important in sales terms than the contents of the comic itself.

The knock-on effect of this was to open up the prospect of more self-motivated work, and the chance for writers and artists to think of themselves more as 'creators' (in the now-fashionable terminology) rather than workers on an assembly-line. Consequently, their newfound bargaining power led to greater freedom to deal with more sophisticated subject-matter, and to utilise more ambitious artistic techniques – notably involving strips that were fully painted.[9]

The other changed relationship was between the industry and fans. Now, a new obsessiveness entered fandom as buying for investment became endemic. This had been an element of collecting since the beginning, of course, but now the practice developed of 'double purchasing' – buying one comic to read plus another to keep in pristine condition in a plastic bag for speculative purposes. To cater to this new fan capitalism, thick 'price guides' were produced, with the latest prices calculated according to rarity; there were even new businesses specialising in comics restoration. For many fans, the hobby of comics collecting now became the business of comics investment. This caused a certain degree of hostility among the old-guard, and indeed from creators themselves. A new name was coined for the more blinkered fans

– 'fanboys', a contemptuous term implying attitudes that were anal-retentive, adolescent and emotionally arrested.

But paradoxically the fanboys were bread and butter to the industry, and publishers increasingly played up to them. Comics were produced in limited editions with free posters and badges, with embossed covers and so on – all gimmicks that were guaranteed to sell. Some titles were published with several different covers, a device designed to encourage fans to buy numerous issues of the same comic. Virtually every new title aimed at this market was published with some kind of hype.

But whatever the negative side of direct sales, it initiated a boom in America which was unprecedented since the early 1950s. The new comics demonstrated a previously unimagined variety of subject-matter in a wide selection of formats. Nevertheless, it was still very much the superheroes who ruled, which meant that Marvel and DC retained market-primacy: new fan favourites included the *New Teen Titans* (DC) and the 'mutant superhero' titles, such as the *X-Men* (Marvel).[10] The retail end of the market in America expanded accordingly. The shops multiplied exponentially to deal with demand – shooting up to around 2,000 by 1986. Conventions got bigger and more sophisticated, with artwork displays, discussion panels, special guest appearances and so on (the San Diego con was by far the biggest by the mid-1980s). Similarly, fanzines became more professional, with artwork illustrations, in-depth interviews, plus 'collecting' information (prominent examples were the *Comic Reader* and the *Comics Journal*). The success of the new system marked an incredible recovery from 'the bad old days' of the 1970s, and by the mid-1980s over half of all industry sales were accounted for by those to collectors. In short, direct sales had meant the consolidation of American fandom into the driving-force of the entire industry.

What all this meant for the British fan scene can be summed up very briefly. Events followed a very similar pattern with only a short time-lag. The idea of direct distribution was copied by entrepreneurs Nick Landau and Mike Lake, who set up Titan Distributors in 1977 (both men had been long-term fans, with Landau having set up his first importing business while still at college).[11] The number of shops went up to around fifty by 1986 – a more than six-fold increase from the decade before. Although not every American title was imported, Britain did see a similar expansion in range and variety. Once again, the new best sellers followed trends across the Atlantic (*X-Men* and *New Teen Titans* were similarly top titles).

Direct sales also meant the growth of new British companies to feed the new market. The two giants, IPC and DC Thomson, had viewed the growth of the fan scene with suspicion from the start, and showed no inclination to become involved now – sticking instead to their traditional base in the newsagents. So, in their place, others stepped in: Marvel, for instance, set up a subsidiary company, Marvel UK, to reprint material for the direct sales market (thereby avoiding freight costs) and also to originate titles – which they did during the 1980s with some success. Meanwhile, DC came to a similar reprinting/republishing arrangement with Titan Books, the publishing arm of Landau and Lake's wholesaling and retailing empire – a deal which was primarily responsible for making Titan Books the third biggest comics publisher in Britain by 1986.[12] There were also one or two British independents, notably Valkyrie, Acme, Escape and Harrier.

Fandom was similarly boosted: indigenous fanzines flourished (*Speakeasy* becoming the most well-known), while American examples were now imported on a regular basis. The site of the chief annual convention now moved to London, and took the name UK Comic Art Convention (UKCAC): by 1986 it was attracting around 500 people and could afford to bring over large numbers of 'star' names from America as special guests. Smaller gatherings, called 'marts', which concentrated on dealing, now took place in various parts of the country throughout the year. Price guides were now produced purely for the British market, and American vintage comics were imported in numbers to satisfy demand (including comics that had never before been available in Britain).

Thus, by the mid-1980s the British fan scene had blossomed into a self-sustaining culture, based on fifty shops, with new publishers – British and American – feeding it. Direct sales had consolidated the rise of the American comic in Britain, latent since the 1960s, and found a teenage readership out of the reach of traditional British comics. In Britain, as in America, the specialist market thrived while the rest of the industry slumped.

The comics

Having looked briefly at the evolution of this new culture, it is now time to turn our attention to the adult comics that were a part of that evolution. For even though the shops were primarily adolescent in orientation, and sold a majority of superhero titles, they also provided an outlet for a surprising variety of adult comics; after all, the older collectors could be expected to interest themselves in something a little more sophisticated than *Spider-Man*, while the adolescent clientele were getting older all the time.

The new adult comics built on the innovations of the underground, and applied them to areas of fiction and non-fiction previously thought the domain of novels and film. They tended to distance themselves from the counter-cultural emphasis on sex, drugs and radical politics, and to adopt a broader approach, drawing not from this one creative source like the underground, but from many. They are therefore difficult to categorise, but fall into three separate but overlapping groups: comics inspired by the science fiction renaissance; comics generated by direct sales; and titles which originated from alternative creative sources but which publishers found expedient to sell from the specialist shops. Our survey will conclude with a brief consideration of the role of sections of the fan press in encouraging their collective growth.

The first group, and the first to emerge chronologically, were adult comics concerned thematically with science fiction. They appeared during the transition period between the underground and the new fan culture in the mid-late 1970s, and were therefore – initially at least – orientated towards the news-stand market (since the head-shops were dying out, and the specialist shops were only gradually becoming established). They were thus often very similar to the undergrounds, and utilised many of the same creators, with the same arrangements for royalties, copyright and so on.[13]

They also grew out of the natural intersection between comics culture and science fiction culture. The interest of the hippie–underground readership in SF was widespread, and the same was as true, if not more so, for the fan collectors – the two groups often overlapped. We have seen how early comics fandom drew from the SF fandom tradition, how the early fanzines were SF fanzines also, and most of all, how the early comics shops tended to be SF bookshops as well.

Indeed, science fiction as a genre had been going through something of a renaissance in the late 1960s and 1970s. In 1969 America had put a man on the moon, an event generally recognised as inspiring a new era of 'space age' SF, with authors like Michael Moorcock and Philip K. Dick producing some of their best work, and movies like Stanley Kubrick's *2001* and (later) George Lucas's *Star Wars* exciting renewed attention in the field.

This coincided with the flowering of 'fantasy' and 'sword and sorcery' as sub-genres. The former was rooted in the hippie 'rediscovery' of the works of J.R.R. Tolkien, and involved stories more closely related to fairy-tales and romantic fiction than traditional technologically-based SF: typical ingredients were elves, wizards and quests set in odd medieval surroundings. 'Sword and sorcery' was tangentially connected, and had its basis in the rehabilitation of a lesser writer – American Robert E. Howard, creator of the 1930s pulp hero Conan the Barbarian. Again, distant pseudo-historical settings and magic were features, but usually only as a backdrop to gory tales concerning impossibly-muscled barbarians, bare-breasted amazons and sundry mythological monsters.[14]

The most influential SF comic came, unexpectedly, not from

Figure 5.2 Cover to *Métal Hurlant*, no. 1 (1975). Comics would never look quite the same. Art: Moebius. © 1975 Moebius/ Les Humanoides Associés

America, but from France. Here, an adult comic boom of a quite unique character had been occurring, itself partly inspired by the liber- ating ideals of the American underground. *Métal Hurlant* (1975), which literally translated means 'screaming metal', was a glossily- produced monthly showcasing the openly erotic and visually stunning work of a number of European creators. They included Phillippe Druillet, Enki Bilal and, above all, 'Moebius' (the pen-name for Jean Giraud), whose richly surreal strips 'Arzach' and 'The Airtight Garage' were instantly recognised as adult classics. Although, being in French, the comic could not be expected to be a commercial success, it was imported in small numbers into the headshops and specialist shops where it found an appreciative audience.[15]

    Métal Hurlant was quite unlike anything seen in Britain before, and made an impact on adult comics' creative development second only to the original undergrounds. Although the quality of the artwork often disguised a shallowness in storytelling (too often reliant on dramatic set-pieces and gratuitous sexism), it was clearly aimed at a relatively sophisticated readership. The tone aspired to be middle-brow and the adverts included the latest philosophical works of Roland Barthes, among others. Above all, its production-values were a revelation – many strips were fully-painted, often using a glossy 'airbrush' technique,[16] and it was printed on high quality magazine paper. France, it seemed, was prepared to treat comics with a respect they lacked in Britain and the US.

An American version of the comic was not long coming. *Heavy Metal* (a poor translation of the name, and nothing to do with the brand of rock music) appeared in 1977. Touted as 'The Adult Illustrated Fantasy Magazine', it sought to retain the high standards of its progenitor, and reprinted many of the best strips. Later, more space was given to American creators working in a similar vein – notably Richard Corben, Howard Chaykin and Vaughn Bodé.

Unlike the French version, *Heavy Metal* did get news-stand distribution, thus introducing talents like Moebius and Druillet to a much wider readership, and opening the way for similar magazines to follow. Nevertheless, because of its sex content (acceptable on the continent, but not in Britain), it tended to be displayed on the top shelf with the pornographic magazines. In the headshops and specialist shops, however, it was a cult favourite, and the spin-off albums of collected stories were correspondingly popular.[17]

Marvel were next to cash in, with their own glossy entitled *Epic Illustrated* (1980), which attempted to broaden the adult SF market by toning down the sex. Here American creators were given precedence, among them more mainstream names like Jim Starlin. It heralded a new adult imprint from Marvel, also called Epic, which began by reprinting in album-form stories from the magazine. (The new line was creator-owned – a major concession from the company, clearly inspired by the underground.) Although individual albums sold well, however, the anthology itself was an increasingly lacklustre affair, and never developed the same reader-loyalty as *Heavy Metal*. It was eventually cancelled in 1987.

Finally, Britain produced its own variation on the formula in the form of *Pssst!* (1982), which stuck more faithfully to the European paradigm, with lots of sex(ism), plenty of airbrush art and very high production standards. It was even financed by a wealthy Frenchman. But, despite the more liberated approach, there was a fatal flaw: the comic was edited by committee, resulting in a mish-mash of strips that failed to satisfy anybody. It did boast one truly worthwhile contribution, however, in the guise of 'The Adventures of Luther Arkwright', an epic-length story by Bryan Talbot, about an 'intra-dimensional agent' and his battle against the Puritan rulers of a fascistic Britain. The strip's sheer complexity and use of allegory marked it out as a major innovation in extended narrative.[18] But alas 'Arkwright' alone was not enough to redeem *Pssst!*, and having failed to gain widespread news-stand distribution the comic folded after only a year, with reported losses of £100,000.

Coming out simultaneously with these high-grade SF magazines were the so-called 'ground level' comics. These were much closer to the undergrounds in terms of production-values, and were usually in black and white. However, they too featured SF, and were often influenced by the work of European artists. The phrase 'ground level' itself was a marketing term meant to imply something half-way between 'under-ground' and 'above ground' (and did not really catch on among fans).[19]

American ground levels included the anthology *Star*Reach* (1974), notable mainly for attracting 'above-ground' creators disen-chanted with the financial arrangements at Marvel and DC, and *Elfquest* (1979), by Wendy and Richard Pini – a surprisingly gripping, densely-plotted drama about various communities of elves, very much in the Tolkien vein. There was also a major Canadian success in the form of *Cerebus the Aardvark* (1977) by Dave Sim, which began as a clever parody of the sword and sorcery genre in general, and Conan the Barbarian in particular, and developed into a complex satire on every-thing from state power to organised religion (see pp. 239–40). These comics were imported in small numbers and sold in the headshops and specialist shops, but did not receive wider distribution.

The British ground levels were slightly different in that they did attempt to follow the glossies on to the newsagents' shelves. They included *Brainstorm Fantasy Comix* (one issue only, 1977), a new direction for the *Brainstorm* stable, edited by Mal Burns, which fea-tured the first-published work of John Higgins; *Graphixus* (1977), also edited by Mal Burns, which included work by Brian Bolland, Hunt Emerson and Angus McKie, plus reviews of both underground and mainstream comics, and interviews with 'hot' creators (notably Moebius); and, finally, *Near Myths* (1978), 'Scotland's First Alterna-tive Comic', edited by Rob King, which was not only the first comic to serialise Luther Arkwright but also the first to feature the work of Grant Morrison (a sword and sorcery tale entitled 'Gideon Stargrave'). However, none of these titles managed to break into the W. H. Smith chain, and none lasted longer than five issues.

The second category of adult comics in our survey are those which emerged expressly out of the direct sales explosion of the late 1970s and early 1980s, and which were orientated specifically towards the specialist shops. These had less to do with the underground tra-dition (although in broad terms were obviously a product of the breaking down of barriers the underground represented), and were of two main types: those produced by the new independent companies, and those published by Marvel and DC.

Figure 5.3 Cover to *Near
Myths*, no. 5 (1980). Art:
Tony O'Donnell. © 1980
The creators

For the independents, competition in the specialist market led to
new initiatives being taken in subject-matter, and this could occasionally mean forays into adult material. Of course, there was a great deal
of variation in the lists of the new companies. Most imitated the Marvel
and DC product and tried to be as commercial as possible (for example,
Comico, First), while others could be almost as underground as the
underground (for example, Fantagraphics). Sometimes (for example,
in the case of Eclipse), lists would span the two extremes.

The first adult titles were very much influenced by earlier SF
comics (*Elfquest* and *Cerebus* can also be considered pioneering early
independents). However, some made efforts to get away from the
'undergroundy' feel of the ground levels, and attempted to raise
production standards. Crucial in this respect was *American Flagg!*
by Howard Chaykin (late of *Heavy Metal*, *Star*Reach* and *Epic*

Figure 5.4 A page from *American Flagg!*, no. 2 (1983). Art/script: Howard Chaykin. © 1983 The creator/First Comics

Illustrated), which was a success for First in 1983. It portrayed the high-octane adventures of a Jewish lawman, Reuben Flagg, in 2035 Chicago, and it mixed sex, action and satire in about equal measure. The design was very high quality, and featured dynamic panel layouts and a little-seen illustrative technique called 'duotone'. By upping the production stakes, the comic set a formula that would be frequently plagiarised in the future.

Increasingly, though, the independents came out with more personal and less fantastic work. A particular favourite in Britain was *Love and Rockets* (1982, Fantagraphics), which despite the fantasy and SF elements of its early issues (hence the 'Rockets' in the title), soon developed into one of the more 'realistic' comics on the market. Created by the three Hernandez Brothers – Jaime, Gilbert and, to a progressively lesser degree, Mario, it featured two main stories, both with women as the lead characters: one set in post-punk Los Angeles (by Jaime), and one in a mythical village in Mexico (by Gilbert). The comic was well-received critically, especially Jaime's crisp, hard-edged art and Gilbert's empathetic writing, which was compared frequently to that of Gabriel García Marquez. Quite unexpectedly, *Love and Rockets* became a bigger hit in Britain than in America.

The other most popular non-SF independents tended to fall broadly into the humour category. They included *Neat Stuff* (1985, Fantagraphics) by Peter Bagge, an hilarious variant on underground themes featuring 'The Bradleys', about a redneck Midwestern family; *Tales of the Beanworld* (1985, Eclipse) by Larry Marder, an entertaining metaphor for man's relationship with the environment, told in terms of a community of beans and including every issue a 'map of the known beanworld'; and *Flaming Carrot* (1984, Aardvark/Renegade), Bob Burden's delightfully surreal comedy about a half-man, half-carrot. The biggest seller was undoubtedly *Teenage Mutant Ninja Turtles* (1984, Mirage), by Kevin Eastman and Peter Laird. Originally an in-joke for adult collectors (parodying the teen-mutant titles – *X-Men* and the rest – and funny animal comics among others), the concept was later super-commercialised as a craze for children.[20]

Finally, some independents experimented with translating wider

Figure 5.5 Panel from 'Locas', *Love and Rockets*, no. 13 (1985). Art/script: Jaime Hernandez. © 1985 The creator

fiction from Europe that did not fit easily into the conventional SF mould. NBM (Nantier-Bell-Minoustchine) reprinted several albums starring *Corto Maltese*, by the Italian Hugo Pratt, about a seafaring adventurer who sided with the underdogs against colonialists in the 1910s. Catalan favoured more offbeat material including *Anarcoma*, by the Spaniard Nazario, a truly bizarre *noir* thriller which starred a transvestite gay detective; *Ranxerox*, by the Italians Stefano Tamburini and Gaetano Liberatore, an ultraviolent black comedy which starred 'a half-man, half-photocopier'; and *Click!*, by the Italian Milo Manara, an exquisitely-rendered slice of soft porn. Such albums were few in number and had a very limited following, but were nevertheless a continuing reminder of the sophistication of the comics scene in Europe.

But while the independents concentrated on carving out their ground, the American giants, Marvel and DC, had their own ideas about adult comics for the direct sales market. Rather than concentrating on creating new characters and comics, they revamped some of their existing titles to give them an adult 'edge'. (The main exception to this rule was Marvel's Epic line.) In this way they could re-use characters over whom they already owned copyright with the minimum extra expense. Although historically it had been the practice to modify characters in accordance with audiences' tastes, this was the first time it had been done with adults so much in mind.

The ground-breaking comic in this respect was *Daredevil*, an old Marvel superhero title with declining sales which was taken over by rising star Frank Miller in 1981. Miller had already made a name for himself doing the artwork for *Daredevil*, but now took over the writing as well. With more or less full artistic control, he remoulded what was an essentially run-of-the-mill vehicle into a fast-moving thriller, much influenced by the Dirty Harry movies of the time. Explicit violence, mixed with a clever use of 'white space' and shadow, gave it a spectacular intensity and filmic quality (not unlike *American Flagg!* on occasion). In terms of the character, 'The Man Without Fear' (his old sobriquet) became 'The Man Without Scruples'. *Daredevil* clawed its way back up the sales charts to become one of the industry's best selling titles, with sales of over 200,000 per month in Britain and America.

DC followed a similar path with *Swamp Thing*, another old title, about a half-man, half-plant swamp monster. Writer Alan Moore (head-hunted from *2000AD*) re-located the character firmly in the 1980s by turning the story into an ecological fable – the Swamp Thing becoming a symbol for Green consciousness, a sort of 'god of vegetation'. Unlike Miller, Moore was less interested in movies than in contemporary politics, and used the comic to comment upon US gun laws, feminism and multinational economics. It was, in the words of one

Figure 5.6 Cover to *Daredevil*, no. 184 (1982). A superhero with a .44 magnum. Art: Frank Miller. © 1982 Marvel Comics Group

critic, 'as intelligent as a comic about a swamp monster can get',[21] and achieved widespread success.[22]

    Daredevil and *Swamp Thing* were particularly popular because, more than any other adult titles, they appealed to the ever-increasing pool of post-adolescent American comics fans. Many of these undoubtedly felt a little embarrassed about continuing to buy *X-Men* and *Spider-Man*, but were reluctant to give up on the genre they loved. Thus giving a sophisticated kink to a familiar formula proved the perfect answer. Many other revamps were to follow, and both Miller and Moore were to notch up blockbuster hits in 1986 and 1987 with *Dark*

Knight and *Watchmen* respectively (these will be discussed in greater detail in chapter 6).

The third and final category of 'mature' work to be sold from the specialist shops were comics which were not strictly a development of fandom, but which publishers were satisfied to sell from the fan-shops in any case (in other words, they 'piggybacked' into the network). These included the avant-garde, the small press and the continuing underground.

The avant-garde was a misnomer in many respects. It was a label fanzine critics tended to apply to work that was 'not commercial' – though in fairness the comics were often sufficiently unlike anything else on the market to describe them any other way. If there were characterising features to them, they included a willingness to experiment, a commitment to self-motivated work and often a 'fine-arts'

Figure 5.7 Cover to *Raw*, no. 2 (1980). Art: Joost Swarte. © 1980 The creators

orientation (some were also sold in arts centres and art galleries). They were the antithesis of the mass-produced superhero comics, and at the same time a reaction against the fantasy vogue in adult comics, and were associated with two publishing houses in particular: Raw in America and Escape in Britain.

Raw Books and Graphics took its name from the archetypal avant-garde title *Raw* (1980), an anthology co-edited by Art Spiegelman and Françoise Mouly. Publicised as, among other things, 'The Graphix Magazine for Damned Intellectuals', it wore its art influences on its sleeve, and came in a large (10 inch by 13 inch) format to emphasise the visual ('so that people literally had to take the comic's measure', as Spiegelman later explained).[23] The strips were a mixture of work by those underground creators who were still working, unorthodox material by new American talent (who were often unable to find a platform anywhere else) and experimental or artistically interesting work from Europe.

Kim Deitch and Spiegelman, both representing the old underground, were regular contributors (Spiegelman's story 'Maus', about the Nazi holocaust was the anchor-strip, and will be discussed in more detail in chapter 6), while newer names included Drew Friedman, whose mesmerising pointillist parodies were often incomprehensible to anybody without a detailed knowledge of Hollywood 1950s B-movies, and Mark Beyer, whose abstract 'rag-doll' art style contrasted strikingly with the often quite conventional nature of his narratives. Meanwhile, Jacques Tardi from France and Joost Swarte from the Netherlands showed that there was a very different side to European comics to that portrayed in either *Heavy Metal* or the non-SF albums. *Raw* was thus an eclectic, classy – if often self-indulgent – mixture and garnered a small but devoted readership, rising from an initial 5,000 to 20,000 by 1986. These sales were miniscule compared to those of the *Daredevils* and *Swamp Things*, but, against this, the comic stood unquestionably as the most innovative title of the 1980s, and its influence was far-reaching.

In time *Raw* gave rise to a number of 'one-shots', which included some of the best and most experimental comics of the period. Among them were Gary Panter's *Jimbo*, a collection of scratchily-drawn 'punk' parables; Jerry Moriarty's *Jack Survives*, a minimalist homily on small-town living; and Charles Burns's *Big Baby*, drawn in a disturbingly skewed 1950s style, in which a child's imagined fear of monsters is juxtaposed with the real fears of the adult world.

Across the Atlantic, Escape Publishing represented Britain's home-grown contribution to the avant-garde. Again the company had its origins in a comic, *Escape*, founded by Paul Gravett and Peter Stanbury in 1983.[24] Openly inspired by *Raw*, it too had its underground contributors (Hunt Emerson appeared in early issues), and also

Figure 5.8 Cover to *Escape*, no. 3 (1983). A major step forward for British comics. Art: Chris Long. © 1983 The creators

exhibited a commitment to publishing new European material (like *Raw*, featuring the work of Tardi and Swarte).

But *Escape* was different in several important respects. Unlike *Raw*, it did not just republish European material, but took its stylistic cue from European comics. Its opening editorial encouraged readers to think of it as 'UKBD' – 'United Kingdom Bandes Dessinées' (the French word for comics) – and critical articles and reviews, which were often of a high standard, were introduced in the manner of European critical journals. Additionally, it increasingly featured home-grown material by a post-underground wave of creators. This included the earthy autobiographical vignettes of Myra Hancock, the dark and disturbing anthropomorphics of Tim Budden and the ethereal adult fairy-tales of Ed Pinsent. In tapping into this well-spring of previously

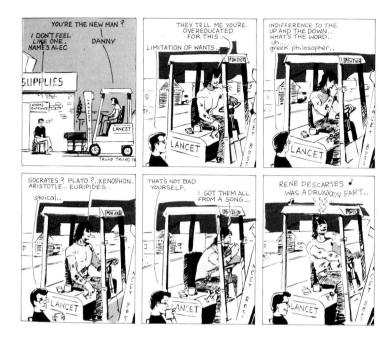

Figure 5.9 Panels from *Alec* (1984). Art/script: Eddie Campbell. © 1984 The creator

undiscovered talent, *Escape* marked a quantum leap from *Pssst!* and the other British SF comics, and represented the most progressive indigenous title since the underground. Like *Raw*, its influence was in inverse proportion to its sales.

Escape also had its one-shots, including Dave Thorpe's *Doc Chaos* (art by Phil Elliott), a politically-aware thriller about a character who was able to inhabit different people's bodies; Phil Laskey's *Night of the Busted Nose*, a 'modern love story' set in a Midlands town; and Eddie Campbell's *Alec* trilogy, a series of superbly vivid (if sometimes averagely drawn) semi-autobiographical stories about an apathetic bar-philosopher – a clever comic about a smart alec.

The 'small press' was another catch-all term, this time for comics with small print-runs which usually meant that they were self-produced photocopies. These emerged in the late 1970s as a result of advances in xerox technology, in the wake of the punk fanzine explosion, and ranged in subject-matter from adventure and comedy (*Viz*, a comic we shall be looking at in detail in chapter 8, was originally a small press comic) to more avant-garde work. Issue runs were usually minute (sometimes in the tens), and titles tended to be sold through the post, via ads in fanzines and elsewhere, or at cons and marts – though the more enlightened specialist shops did allow them a shelf or two. The small press was thus truly the heir to the original underground Do-It-Yourself ethic.

Very few small press comics were American as it was simply not profitable for distributors to import them. As for the British scene, the

Figure 5.10 Cover to *Fast Fiction*, no. 12 (1984). Art: Ed Pinsent. © 1984 The creators

most visible aspect was the 'Fast Fiction' mail-order service, which began as an ad hoc organisation founded by Paul Gravett in 1981, and had as its principal meeting-place the regular London marts. Eventually *Fast Fiction* became an anthology comic in its own right, showcasing some of the best of the small press talents. Many of *Escape's* future stars received their first exposure there.

Finally, no survey of the adult comics in the specialist shops would be complete without some mention of the undergrounds. Although, as we have seen, the underground went into a steep decline in the late 1970s, it continued to be a force in the 1980s: the headshops may have gone, but the fan-shops provided a new outlet (the division between the two cultures should therefore not be exaggerated). One British company in particular kept the flame burning: Knockabout, founded and run by Tony and Carol Bennett, which imported American comix as well as originating material, including the eclectic and often hilarious *Knockabout* anthology (1980).

Indeed, many creators from the original comix boom produced some of their best work in this period. Robert Crumb, for example, made something of a comeback in 1981 as editor and chief contributor to the anthology *Weirdo*, taking his 'confessionals' to sublime heights; while in 1985 Gilbert Shelton, in collaboration with Paul Mavrides, produced the first instalment of the excellent *Idiots Abroad*, in which the Freak Brothers travelled the world and discovered that hippie values still had a place in the materialist Reagan–Thatcher era. Although, in Britain, many of the original creators had gone into

Figure 5.11 Panels from 'Uncle Bob's Mid-life Crisis', *Weirdo*, no. 7 (1983). Art/script: Robert Crumb. © 1983 The creator

mainstream comics, some continued to produce their best work for the underground: Hunt Emerson, for example, was the subject of much media attention in 1986 for his best-selling *Lady Chatterley's Lover*, a slapstick interpretation of the once-banned D. H. Lawrence classic.

Unfortunately, it was also true that of all the comics sold from the specialist outlets, the undergrounds were the ones that attracted the negative attention of the authorities.[25] Knockabout were subject to numerous police and customs seizures during the period, and in 1983 went on trial at the Old Bailey charged with obscenity. As had happened in the earlier *Nasty Tales* trial, the defendants were found not guilty, though the episode was financially damaging for the company in the long run.[26] In true underground fashion, the victory was subsequently celebrated in a comic, the *Bumper Knockabout Trial Special*, the proceeds of which went towards the company's costs, while *Lady Chatterley's Lover* (published by Knockabout) was another oblique comment on the issue of censorship.

These, then, were the three main categories of adult comics. As has been intimated, the crossover between them was enormous: some independents published the same creators as titles by Marvel and DC, some undergrounds the same as the independents, some small press the same as the avant-garde, and so on. (An in-demand creator like Hunt Emerson could quite happily turn up in just about any subgroup, and indeed did.) Yet, for all that, there were as many differences as similarities: ultimately a *Raw* fan was unlikely to get very excited about *Daredevil*, and vice versa.

The only thing that all the comics had in common was their adult nature, and this was something that was increasingly recognised by sections of the fan press over the years. Duly, with the progressive growth in numbers of adult comics, it became possible for fanzines to concentrate less on traditional adolescent fare and to take a much more selective line – to adopt a more critical perspective on the monthly product, and to review the *Daredevils* and *Raw*s on their own merits as part of the same 'adult' milieu. This restructuring of certain fanzines' agendas was often portrayed as simply 'raising the standards of criticism', but what it meant in practice was turning them into 'adult comics fanzines'.

The pioneering title in this respect was the American *Comics Journal*. Under the editorship of Gary Groth, superhero and 'collecting' stories were progressively eschewed in favour of evaluative criticism of the more mature titles, coupled with a campaigning attitude to creators' rights and a scholarly approach to comics history. Although the style was often verbose, the *Journal* was in effect a new kind of fanzine, and provided much-needed proof that such publications need not be mindlessly sycophantic and uncritical.[27]

Other fanzines were clearly influenced by its direction –

notably, in Britain, *FA* (previously *Fantasy Advertiser*) and to a lesser extent *Speakeasy*. (The articles in *Escape* were comparably analytical, but drew inspiration more from the European *Cahiers de la bande dessinée*.) At conventions, too, it was noticeable that a more critical element was creeping in, manifested by the introduction of panel discussions on topics such as censorship and women in comics.

These trends should not be exaggerated. Most fanzines were more than happy to continue as before, catering for the traditional fan readership in the traditional way. It would also be wrong to give the impression that conventions were suddenly transformed into campaigning literary workshops. But, the new awareness of the possibilities of serious criticism did have an impact, and was undoubtedly to the good in terms of raising standards in comics generally.

In this way, adult comics became more and more a part of fan culture in the 1970s and 1980s. In terms of their development, this was both a strength and a weakness. A strength because without the institutions of fandom – the shops, the marts, conventions and so on – the new material would have had no other outlet; a weakness because the new adult comics were inevitably restricted by being part of a larger comics culture – obsessive, insular and based on collecting adolescent superhero titles. If the new adult comics were ever to find a wider audience outside the specialist shops, the crucial question was how to escape the 'fanboy' image. The answer was to come in the form of three outstanding titles, and a new name for an old concept: the 'graphic novel'.

Further reading

Sadly, there are no histories of fandom as such. However, Gary Groth and Robert Fiore (eds), *The New Comics* (New York: Berkley 1988) includes illuminating interviews with many prominent creators. Back issues of fanzines from the period, and of price guides, are another useful source. Especially recommended are the *Comics Journal*, *FA*, *Speakeasy* and also articles in *Escape*. For background information on the nature of science fiction culture, and the SF renaissance of the 1960s and 1970s, see Brian Aldiss's *Trillion Year Spree* (London: Paladin 1986).

'Comics grow up!': dawn of the graphic novel

There was a marketing opportunity ... My job was to develop a semantic the general public and the book trade could understand.

(Igor Goldkind, ex-Titan Books PR)[1]

Between the summer of 1986 and that of 1987 adult comics, as they had developed in the specialist shops over the previous decade or more, were discovered by the mainstream press. The result was a flood of articles to the effect that comics had suddenly 'grown up' – an erroneous interpretation, but one which nevertheless brought them to the attention of a new audience outside the narrow confines of fandom. An unprecedented boom in production was initiated, and comics found a wide market among older readers for the first time since the First World War.

The explosion was sparked by three titles in particular (hereafter referred to as 'the Big 3' for convenience's sake). All were American in origin, all had their roots in direct sales and all were published in book form in Britain within a year of each other. We can look at each in turn.

Batman – The Dark Knight Returns (1986) by Frank Miller

Originally in four parts, this was published as a single volume in America by DC and in Britain under the Titan imprint. This was the revisionist superhero story to top them all – not of a minor character this time, but of one of the best-known: Batman, a.k.a. The Caped Crusader, a.k.a. The Dark Knight. Frank (*Daredevil*) Miller took the myth back to its macabre 1930s origins, while at the same time giving it a cynical 1980s sensibility. Thus Batman was portrayed not as the square-jawed law-enforcer of earlier comics, nor as the camp, pop-art figure of the classic 1960s TV series, but as a brooding psychopath, 50 years old and still traumatised by the death of his parents. This was Batman as the avenging vigilante, and, in characteristic Miller fashion, the comic was often shockingly violent: for example, Batman actually tries to kill the Joker (as opposed to turning him over to the authorities) and at one point blinds him in one eye. 'Batman is an absolute control freak', Miller later explained, 'the Joker ... represents the chaos Batman despises, the chaos that killed his parents.'[2]

Imaginative and viscerally appealing it may have been, but the

politics of the story were more than a little confused. Whereas *Daredevil* had been a more-or-less straightforward superhero story plus violence, here there were added satirical elements. For instance, President Reagan is shown condoning the American invasion of a small country (not unlike Nicaragua), while Superman makes an appearance as an agent of the American government there. Yet at the core of the story is the figure of Batman and his bloody crusade, outside the law, against crime: essentially a fascist personality (very much in the vein of the Dirty Harry movie character Miller so admired) but without the irony that characterised, say, Judge Dredd. It was a dubious mix, and some critics would later condemn the comic for its parallels with the true-life case of Bernhard Goetz, the New York vigilante subway killer. At best it made for an uncertain tone.

Watchmen (1987) by Alan Moore and Dave Gibbons

Another superhero revisionist story from DC, originally in twelve parts, again this was published as a book in Britain by Titan.[3] Moore and Gibbons had first worked as a team at *2000AD*, and here resuscitated the partnership for an epic story about a group of aging superheroes (the Watchmen) who are forced out of retirement when one of their number is assassinated. The plot, structured like a Chinese puzzle, leads them to the killer, but only after the conflicting world-views of the main protagonists have been juxtaposed. There were many similarities with *Dark Knight*. *Watchmen* also dealt with

costumed characters in the 'real' world, and also contained moments of
extreme violence.

   But unlike *Dark Knight*, *Watchmen* questioned vigilantism –
'Who Watches the Watchmen?' was one of the comics' key conun-
drums. It also went deeper into other aspects of superhero lore (often
with understated wit): the Night Owl character was sexually impotent
without his owl costume; Dr Manhattan originally got his astounding
powers by being zapped in a nuclear accident (in the established
superhero/SF tradition), but found that the radiation he emitted was
apparently giving friends cancer; Rorschach was a psychopath, and
lived by an extreme code of retributive justice;[4] Sally Jupiter, the main
female character, was forced into the 'glamorous' life of a superhero by
her domineering mother. In commenting on these various issues and
psychological impulses, Moore's work was clearly in a much more
liberal vein politically than *Dark Knight*. 'All comics are political',
Moore said later, 'all I was doing was commenting from an alternative
perspective to the majority.'[5] Though undoubtedly pretentious in
places, *Watchmen* still remains the most accomplished of the superhero
revisionist comics.

Maus (1987) by Art Spiegelman

Originally a continuing story in *Raw*, in six parts, this was collected as a single volume by Penguin Books.[6] It told the true story of Vladek Spiegelman's experiences of the Nazi holocaust, as recorded by his son, Art, and presented in anthropomorphic terms, with Jews as mice, Germans as cats and Poles as pigs. It was also an autobiography in the sense that the story partly concerns the author's relationship with his father in the present-day, and the way in which the legacy of the holocaust affects that relationship. The historical period covered spans roughly from 1935, when Vladek ran a business in Poland, to 1944, and his arrival at 'Mauschwitz'. His experiences in the final year of the

Figure 6.3 A page from *Maus* (1987). Art/script: Art Spiegelman. © 1987 The creator

war were recounted in continuing episodes in *Raw*, and published as a second volume in 1992.

A disturbing and intensely honest work, Maus ran the obvious risk of being accused of trivialising the holocaust. But instead, the characterisation of Jews as mice only added to the sense of their isolation and victimisation. Spiegelman explained later that

> the preface quotes Hitler's words that 'The Jews are undoubtedly a race, but they are not human', and it was just a metaphor that kept coming back to me: it was clear to me that drawn as people, the comic would not have worked so well. [7]

These 'funny animals' certainly were not funny, and far from being exploitative, the device opened up a new way of dealing with an 'impossible' subject. [8] *Maus* was unquestionably a landmark comic, and was also acclaimed as a major work in holocaust literature generally.

These three titles had in common their large scale, their quality and above all their adult nature (which is not to say that they were not bought by younger readers). Published almost simultaneously, they were perceived by a naive press not familiar with comics fandom (the author of this book included, it should be admitted) as constituting a new and historically unique trend. It was as if an 'adult comics revolution' had taken place, with a 'new breed' taking this quintessentially juvenile medium into hitherto unexplored areas.

'Comics Grow Up' became a regular headline on the arts pages, with a flood of articles on the Big 3. Sometimes the pieces would be general in tone, and take in other titles like *Swamp Thing* or *Raw*; sometimes *Maus* would be treated separately due to the fact it was published by Penguin, and therefore automatically had a status the others did not; sometimes *Watchmen* and *Dark Knight* were the focus due to the similarity of their subject-matter. Whatever the angle, inevitably the coverage tended to concentrate on the novelty aspect – analysing the comics for how they were different rather than for what they were (at times, it was almost a case of 'wow! comics about holocaust victims and psychopathic superheroes!').

Everybody from the *Observer* to the tabloids took up the story, though, as ever, the music press and newer 'style press' were generally first off the mark (having maintained contact with what was going on in comics since the early days of *2000AD*). [9] During this period it seemed impossible to pick up a printed publication without some mention of 'the adult revolution' in comics. Later, the story would be taken up by radio and TV.

Figure 6.4 The press
discover a fresh arts story,
1986–7

The willingness of the newspapers to cover comics, when previously the medium had been ignored except for occasional 'scandals'
(the horror comics, the underground, *Action*), can also in part be
explained by the much wider intellectual debate occurring at the time
on the nature of culture – which caused no end of confusion among
arts editors as to what to include in their pages. Very simplistically,
with the growth of cultural studies in tertiary education and the
fashionableness of post-modernist theory (which nobody in the media
seemed properly to understand), it became increasingly acceptable to
think of 'culture' as including not just the 'high arts' – opera, prose
literature, fine art – but also areas such as television, video, rock music
and 'pop' culture generally. The barriers between 'high' and 'low' culture, it seemed, were, if not breaking down, then leaking badly, and
there was pressure on the 'arbiters of taste' to expand their horizons.[10]

    This was the point at which the industry PR stepped in to exploit
the situation. Once it became clear that there was an opening in the
media for comics coverage, and that the idea of comics growing up was
being taken seriously, publishers began to work to sustain the story in

order to keep the profits flowing. Thus the concept of a 'new breed' of adult comics was nurtured from within the industry itself, sometimes quite cynically, via massive advertising and PR. For the first time in a decade, the industry stopped concentrating solely on fandom and lifted its eyes to the potentially bigger audience outside.

A major part of this PR hype was the marketing of the Big 3 as 'graphic novels'. The term had several advantages from a publicity perspective. First, it was used as a device to mark them out as something new, to distance them from the childish connotations of the word 'comic'.[11] By the same token it hopefully elevated them to the status of novels.[12] Second, it had the added advantage of associating them with the European comics scene, where (as has been intimated, and as we shall see in more detail in chapter 15) album-format comics had long been culturally respectable and read by all ages. Third, it was even suggested that the graphic novel might be the next stage in the evolution of literature, and could take over from the novel entirely. The novel was dying, it was argued, while at the same time forms of visual communication were growing (as was shown by the popularity of video games, and advances in the technology of Virtual Reality). Graphic novels therefore fitted neatly into a 'self-evident' historical progression: they were, in the fashionable phraseology of the time, 'literature for the post-literate generation'.[13]

Particularly important in this resculpting of comics' image in Britain was Igor Goldkind, a talented PR consultant with no previous experience in the comics field. In a bold move, he had been hired by Titan Books (publishers of two of the Big 3 in Britain) with the specific aim of promoting comics to a wider public. This he did with some vigour, sending out press releases, setting up press conferences and generally boosting the idea of adult albums. (Goldkind's auxiliary significance, therefore, was to bring to comics a PR sensibility previously thought to be characteristic of other areas of publishing.)

Here was more grist to the press's mill. Not only were the comics different in quality, but also in form. With prompting from Goldkind and others, journalists began to suggest that Britain was moving towards Europe in terms of its attitude to comics, and that it would not be long before a 'general' readership would be picking up graphic novels as readily as any other kind of fiction. Indeed, some went further, arguing for the special 'importance' of graphic novels as the heralds of a new era in visual literacy. All the signs were there, in short, that the British public was on the verge of accepting comics as a valid medium of expression. Very soon, it was confidently predicted, it would be no embarrassment to read a comic on the bus.

However, the graphic novel hype created a false impression in certain crucial respects. Certainly the 'graphic novel' did exist: it is a definable category of comic – a longer than usual work, in book form, with a thematic unity. Each of the Big 3 could therefore be justifiably described as such. Where PR strayed from the truth, however, was in suggesting that the form was something new. This was certainly not the case: graphic novels can be traced to children's comics of the 1940s, while the term as such had been in use in fandom since the late 1970s (the history of the graphic novel will be discussed in greater detail in chapter 18).

As for the idea that the graphic novel was somehow on the verge of taking over from the prose novel as the reading matter for a post-literate society, this too was manifestly far-fetched. The twin concepts of 'the death of the novel' and 'the growth of visual literacy' were both open to attack on a number of levels. [14] Interestingly, the theory echoed similar claims that had emerged during the early years of cinema in the 1900s, and of television in the 1950s: neither of those mediums had sounded the death-knell for the printed page, so the prospect of comics doing so was equally remote.

But whatever the true situation, as a PR exercise the idea of the graphic novel as a dynamic new form worked perfectly. This, coupled with the fortuitous timing of the publication of the three comics (both in terms of coinciding with each other, and with the new readiness of the press to treat popular culture seriously), and their obvious quality, served to open up a whole new market.

The immediate result was to attract a new kind of reader into the specialist shops. Often, these customers had little or no knowledge of fandom, and exhibited little interest in buying the traditional bit-part comics, but instead went for the media-hyped albums (this was especially true of *Dark Knight* and *Watchmen*, which had already been huge hits in their original form, and were now sold over again). As one London shop-owner explained, 'in the old days, if non-fans had come into the shop at all, they were very embarrassed – I've had to put comics in brown paper bags like pornography. But the new book format seemed to short-circuit that psychological barrier'. [15] Later, a proportion of this new clientele did develop a more wide-ranging interest in comics, and formed the basis for an expanded collector culture in the late 1980s and 1990s.

But more significantly, an entirely new outlet for comics was opened up – mainstream bookshops. *Maus* was published by Penguin, and so was taken up automatically; but *Dark Knight* and *Watchmen* also had few problems getting stocked. Of course, bookshops had sold certain kinds of picture books in the past – most notably children's albums and Christmas stocking-filler cartoon compilations like *Garfield* and *Andy Capp*. However, this was the first time comic books *per se* had been taken on board in any numbers. [16] It was a major step forward, not least because it made them accessible to a public who may either have felt intimidated by the fan shops (this applied particularly to women), or who may never have otherwise come across them. Igor Goldkind later summed things up:

> Now there was a possibility of reaching readers who had no preconceptions about comics, who hadn't read twenty years of Marvel and DC output. From a publishing point of view, we could now attempt to sell something a little bit more sophisticated than knock 'em down violence.[17]

In this way, each of the Big 3 became bestsellers. *Dark Knight* did the best business – mainly because it was about a character familiar to most people from TV – selling approximately 50,000 copies within a year in the UK and remaining on the *Sunday Times* bestseller list for 40 weeks; then came *Watchmen* (40,000 copies); then *Maus* (20,000 copies).[18] The respective authors and artists became celebrities, and because they were supposedly involved with 'graphic novels', and not 'comics', they were often treated with a hitherto unprecedented seriousness. It was a long way from the days when the key characteristic of a comics creator was anonymity.

Indeed, one creator in particular was focused upon by the media: Alan Moore. Although all the comics were American in origin, Moore represented a British 'stake' in what was going on (something which neatly disguised the fact that there had been hardly any British investment in direct sales over the previous decade). He was adopted as a kind of spokesperson for adult comics – a task he fulfilled with great patience, as virtually every interested journalist buttonholed him for his views. He was soon dubbed 'Britain's First Comics Megastar', and for once the media analysis rang true.

Further reading

The best general source on *Dark Knight* is Roberta Pearson and William Uricchio (eds), *The Many Lives of Batman* (London: BFI Publishing/Routledge 1991), which contains an insightful interview with Frank Miller. For *Watchmen*, the video *Watch the Men – Dave Gibbons and Alan Moore* (London: Acme Video/CA Productions 1988) consists of useful interviews with the two creators. Both titles are key texts in Richard Reynolds' *Superheroes* (London: Batsford 1992). *Maus* is covered in some detail from a literary perspective in Joseph Witek's excellent *Comic Books as History: The Narrative Art of Jack Jackson, Art Spiegelman, and Harvey Pekar* (Jackson, Mississippi: University of Mississippi Press 1989); and from a semiotic viewpoint in Steve Baker's *Picturing the Beast* (Manchester: Manchester University Press 1992). Additionally, all the creators of the Big 3 are interviewed in Gary Groth and Robert Fiore (eds), *The New Comics* (New York: Berkley 1988).

From boom to bust

Yet how healthy is the state of this long-awaited New-foundland? Comics have got themselves a good press over the last few years after years of ridicule . . . but how many are actually worth reading?

(Editorial, *Speakeasy* fanzine, 1989)[1]

The events of 1986–7 burst the dam for adult comics. The period that followed saw a flood of new material orientated at the market opened up by the Big 3, as publishers new and old rushed to cash in. Unfortunately, but perhaps inevitably, the keynotes of the boom were greed, haste and over-production. As a result, very few of the new comics were of a comparable quality to the Big 3, and a sort of comics South Sea Bubble was created as they became the fastest-growing area in both British and American publishing. It could not last, and the bubble eventually burst in 1990–2, precipitating a rapid decline, and leaving public perceptions of the medium largely unchanged.

There were three main areas of expansion: fandom, the book-shops and the newsagents. Because the boom had originated from within fandom, trends tended to amplify those outlined in chapters 5 and 6: most new titles were aimed at the 16–24 age-range, and were American in origin – although British creators were still very much to the fore (as we shall see, names from *2000AD* constantly reappear). Moreover, the 'graphic novel' now became ubiquitous, as virtually everything was now published in, or repackaged into, the now-fashionable format. The sheer scale of the boom, however, meant that comics publishing in general lost its focus: if the following survey seems somewhat sprawling, therefore, that is because it is a reflection of the way the situation seemed at the time. For the same reasons, it is also necessarily more selective.

To look at fandom first. The boom here was undoubtedly the most dramatic and the most sustained. The number of shops rocketed from around fifty in 1986 to approximately 300 in 1992. (This number included 'chains' of several branches such as those owned by Virgin and Forbidden Planet.) It was a gigantic leap, and meant that now every major town in the country had its own comics shop – with many boasting several. At the same time, attendance at UKCAC grew from 500 to around 3,000, leading to the institution in 1990 of another major annual convention in Glasgow – 'GlasCAC'.

There were also more publishers, as yet more independents

joined the fray. Big players included, from America, Tundra (founded by Kevin Eastman from the profits made from the *Teenage Mutant Ninja Turtles*), and Dark Horse (who specialised in comics about characters licensed from movie companies). In addition, there were roughly fifty others. From Britain, new publishers included Trident in Leicester, Sideshow in Sheffield and Mad Love in Northampton (founded by Alan Moore in an effort to side-step the disadvantages of working for the major companies).

This expansion of fandom was not entirely due to the influence of adult comics, but was instead more an indication that increasing numbers of adults were becoming collectors. In the immediate post–1986 period, collecting was reckoned by some sources to be the fastest growing hobby in the world. Thus it should be borne in mind that the regular superheroes – *Spider-Man*, *X-Men* and the like – continued to outsell the adult titles in this market. As a corollary, buying for investment was being taken much more seriously, with prices for vintage titles reaching stratospheric levels, and comics being recommended by some financial analysts as the 'fourth most reliable movable commodity investment'.[2] Having said that, adult comics were a far greater proportion of the total production than before.

The main companies to benefit were Marvel and DC, primarily because they were in a position to capitalise on the vogue for revisionist superheroes set in motion by *Dark Knight* and *Watchmen*.[3] Both companies were now part of much larger media corporations – New World Pictures and Warner Communications respectively – and were able to consolidate on the economic advantages this could bring. This was especially true in the case of DC, and in 1989 the movie *Batman*, inspired by the success of *Dark Knight*, was produced by Warners. This not only became the fastest-grossing movie of all time, but was also the subject of an unprecedentedly successful merchandising campaign (see also pp. 216–20).

Thus, in terms of newly-originated material, the revisionist superheroes were by far the biggest bandwagon. The best of the new Batman titles included *The Killing Joke* (Titan/DC 1988) by Alan Moore and Brian Bolland, a sadistic exploration of the psychology of the Joker, and *Arkham Asylum* (Titan/DC 1989) by Grant Morrison and Dave McKean, a similarly dark psycho-drama involving all the Bat-foes locked up in the eponymous institution. These were followed by more gimmicky titles, such as the computer-generated *Digital Justice* (Titan/DC 1990), the self-explanatory *Batman 3D Graphic Album* (with 3D spectacles supplied) (Titan/DC 1990) and the pitting of Batman against Judge Dredd in the best-selling *Judgement on Gotham* (Fleetway/DC 1991).[4]

There were numerous other revisions of the superhero genre, and of established superhero characters. Commercial hits included *Marshal Law* (Marvel 1989) by Pat Mills and Kevin O'Neill, an ultra-violent, ultra-cynical satire, and *Animal Man* (DC 1989) by Grant Morrison and Charles Truog, a kind of superhero-as-embodiment-of-animal-rights fable. Others numbered *Black Orchid* (DC 1988), *Black-hawk* (DC 1989), *Green Arrow* (DC 1988) and *Brat Pack* (King Hell/Tundra 1990). The list is endless.

Clearly, instead of being 'the last word in superhero comics', as some pundits had suggested, *Dark Knight* and *Watchmen* had completely revitalised the genre. Certainly some titles were imaginative and had something to say; most, however, were dire plagiarists that rightly drew criticism for being obtusely self-referencing and only spuriously 'adult'. As Alan Moore commented at the time: 'It doesn't matter how sophisticated they are, they're still about men with their underpants over their trousers.'[5]

Other genres that had been popular in fandom before 1986 also found a wider audience. This was especially true of humour, with the continuing underground and independents putting out some particularly amusing material: *Yummy Fur* (Vortex 1987), by Chester Brown, featured the blackly hilarious adventures of the cruelly victimised Ed the Happy Clown; *Eightball* (Fantagraphics 1989), by Dan Clowes, was another offbeat satire, dealing in a kind of heightened reality, reminiscent of the films of David Lynch; and *Hate* (Fantagraphics 1990) was Peter Bagge's follow-up to his *Neat Stuff*, and charted the progress of one of the more repellent characters from that comic, Buddy Bradley, in his quest for beer and true love. There were also several outstanding anthologies: the Canadian *Drawn and Quarterly* (Drawn and Quarterly 1990) carried on in spirit where *Weirdo* had left off, and was remarkable for the entrancingly personal work of Julie Doucet (touted by critics as 'the female Robert Crumb'). Finally, Knockabout continued to put out a range of funnies, including new work by Hunt Emerson and Gilbert Shelton, plus a curiosity in the form of *Thrrp!* (1987) the first excursion into underground-style humour for the great ex-*Beano* creator Leo Baxendale.

Horror comics also boomed, now revamped to bring things up to date with trends in cinema and novels.[6] Two of the most intelligent titles were *Hellblazer* (DC 1987) by Jamie Delano and John Ridgeway, about a 'psychic investigator' and the supernatural crimes he discovers in contemporary, socially-riven Britain; and *Sandman* (DC 1989) by Neil Gaiman and various artists, concerning the macabre adventures of a mythic 'Master of Dreams'.[7] Additionally, there were numerous adaptations of the work of top horror author and film-maker Clive Barker (for example, *Hellraiser*, *Nightbreed*, *Tapping the Vein* – all 1989), none of which were satisfactorily realised, and a quantity of film

adaptations, the most successful of which was the series based on *Aliens* (Dark Horse 1988). Finally, there were a number of ground-breaking anthologies, headed by *Taboo* (Spiderbaby Grafix 1988), which showcased a darker side to the work of big names such as Moebius and Alan Moore (whose continuing story 'From Hell', illustrated by Eddie Campbell, about the Jack the Ripper murders, has been acclaimed as his best post-*Watchmen* work).

But within the horror genre there were also comics that were the equivalent of hard-core movies (so-called 'splatter movies' and 'video nasties') – a category that tended to be the province of small-scale publishers willing to exploit areas the majors would avoid. *Faust* (Northstar 1988), by David Quinn and Tim Vigil, set the tone, and concerned the excessively bloody adventures of a schizophrenic costumed vigilante who eviscerates victims with foot-long knives that issue from his gloves. It was followed by a number of others, including the imaginatively-named *Splatter* (Northstar 1991). On a slightly different tack, the British *Lord Horror* (Savoy 1989) was a bizarre, satirical piece of excess designed, in the words of its author, 'to provide an insight into the mind it would have taken to erect a concentration camp'.[8] Though it is a generalisation, this sub-genre tended to specialise in the sadistic dismembering of women – with every globule of blood lovingly depicted.

War comics also went through a revival, and were similarly updated to take account of trends in cinema, especially Hollywood's obsession with Vietnam.[9] *The Nam* (Marvel 1986), which was particularly popular, was a fictionalised autobiography by combat veteran Doug Murray which inexplicably attained Code approval. *Vietnam Journal* (Apple 1987) was in a similar vein, again by a combat veteran, Don Lomax, but was much more realistic – and better for it. Both comics were highly reactionary readings of events, and laid the ground for a spate of similarly slanted adult war comics, featuring not just Vietnam, but also the Second World War and the 1991 Gulf War – notably another title by Don Lomax, *Desert Storm Journal* (Apple 1991).[10]

Other kinds of broadly 'adventure' comics included thrillers, which were generally of the *noir* variety, often with added cinematic violence. *Violent Cases* (Titan 1987) by Neil Gaiman and Dave McKean, was an atmospheric tale of Chicago gangsters told in grainy flashback; *Fast One* (No Exit 1991), illustrated by Geoff Grandfield, adapted Paul Cain's 1932 hard-boiled novel; *London's Dark* (Titan 1989), by James Robinson and Paul Johnson, concerned a murder mystery set in London during the Blitz. In a more contemporary vein, the eclectic *Trident* anthology included the extraordinary 'St Swithin's Day' by Grant Morrison and Paul Grist, a tense semi-autobiographical story of an alienated young man's preparations to assassinate Mrs Thatcher.

At the other end of the fiction spectrum, sex comics now became an established genre. They were sometimes sold shrink-wrapped, with prominent 'warning' notices, precautions guaranteed to arouse the maximum curiosity. *Black Kiss* (Vortex 1988) by Howard Chaykin defined the territory; sleazy, misogynist and supposedly humorous, it was originally given away free in *Hustler* magazine. Other notable examples included *Leather and Lace* (Aircel 1989) by Barry Blair, and the 'Eros' line (Fantagraphics 1990). They were no more explicit than many underground comix, but aimed to titillate rather than to make

Figure 7.2 Page-panel from *Vietnam Journal*, no. 4 (1989). Art/script: Don Lomax. © 1989 The creator

any broader counter-cultural statement. By 1992 there were over seventy sex titles being published in America, though, as we shall see below, by this date very few of these were being imported into Britain.

Non-fiction comics also became much more visible, as, in the wake of *Maus*, autobiography and biography came more to the fore (reviving a tradition which went back to the Crumb confessionals). *Spiral Cage* (Titan 1989), by Al Davison, told the story of the (British) author's battle with spina bifida; *Melody* (Kitchen Sink 1988) was Sylvie Rancourt's account of how she became a stripper in Ontario;

Figure 7.3 Cover to *Black Kiss*, no. 1 (1988). Art: Howard Chaykin. © 1988 The creator/Vortex Comics

American Splendor was self-published by Harvey Pekar and concerned his wry views on working-class life in Cleveland (an outstanding title which had strictly speaking been going since 1976, but which only now attracted the critical acclaim it deserved). Biographies included *The Wilderness* (Four Winds 1989) by Tim Truman, a copiously-researched historical profile of the American Revolution renegade Simon Girty, and, less impressively, the various life-stories of rock stars published by Revolutionary Press (including *Iggy Pop* and *Ozzy Osbourne*).

Non-fictional 'political journalism', often in dramatised

documentary form, also made an impact (a tradition once more going back to the underground and the 'cause comix'). The most impressive example was *Brought to Light* (Eclipse 1988), in which the lead story 'Shadowplay', by Alan Moore and Bill Sienkiewicz, detailed the history of CIA covert operations around the world (using the powerful recurring image of swimming pools full of blood to symbolise the results).

Figure 7.4 A page from 'Shadowplay', *Brought to Light* (1989). Art: Bill Sienkiewicz. Script: Alan Moore. © 1989 The creators

Others included the anthologies *Breakthrough* (Titan 1990), about the fall of the Berlin Wall, *Strip AIDS* (Willyprods 1988), aimed at raising AIDS-awareness; and *AARGH!* (Mad Love 1988) – an acronym for Artists Against Rampant Government Homophobia – protesting the British parliamentary bill containing Clause 28, which aimed to ban the 'promotion' of homosexuality.

Finally, no discussion of the comics within fandom would be complete without some mention of reprints. Or, to be precise, the biggest reprint boom in the history of the medium. Again, the target was the post-Big 3 readership, in order to acquaint them with some of the masters of adult comics both from the past, and from abroad. Reprints had the obvious advantage for publishers of already being in existence, and therefore cheaper to produce. Additionally, many foreign examples had originally been published in album form, which made the transition to the graphic novel format very easy. In short, it was a cheap and convenient way of feeding the new market.

Titles and stories from direct sales before 1986 made a spruced-up reappearance: these included *Luther Arkwright* (completed, and published in three volumes), *Love and Rockets* (split into volumes of individual stories) and *V for Vendetta* (completed and published in colour). New volumes of other previously collected favourites continued to appear, including *Cerebus*, *Daredevil* and *Swamp Thing* (which now ran to an impressive eleven volumes in its Moore incarnation). From the more distant past, the new British readership was introduced to American innovators of the form. These included Winsor McCay and George Herriman, whose newspaper strips from the 1900s were collected into handsome coffee-table volumes, and Will Eisner, whose 'Spirit' stories from the 1940s were relaunched in pocket-book form. In this way, many of the creators who had shaped the form since the beginning of the century were given at least some of the credit they warranted (see also chapters 10 and 11).

The work of top creators from other parts of the world was republished. European album reprints continued to be a staple: including Moebius's obscure 'new age' SF (*The Incal*, *Gardens of Aedena*); the medieval dramas of Belgian Hermann (*The Towers of Bois Maury*); the funnies of Spaniard Max (*Peter Pank*); and the soft porn of Italians Milo Manara and Guido Crepax (*Butterscotch*, *Emmanuelle*). These were joined by work from South America, particularly by the team of José Muõz and Carlos Sampayo (*Sinner*, *Joe's Bar*), and an increasing amount of material from Japan: notably Keiji Nakazawa's eyewitness account of the Hiroshima atomic bomb, *Barefoot Gen*, the Kazuo Koike–Goseki Kojima samurai epic *Lone Wolf and Cub*, and Katsuhiro Otomo's cyberpunk dystopia *Akira*.

It should be noted that although this flood of foreign material was important in that it gave the adult boom an international context (and demonstrated that adult comics were far from new in other parts of the world), in general they did not sell especially well, and from the start assumed a position in comparison to American comics analogous to art-films and Hollywood.

Moreover, reprints generally (either from the past or abroad) did not always convey the entire historical 'truth'. To be specific, usually only the very best output of a particular artist or country was on show; the less good, less acceptable and less accessible material was necessarily edited out (Britain was spared, for example, the 4,000-page Japanese comics on car maintenance, the tackier Euro-porn and certain vintage American strips featuring stereotyped images of black people). This editing sometimes misled critics into taking a somewhat rosy view of things when compared to the modern-day warts-and-all American and British output.

Moving on to the markets outside fandom, there were also dramatic changes. In the mainstream bookshops, comics albums were increasingly stocked. The Big 3 had sold well, so there was a willingness to follow-up. W. H. Smith, and other chains set up graphic novel shelves, while Dillons even instituted autonomous comics departments (called 'Light Years'). The bookshops did not take up everything produced within fandom by any means: there was a strict selection process that immediately cut out the more extreme sexual and violent material, and also the more politically controversial fare. Generally, however, if a comic was in a square-bound format it stood a chance of being distributed.

With this commitment to comics by the bookshops, and with the large sales of the Big 3 in mind, mainstream book publishers began to enter the field (and to orientate their output principally towards this market). This trend was started in earnest by Penguin in 1989. They had published *Maus*, of course, but this had been a one-off; now, they made a pledge to bring out a comic book approximately every month – mainly, though not exclusively, graphic novels. Penguin's eclectic list included the aforementioned *Barefoot Gen* (an obvious follow-up to *Maus* by virtue of its subject-matter), *Raw* (taken over in 1990) and *Give Me Liberty* by Frank Miller and Dave Gibbons (1991) (a futuristic adventure previously serialised by Dark Horse). The next to follow suit were Gollancz, who kicked-off with two original titles: *A Small Killing* by Alan Moore and Oscar Zarate, the story of an advertising executive's spiritual redemption; and *The Luck in the Head*, by M. John Harrison and Ian Miller, an obscure Gothic SF fantasy. The entry of these two publishers was followed by reports in book trade magazines and elsewhere of many more about to take the plunge.

It should be noted that the book publishers were not subject to the same sort of vetting in the bookshops as the comics publishers, and could rely on their reputations and established distribution channels to get books stocked. As Penguin's commissioning editor commented at the time: 'We don't have a history of publishing superheroes, and so we don't have that barrier to overcome. Our books are for an adult, literate readership, and so perhaps book-stockists – and hopefully people generally – will take us more seriously.'[11]

Closely connected to these developments in the bookshops was the decision of some public libraries to stock graphic novels. Once again there was a selection process, but the major advantage for the public was that it brought the more expensive examples into the range of everybody. It was no coincidence that the site chosen for the period's most important exhibition of comics art ('Strip Search') should have been a London library.[12]

Finally, the third market, the newsagents, saw a spectacular but short-lived boom. This was, of course, the traditional British market for comics, but until now had been largely ignored for adult fare (*2000AD*, *Warrior* and *Heavy Metal* having been the only examples to make significant inroads). Thus, it was up to the new titles to literally make space for themselves – above the bottom shelf and the children's comics, but below the top shelf and the porn magazines.

Most significantly, Fleetway, the publisher of *2000AD* and one of the British giants (at the time, part of the Maxwell empire), committed themselves to adult material. At the same time, they at last agreed to pay royalties to creators – something that had previously been staunchly resisted. This was seen as a major step forward for creators' rights, even though the question of copyright was left unchanged (see also p. 60). Not only were the newsagents to be targeted, but stories from the new comics line were to be filleted out and sold as graphic novels to the direct sales and bookshop markets – another first for Fleetway. Significantly, the company's historical rival, DC Thomson, declined to follow any of these leads.

Fleetway's flagship title, *Crisis* (1988), thus marked a landmark as the first specifically adult comic to be put out by a mainstream/newsagent British publisher. It was also unusual in that the subject-matter was overtly political, including stories such as 'Third World War' (by Pat Mills and Carlos Ezquerra), which attacked, among other things, multinationals in the developing world and police racism, and 'Troubled Souls' (by Garth Ennis and John McCrea), a drama set against the background of the ongoing war in Northern Ireland. When in 1988 Amnesty International came up with the idea of using the new adult comics to push their cause, *Crisis* was the natural title to approach, and a special issue was produced, based on true case-histories (Figure 7.5). But despite good intentions, the title attracted only a limited following, and was frequently criticised for being 'worthy but dull'.[13]

Revolver (1990), was Fleetway's less serious-minded follow-up

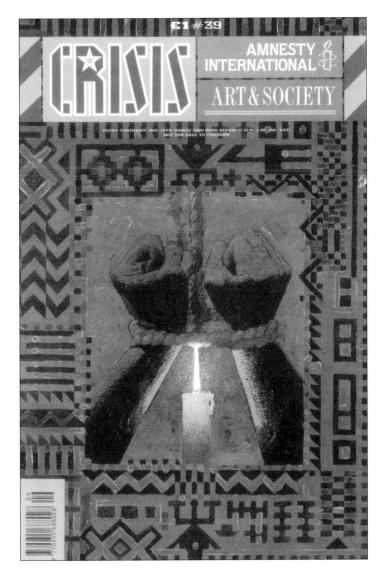

to *Crisis* (in part intended as a response to criticism of that title), and featured a mix of humorous and offbeat strips – including a biography of rock guitarist Jimi Hendrix by author/journalist Charles Shaar Murray (with art by Floyd Hughes), and a revisionist reworking of Dan Dare, by Grant Morrison and Rian Hughes, in which the 1950s hero's imperialist past comes back to haunt him.

These were joined by other titles in the broadly 'adventure anthology' mould from other publishers. *Strip* (Marvel UK 1990) featured reprints of successful direct sales stories, including Marshal Law; *Blast!* (John Brown 1991) also contained reprints, plus new strips,

Figure 7.6 Panel from 'Dare', *Revolver*, no. 4 (1990), showing a somewhat different take on the Dan Dare myth. Art: Rian Hughes. Script: Grant Morrison. © 1990 Fleetway Publications

including the humorous cyberpunk thriller 'The Virtual Kiss' by Warren Ellis and Matt 'D'Israeli' Brooker; *Toxic* (Apocalypse 1991) attempted to resuscitate the spirit of the classic period *2000AD* and included new strips by, among others, Pat Mills, Alan Grant, John Wagner and Mike McMahon. The latter title was characterised by a somewhat infantile desire to shock, and parodied the adult comics hype in its tag-line: 'The Comic Throws Up!'

Additionally, there was a wave of other titles from smaller independent companies which became known as 'style comics', due to their blend of strips and elements from the style magazines – notably, modish presentation and music coverage. *Heartbreak Hotel* (1988), captioned 'Where Music and Comics Meet', was the most ambitious, featuring strips based on songs. *Deadline* (1988) prospered due largely to the cult popularity of its main strip character 'Tank Girl' (by Jamie Hewlett and Alan Martin), a sort of female Mad Max. *Sphinx* (1990) was a late addition to the roster, calling itself 'The Magazine of Black Music, Culture and Comics', a lively mix of rap coverage, black nationalism and *Crisis*-style polemics.

Other independents included comics that had been going for many years but which now attained widespread newsagent distribution: *Escape*, for example, now in a glossier incarnation, brought a taste of the avant-garde to a wider public. *Viz*, at the other end of the spectrum, was a vulgar but truly amusing humour title, founded in 1979, which only began to sell outstandingly after 1986 (the story of its success, and the emergence of its many copyists, will be dealt with in the next chapter).

Finally, the newsagents continued to stock a limited number of regular Marvels and DCs – some of which now dealt with adult subject-matter. The range was far fewer than in the specialist shops, and issues would generally take much longer to reach the shelves. But it is still worth noting that it was now possible to pick up the likes of *Hellblazer* and *Sandman* from this source.

Thus in three separate markets, adult comics were booming. As a result, media interest continued to be intense. Some magazines instituted regular comics review columns, while coverage spread to TV and radio. The 'adult comics revolution' story was repeated ad nauseam in this period, with the first national TV documentary on the subject titled, inevitably, 'The Day Comics Grew Up!'.[14] There was no shortage of interviewees from among publishers and creators to give substance to the story.

In the process of the media overkill, new 'stars' were discovered. These included the British writers Grant Morrison and Neil Gaiman, both of whom were highly-versed in comics lore, and produced some impressively literate work for both American and British publishers,[15] and artists Dave McKean, another Briton, who specialised in a highly-stylised photo-realism, and, from America, Bill Sienkiewicz, whose design-conscious montage work was acknowledged as a major innovation. None of the new names, however, garnered the same celebrity status as Alan Moore.[16]

Partly through the media, comics' relationship with youth culture was reaffirmed. As ever, the music and style press took a particular interest in events, and in this period the *Face*, *iD* and the *Cut* all commissioned integral adult comic strips (a trend mirrored by the growth of the 'style comics').[17] Comics were frequently cited in rock and rap songs (one immortal lyric ran 'Alan Moore/knows-the-score'),[18] while comics-art made its way on to record-sleeves, gig-flyers and posters (the smiley face design that had featured in *Watchmen* now became the motif for the Acid House dance-craze). There was no getting away from it – in the late 1980s, comics were hip once more.

And yet, for all the trendiness, for all the media attention and for all the sheer quantity of comics, it gradually became apparent that the boom had limits. In particular, media acceptance of adult material did not necessarily equate with public acceptance. Thus a situation developed whereby, while the industry was busy congratulating itself on its spectacular progress, serious problems became apparent due to different rates of growth in the various markets.

On the one hand, the fan market was generally sound, and growth was sustained throughout the period, albeit on a decreasing scale. To put it simply, comics were a passion for fans, and money would always be found for their hobby (in the words of Dez Skinn, 'it's like alcohol or tobacco – it's an addiction, and you can't easily stop').[19] Thus, it was possible for adult comics to be successful simply by targeting the already-available fan market.

However, it is important to note that although the market was buoyant as a whole, there were significant changes over time in who published what. In particular, the independents were squeezed as Marvel and DC adopted ever-more aggressive marketing strategies. (For example, in 1990, *Spider-Man* was relaunched by Marvel in four covers, and sold a staggering 250,000 copies in the UK alone.) Hence, although there were numerically more independents, they were competing for proportionally less market share. Under this pressure, some filed for bankruptcy (for example Now, First, Comico); some concentrated on other areas of publishing (Eclipse); and some moved into sex-erotica to stay afloat (Fantagraphics). Whether this ultimately meant that there were less adult comics on the shelves in toto is debatable.[20]

On the other hand, in the markets outside fandom the story was very different. In the bookshops it was clear by 1990 that sales of comics were not what had been expected. Sales of graphic novels and albums were very disappointing, and there was nothing that could remotely compare with the success of the Big 3. During 1990–2, the chains reconsidered their orders, and rationalised shelf-space. Dillons, for example, dropped its autonomous comics departments after barely six months. In response, Penguin cut back its output, and some book publishers who had been considering joining the field now had second thoughts.[21]

In the newsagents, too, there were major problems. Aside from the (by now) million-selling *Viz*, the other adult comics simply did not sell. By 1992 *Crisis, Revolver, Heartbreak Hotel, Escape, Strip, Blast!* and *Toxic*, had ceased publication, and most of the others were clinging on by the skin of their teeth. It was a dismal performance, and led Fleetway and several others to turn their backs completely on adult comics, and to either concentrate on children's comics or on other areas of publishing altogether.[22]

The question was, why did adult comics so manifestly fail to take off with a wider public? The simplest, and most convincing, explanation is that, despite the huge media coverage, there was widespread ambivalence about the whole phenomenon. On the most alienated level, most adults did not read comics on a day-to-day basis, and remained ignorant of their potential range. For this group, the old prejudices were still firmly in place, and the idea of 'a comic' remained inexorably linked with juvenile *Beano*-style buffoonery. Something of their attitude was captured in a review of *Raw* that appeared in the *Sunday Times* in 1989. It concluded: '*Raw* is not even funny ... *Beano* and *Dandy* have nothing to fear.'[23]

Even those general readers who had been attracted by the Big 3 were not necessarily convinced. These comics had sold well, certainly, but they were an exception because (notwithstanding their inherent quality) they appealed on the basis of their novelty value, had been hyped to the nth degree and were fêted by the media for these reasons. Faced with a plethora of follow-up comics that were rarely of the same standard, and were no longer novelties, the audience won by them was bound to dissipate. Indeed, it could be said that for this group, the generally puerile and fan-based content of most comics produced in the boom only convinced them that the medium was the preserve of a highly-specialised and obsessive subculture. This was summed up in the memorable comment by columnist Julie Burchill that 'Comic books for adults is a complete contradiction in terms, as anyone who reads comics is *not* an adult and should have their voting rights removed ASAP.'[24]

This seemingly unshakable public indifference made it possible for a backlash to gain currency. In the first place, the media increasingly lost interest in comics, and in some cases became positively hostile to them. They were not a story anymore, and coverage gradually dwindled between 1990 and 1992. Even the style and music presses, the traditional champions of the medium, were less keen: occasional features continued to appear, but the days of strips being specially commissioned for the glossies were long gone. By 1992 it was fair to say that comics were not hip anymore.

The more hostile press adopted two lines of attack. First, there were generally critical articles, which argued that adult comics *per se* were a 'bad thing', intrinsically lowbrow and possibly even a threat to literacy. An early example was a piece in *The Independent* entitled 'Traditional Novel in Danger as Teenagers Turn to Comics' (a curious twist to the comics PR hype), which quoted a National Union of Journalists official, who suggested that comics were a malevolent manifestation of the modern trend for shortening attention spans. There were several other similarly-slanted pieces in the quality and tabloid press.[25] These complaints might seem familiar: they were identical to those made against children's comics for decades, now dusted off and applied to their adult counterparts. They can also arguably be interpreted as part of a wider push by certain journalists for a 'return to standards' after the expansion of the concept of 'culture' in the 1980s (see p. 92).[26]

The second avenue of criticism, connected to the first, was to sensationalise the sexual and violent content of some titles, and brand adult comics generally as 'perverted', 'disgusting' and beyond the pale. This played on the historical association in Britain of the word 'adult' with 'sexual' (as in 'adult movies' or 'adult magazines'), the two being synonymous since roughly the turn of the century. Again there was a precedent for this kind of attack in the backlash against the underground in the 1970s.

But the counterblast did not stop with the media. In time-honoured fashion, their 'concern' was then taken up by the authorities. The first half of 1991 saw a spate of raids on comics shops across the country, together with customs' confiscations. Titles like *Black Kiss*, *Leather and Lace* and various 'Europorn' albums were taken (plus a quantity of non-exploitative material that happened to contain sex-scenes). In Manchester the satirical horror comic *Lord Horror* was also seized. None of the raids has yet resulted in a successful prosecution.

The intervention of the authorities inevitably led to a much greater degree of self-censorship within the industry. Just as the underground became more cautious after its brushes with the law, so now more mainstream publishers cut back on comics involving 'strong' subject-matter, while distributors also shied away from importing such material. Notable instances of self-censorship included the axeing of the strip 'Skin', by Peter Milligan and Brendan McCarthy (about 1970s skinhead culture), from *Crisis*, and its subsequent failure to find a publisher,[27] and the pulping of the graphic novel *True Faith* by Fleetway after complaints from Christian fundamentalists. By 1992 it was also true that there was very little sexually-explicit material making its way into the specialist shops.

Whether the backlash will continue is unclear. Naturally, bearing in mind the histories of the 1950s horror comics, *Action* and the underground, fears have been expressed that the events of 1991 are a prelude to much wider censorship of what can and cannot be said in a comic, and, in particular, that once again sex and violence will be a mcguffin for the censorship of more politically-orientated work. (Was it really such a coincidence, for example, that *Lord Horror* was seized when it contained a satirical attack on the police force?).

The clampdown was further proof, if it were needed, that comics were still not accepted as a medium in Britain. Almost all of the material objected to would have gone unnoticed in a novel, and while much of it might arguably have been indefensible on aesthetic grounds, it was clear that freedom of expression did not extend to comics to the same degree it did to other media. The fact that the complaints were of the same nature as those made against earlier comics showed how little had changed.

But even with the negative forces at work between 1990 and 1992, it might still have been possible for adult comics to have made a significant impact if it had not been for the worst economic recession in Britain for sixty years. This really took hold in 1990–2, and magazine publishing was hit particularly badly. As we have seen, the fan market was a special case because collectors managed to find a disproportionate percentage of their income for their hobby.[28] But in the bookshops and newsagents, there was no such economic buffer. Consequently, comics in these markets suffered with the rest of the publishing trade – which in 1992 estimated that sales were down by 30 per cent on 1989.

The comics producers and retailers pointed to all these outside pressures as excuses for failure. But they had themselves to blame too. In particular, too often they made no distinction between what was acceptable for the fan market and what for the bookshops and newsagents. Thus, in terms of subject-matter, far too many comics were concerned with fan themes that simply did not have a wider appeal. The obvious examples to cite were the superhero revisionist titles – comics that often required a detailed knowledge of the mythology of an American genre. They dominated bookshop space just as they did the specialist shops; moreover, many of the new newsagent comics included revisionist superhero strips (*Strip*, *Blast!*, *Crisis* and *Toxic* among them). As intimated above, it is easy to argue that such fare was not just unfamiliar to bookshop and newsagent audiences, but positively off-putting.

Moreover, the new comics were often much too expensive. Sometimes this was the result of pure greed on the part of publishers, but generally it was (again) an expression of inappropriate fan-values: a £20 graphic novel or a £1.65 newsagent comic might have been acceptable to a connoisseur fan who had taught him- or herself to appreciate the medium on a number of levels, and who might read it several times; but for a novice reader who may have been thinking of buying the comic on impulse to read once in half an hour, the price was prohibitive.

Finally, the marketing of the new comics left much be desired. Graphic novels were commonly shelved in a section to themselves – with autobiography, humour, historical drama, etc., all mixed together – without any attempt to separate them out, or to indicate to the readers what their content might be. Again this system might have worked for a fan readership, for whom a degree of knowledge of the comics might be assumed, and who could reasonably be relied upon to know what they were buying. But for the general reader it was at best unhelpful. Similarly, in the newsagents, despite several attempts by publishers to educate retailers on the best place to shelve adult comics, they continued to be displayed either next to children's fare or to porn magazines: either position spelt commercial death.

As the realities of the situation became more obvious with time, so the predictions made by comics pundits and the PR machine in 1986–7 started to look increasingly hollow. The gap between the fantasy of 'sophisticated literature for the post-literate generation' and the reality of yet another superhero revision was often embarrassingly wide. It became evident that Britain was not experiencing a rapid progression in imitation of the rest of Europe. Nor was it the case that the public would soon be picking up graphic novels as naturally as Ruth Rendell novels. Perhaps most tellingly of all, the majority of people did not feel able to read a comic without embarrassment on the bus – perhaps the most often repeated boast of the old-style comics evangelists.

Certainly adult comics had progressed a certain distance since 1986, but there was obviously a limit to what could be achieved. There were now more comics, available from a greater number of outlets, on a wider variety of subjects. Yet the boom had been based on hype rather than demand, and whatever industry PR might have said to the contrary, there were still huge problems of credibility. Over seventy years of conditioning in Britain were not going to be reversed overnight, and whatever else the boom represented, it was not the point historically when comics became 'respectable'.

Further reading

Paul Gravett's *The New Penguin Book of Comics* (Harmondsworth: Penguin, forthcoming 1993) promises to include a wide-ranging survey of the comics from this period. Gary Groth and Robert Fiore (eds), *The New Comics* (New York: Berkley 1988) is once again recommended for its interviews with key creators, including Bill Sienkiewicz. As ever, back issues of fanzines also provide a useful overview, especially the *Comics Journal*, *FA*, *Speakeasy*, plus articles in *Escape*.

Viz 'More fun than a jammy bun!'

I think if future generations look back on the literature of the age, they'll more usefully look back to *Viz* than for instance to the novels of Peter Ackroyd or Julian Barnes . . . simply because *Viz* has got a lot of genuine vitality and a vitality of its own, a vitality which comes up from the society it represents and those novelists don't.

(Auberon Waugh, editor *Literary Review*)[1]

Viz, an hilariously bawdy pastiche of the *Beano* and tabloid newspapers, became a national sensation in 1988 when it became simultaneously the biggest-selling comic in the country, and the best-selling adult comic of all time. Since then it has built on that readership, and in 1992 sold over 1 million copies an issue. For a publication that subtitled itself 'Britain's crappiest magazine', it was a meteoric rise, and represented a rude awakening in every sense for the rest of the magazine publishing industry. In a sense, to understand why *Viz* succeeded is to understand why so many other adult comics that came to prominence over a similar period failed.

In order to place *Viz* historically, however, it is necessary to trace it back to its small press origins in Newcastle in 1979. For crucially, the comic was (and is) unique in its sensibility, and had little to do with mainstream comics, comics fandom or with the underground. With this in mind, we can identify three phases in its development. The first is roughly 1979–85, when it was deeply influenced by the shock-waves of punk; the second is roughly 1985–9, when it acquired national distribution and began to sell in extraordinary quantities; the third is from roughly 1989 onwards, a period marked by a creative (if not a commercial) decline.

Punk is too recent a phenomenon to have been properly historically assessed. Yet clearly it represented the most significant cultural upheaval since the hippie movement. Part youth rebellion, part artistic statement, it exploded on to the British scene in 1976–7, and had its primary expression in music, with bands like the Sex Pistols and the Clash producing some of the the angriest, nastiest rock and roll ever heard. Although punk had no openly expressed philosophy in the same way as the 1960s counter-culture, there were certain defining characteristics – notably an emphasis on themes such as negationism (not nihilism), youth, energy, aggression, spontaneity and working-class 'street credibility'.

Within this, punk's relationship with the old hippie counter-culture was complex. Outwardly, it was a root and branch rejection of it – hippies were the 'enemy', and punk 'anti'-attitudes the response to their idealism and millenarianism. (Speed was the punk drug, not LSD or marijuana.) Yet, in fact, punk borrowed much from hippie culture, most obviously an antipathy to straight society, but also a rejection of the straight media, and similar ideas about 'doing it yourself'.

This was expressed in the various associated manifestations of the scene. Just as hippie culture had had expression in other media, so too did punk: in publishing, fanzines appeared about bands, self-produced on photocopiers and sold for a few pence; in fashion, self-customised clothes and haircuts defined the punk 'look', while in graphics, 'spontaneous' artwork involving montage and 'blackmail' lettering had the same function. In the longer term, punk movies and plays appeared, while musically, the form revolutionised heavy metal and strongly influenced rap and hip-hop. In particular, punk's influence was evident in the emergence of 'alternative comedy', which made its first appearance at festivals and tiny clubs (often with bands on the same bill) in the late 1970s, and featured a new wave of fast-talking, confrontational comedians like Alexei Sayle and Rik Mayall.[2] In short, popular culture post-1977 was a very different prospect to that before.

This was the milieu from whence *Viz* emerged.[3] It was launched in Newcastle in 1979, and was self-produced, like a fanzine, from the bedroom of two brothers, Chris and Simon Donald (aged 19 and 16 respectively).[4] With rock-bottom production values, it had a first print-run of 150, and sold for 20 pence. Unlike the vast majority of other small press comics, *Viz* was cranked-up, brutal, street credible (much of it was in Geordie street-slang) and foul-mouthed – from the start its distinguishing feature was a lack of respect for anyone or anything.

Specifically, *Viz* took children's comics – as we have seen, still symbolic of the sanctity of childhood in Britain – and metaphorically ripped them to pieces. With the new viciousness of alternative comedy their contrived innocence was methodically undermined with lashings of toilet humour, sex, swearing and, above all, violence: as Simon Donald later explained, 'People aren't supposed to die after cartoon violence – in *Viz* they do, and that's the joke.'[5]

Generally, it was children's comics from the 1960s and early 1970s that were targeted (the comics the punk generation had grown up with), and in the first twelve issues, characters were introduced that had identifiable inspirations: for example, 'Billy the Fish', a surreal pastiche of Roy of the Rovers, and 'Johnny Fartpants', a kind of Dennis the Menace with wind. There were also less specific inventions in the

same general style, among them 'Roger Mellie, the Man on the Telly', a TV presenter with an uncontrollable urge to swear on-air, and 'The Pathetic Sharks' who become nauseous at the sight of blood. Early characters that later disappeared, but which were especially notable for their violence, included 'Skinheed', about a mindless bootboy, and 'Paul Whicker, the Tall Vicar', a sadistic cleric. Completing the *Viz* line-up were spoof tabloid newspaper letters pages and articles ('Zoo of Shame – Children Watch as Animals Make Love!'), various parodic adverts, and one-off gag cartoons (including the infamous, and very rude, 'Rude Kid').

Nothing like it had been seen before, and although *Viz* was subsequently placed in the underground tradition by some commentators, it was clearly of a different mettle. The underground had been

Figure 8.2 'Roger Mellie, the Man on the Telly', *Viz*, no. 6 (1982). Art: Chris Donald. Script: the *Viz* team. © 1982 The creators

outrageous and violent, certainly, but never developed *Viz*'s 'killer instinct'. By the same token, *Viz* was not part of the propagation of a coherent ideology postulating an alternative society, and its satire was random rather than focused on 'the establishment' (in Chris Donald's words, 'the only criteria for something's inclusion in the comic is if it's funny'.[6] It is arguably for this reason that there was never a '*Viz* trial' in the same way that there had been a '*Nasty Tales* trial' or '*Knockabout* trial', since it was never considered 'dangerous' in the same sense.

Even as a small press comic, the formula proved a major success. This was despite formidable barriers: most newsagents refused outright to stock the comic, and when Manchester police chief James Anderton saw a copy, he immediately referred it to the Obscene Publications Squad (no prosecution resulted). Nevertheless, the Donalds found a ready audience in student unions and in pubs (indeed, circulation was increased by news of the Anderton incident). Very soon it became economically viable to convert *Viz* into a properly produced comic: advertising was solicited from local businesses, the cover-price went up to 35p and a professionally-printed tabloid format was introduced (in imitation of traditional children's comics).

This more 'professional' approach was accompanied by the hiring of more staff. In particular, Simon Thorp and Graham Dury joined the team, and in time they added fresh characters to the roster – among them 'Norbert Colon' ('He's as Tight as a Gnat's Chuff'), 'Finbarr Saunders' ('and his Double Entendres') and 'Buster Gonad and His Unfeasibly Large Testicles' (so large, in fact, he has to carry them round in a wheelbarrow).

Figure 8.3 Panels from 'Norbert Colon – He's the Meanest Man on Earth!', *Viz*, no. 16 (1986). Art: Simon Thorp. Script: the *Viz* team. © 1986 The creators

With their input, the comic became less 'angry' and more influenced by contemporary trends in alternative comedy. By now the spiky club comedians of the late 1970s had become the stars of their own TV shows – for example, *The Young Ones* and *Blackadder* – and were increasingly rehabilitating the nudge-nudge humour of the 1960s *Carry On* films (albeit within 'ideologically acceptable' limits).[7] This kind of humour also became increasingly evident in *Viz*, with bawdiness taking over from brutality as the comic's stock in trade.

By the mid-1980s the comic was a major cult in the north-east, with sales in the region of 4,000 copies an issue. But its big break came in 1985 when distribution in the south was finally secured. Virgin Books in London struck a deal with the *Viz* team and, despite initial doubts that some of the comic's Geordie colloquialisms might not travel, experimented with putting it on sale in Virgin record shops. (In recognition of this new arrangement, the comic instituted a pop chart in which chart position indicated how much money the particular band had spent bribing the editors.)

The Virgin management need not have worried. Sales in the shops were much better than expected. Indeed, the employee at Virgin responsible for 'discovering' *Viz*, John Brown, now took it upon himself to set up his own company to deal exclusively with the comic, and to broaden further distribution in the rest of the country. 'From the first moment I saw it', he said later, 'I knew that it had the potential to be huge – comedy and sex are the two biggest general-interest subjects in the world.'[8]

With new backing, and a new market to exploit, sales rose exponentially. Even W.H. Smith agreed to stock the comic (arguably further proof that *Viz* was not considered a 'threat' in the same way as the undergrounds). The period from 1985 to roughly 1989 saw *Viz* on peak form: earlier experience had significantly improved the quality of the draughtsmanship and the gags were sharper than ever. By 1988, the comic was selling an impressive 500,000 copies (unprecedented for an adult title), and being profiled with a mixture of amusement and disgust in the arts pages of the quality newspapers.

Why *Viz*'s rise during this period should have been quite so all-conquering is debatable. Possibly, the answer has something to do with its politics – or rather, lack of them. To be specific, although *Viz* took some elements from alternative comedy, it pointedly ignored others. In particular, 1980s alternative comedy had a radical political agenda (which was in large part what made it 'alternative' in the first place): all the comedians associated with it kept to material that was pointedly anti-racist, anti-sexist and anti-heterosexist – this at a time when the majority of humour was still based on just those themes. Some, notably Ben Elton, went so far as to use their comedy as a soapbox for their left-wing political views.

Viz never took this path. Although the comic was hardly a 'serious offender' in the political correctness stakes when compared to most old-wave comedians, it did not make ideological soundness a priority, and certainly never identified itself with the left. (Indeed, the left was as likely to be savaged as anybody else.) It resolutely trod a path that was, if not right-wing, then at least not right-on.

This was arguably its major strength. People who were repelled by the preaching of alternative comedy would not have encountered any such problems with *Viz*. In a sense it was reassuring humour, without strings. There is even an argument for seeing *Viz* as having a 'special relationship' with the Thatcherite consensus that reigned in Britain at the time, and specifically with what has been described as the 'anti-culture culture' that this engendered.[9] This would partly explain the extraordinary range of people who bought the comic, including readers of every political persuasion.

Thus, the years between 1985 and 1989 were characterised by *Viz*-mania. Reports in the press told of financial workers faxing pages of their favourite strips across the City of London, and schoolboys mimicking characters and jokes, in much the same way as a previous generation had done with Monty Python. It was also at this point that several well-known personalities declared themselves fans – among them ex-Python members, staff at *Private Eye* and *Literary Review* editor/*Daily Telegraph* columnist Auberon Waugh. The alternative comedy link was cemented when Harry Enfield appeared in a photo strip (he later returned the compliment by using a stage-routine written for him by Chris Donald, involving a character called 'Buggerallmoney').

The comic did not appeal to everybody. Notoriously, and unsurprisingly, the vast majority of the readership was male (85 per cent according to a survey in 1988 – Figure 8.4). However, it is worth noting that 15 per cent of 500,000 was far more women readers than any other comic, and that 15 per cent was above the usual percentage of female readers for comics.

It was inevitable that during this period of rapidly rising sales the connection would be made by some commentators between *Viz* and the vogue for adult comics generally. On the surface, there seemed to be plenty of connections. For example, chronologically, the fit with the

Figure 8.4 Illustration from a *Viz* readership survey, 1988. © 1988 House of Viz/John Brown Publishing Ltd.

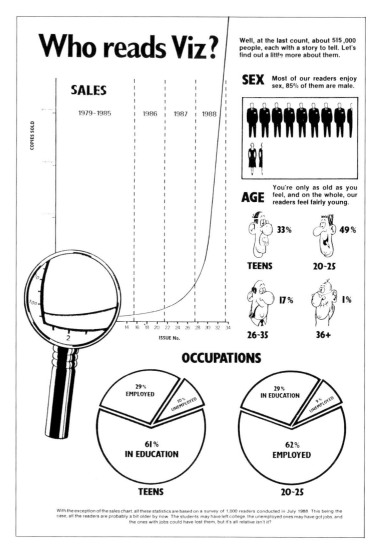

'adult revolution' seemed perfect. Moreover, it was true that the *Viz* team were engaged in imposing an adult sensibility on a childish form, much in the same way that Moore, Miller *et al.* were doing with the superheroes. Also, fandom seemed happy enough to treat *Viz* as just another comic: it was sold from fan shops, and its creators were frequently interviewed by fanzines and guests at conventions.

But, of course, there was a fundamental mismatch with the other comics of the boom. The most relevant point emerging from the unique lineage outlined above was that *Viz* came out of a British tradition rather than an American one. While other comics generally progressed in the direction of flashier presentation, more expensive price and a pervasive 'American-ness' (even when produced by British creators), *Viz* was cheap, produced on low-quality paper stock and traded in a resolutely British brand of punky cheekiness. The difference between a £14.95 hardback Batman graphic novel and the 90p *Viz* could not be more pronounced.

Thus, *Viz* made a completely different connection with the public than other comics. Most of the people who read it did not read any other comics. It was perceived as a 'comedy magazine' (like, say, *Private Eye*) rather than as a comic *per se*. To refer back to an analogy from a previous chapter, it was the only comic in the period that can be said to have passed the 'embarrassment test' on the bus.

But for all its popularity, having made it to the top, *Viz* began to show the first signs of the decline we can identify as the third phase of its history. By the end of the 1980s the creators and publisher were fast becoming millionaires, and a detectable complacency started to set in. The jokes had always been fairly one-note but now there seemed to be less inventiveness within the established parameters. Coinciding with this was an unprecedented level of negative comment in the media as the comic's success also meant it came into the orbit of arts critics who might not otherwise have seen it. The hackles of the left-wing press, especially, were raised by the flagrant sexism of some of the strips. One in particular was singled-out – 'Sid the Sexist', about a Geordie oaf who chats up women with outrageously offensive banter (his motto, 'Tits Oot For the Lads!'). Although the character always ended up being humiliated in the final panel, it was pointed out that much of the humour was intended to come from the language he used.

The *Viz* team were not shamed by the complaints, however, and responded with new strips that were deliberately antagonistic – the best-known being 'The Fat Slags', about two grotesquely overweight office secretary friends forever in pursuit of 'a quick shag an' a bag o' chips', and 'Millie Tant', about a fearsomely ugly feminist and her preposterous 'radical causes' (in one early appearance, she 'maces' an old man in the park for 'raping me with his eyes'). These were mild inventions compared to some of the characters that had appeared in the underground comix, but featuring in a (now) mainstream publication

Figure 8.5 Panels from 'Sid the Sexist', *Viz*, no. 9 (1982). Art: Chris Donald. Script: the *Viz* team. © 1982 The creators

Figure 8.6 Panels from 'The Fat Slags', *Viz*, no. 41 (1990). Art: Chris Donald. Script: the *Viz* team. © 1990 House of *Viz*/John Brown Publishing Ltd.

they cemented *Viz*'s reputation for being outrageous.[10] Their arrival also signalled the entry of a certain self-consciousness in the comic: hereafter, there would be fewer moments of comedic genius and more of gratuitous offensiveness.[11]

Controversy did not do any harm to sales, however. Indeed, the comic's enhanced reputation as a 'yob comic' (there from the start, of course, though in a different sense) drew even more readers to it. The Fat Slags were subsequently licensed to advertise beer (the ad was swiftly binned by the Advertising Standards Authority), while the merchandising of crude T-shirts and other spin-offs became a major money-spinner. By 1990, *Viz* had broken the 1 million circulation barrier, and was the fourth biggest-selling periodical in the country (after *TV Times*, *Radio Times* and *Women's Weekly*). In commercial terms it was a staggering achievement.[12] Very few comics in history can be said to have tapped the national *zeitgeist* in such a way.

In 1992 the sales figures were still rising. Having conquered the newsagents the *Viz* empire diversified into other projects. Two animated TV series have appeared (*Billy the Fish* and *Roger Mellie*), neither of which capture the flavour of the original strips (see pp. 218–9), and there are plans for live-action productions of other favourites, including, incredibly, Sid the Sexist. There are also signs that the comic is becoming a cult in other countries. Australia already has a version of its own, while in America sales are gradually rising. The parochialism of the humour is a potential problem to expansion overseas, of course, but it should perhaps be borne in mind that not so long ago the now world-famous humour of Monty Python was also considered 'untranslatable'. [13]

But the *Viz* story is not quite complete without some mention of the plethora of other comics it has spawned. In the short time since *Viz* has 'come south', it is estimated there have been at least twenty emulators – and there still seem to be more appearing each month. Most commentators have tended to lump them together and dismiss them as '*Viz*-clones', though this is not strictly true.

Certainly, the biggest group has been 'adult humour', with comics stepping into the distribution network that *Viz* took many years to build. Often they are not published by comics publishers at all, but by magazine publishers (often involved with soft porn). Typically, they are very poor copyists – names like *Zit*, *Poot*, *Gas* and *Smut* generally sum up their intellectual content. The artwork is uniformly awful, while in terms of humour they seem to have taken *Viz*'s more gross aspects, and left the punk attitude behind.

Other adult comedy titles have made more effort to carve out their own ground. *Brain Damage* (1988), for example, set out to plug *Viz*'s 'blind spot' for politically-committed satire, and utilised underground creators, including Hunt Emerson and Melinda Gebbie. *Talking Turkey* (1991) also uses underground work, and has attempted to introduce European humourists (notably Frenchman Edika and Italian Carali) to a British audience.

But there have been other kinds of *Viz* emulators. The excellent *Oink!* (1988), for example, was aimed at a children's audience, and took the irreverence and brutality from *Viz*, while eschewing the sex and swearing (it was touted as 'a *Beano* for the 80s'). It folded partly because it was shelved with all the other adult *Viz* copyists – a trap that other similarly-styled children's comics have also fallen into. *Winebibber* was another anomaly, and was published by a fundamentalist group within the Church of England. It included strips like the dismal 'Barry Belf – He Evangelises Himself!'.

Finally one area that should not be underestimated is the small press/self-publishing explosion that *Viz* has inspired. Although the trend has declined in the 1990s, there was a period in the late 1980s when virtually every town in the country, and every campus, had its own cheaply-produced imitation *Viz*. These were rarely distributed beyond their immediate locality, and were often of a fairly lamentable

Figure 8.7 Just a few of the
Viz copyists

quality, but nevertheless represented the biggest self-publishing boom
since the underground.[14] This in itself is testimony to the exceptional
nature and influence of *Viz*—the comic with an unfeasibly large
number of emulators.

Further reading

A history of *Viz* has yet to be written. On the meaning and consequences of punk, the best account is Jon Savage's *England's Dreaming*
(London: Faber 1991). For a basic introduction to how comedy
changed in Britain in the 1980s, see Roger Wilmut's *Didn't You Kill
My Mother-in-Law?* (London: Methuen 1989). For an altogether
more intellectual exploration of 'toilet humour', see Mikhail Bakhtin,
Rabelais and his World (Cambridge, Mass.: MIT 1968).

The future

It is true that nobody in the media is doing 'comics grow up' stories anymore — thank God — but I still think that there are enough truly outstanding comics being published to be optimistic about the future.

(Dominic Wells, comics critic, 1992)[1]

The years 1986 to 1992 have been ones of intense activity in comics publishing. In terms of adult comics, however, this has not always translated into commercial success. In retrospect, it is clear that the hype surrounding the Big 3 raised hopes to a level which the industry had no real chance of satisfying subsequently. (Only *Viz* has managed to garner a sizeable general readership.) But just as it is wrong to exaggerate the rise of adult comics, so we must not overplay their decline. A significant number are still available, and continue to find an audience. We are thus in a period of readjustment and transition: for publishers and readers alike, it is a time for taking stock and for asking 'where next?'.

Fandom is perhaps the most optimistic market, and certainly the least affected by the 1990–2 downturn. It is worth reiterating that, at the time of writing, there are approximately 300 specialist shops in the UK – a larger number than ever before. On the negative side of the ledger, they retain the unattractive aspects of the pre-1986 fan scene; which is to say, they are very male environments, based on a self-referencing culture dominated by collecting superhero comics. On the positive side, the fact that they exist means that there is still a network which publishers of adult comics can use to sell their product.

Thus we can say that in fandom there have been net gains since 1986. Publishers are aware of this of course, and Britain is now seen as such an important part of the anglophone direct sales market that several major American companies have either very recently set up bases here, or intend to do so in the near future. In spring 1992 Tundra launched Tundra UK, while Dark Horse International is scheduled to open in London by the autumn. Even DC Comics are reported to be setting up offices in this country in 1993, though whether this will become a fully-fledged subsidiary of the company is not yet known. (As we have seen, Marvel had already taken this step as early as 1983). How much of these publishers' output will be adult-orientated remains to be seen (though, judging from advance lists, it seems clear that Tundra UK, in particular, are keen to develop in this area).

The bookshop market is much less hopeful. As we have seen, it has experienced severe setbacks with adult comics, but, again, we should not over-dramatise. Comic albums and graphic novels have not disappeared altogether. Rather, they have been marginalised – like, for example, poetry or experimental fiction – and are best seen as a specialist interest as opposed to a source of constant best sellers. Not everybody is necessarily downhearted about this scaling-down of expectations: when asked about the less-than-expected sales for *Raw*, Art Spiegelman joked, 'It's worse than Jackie Collins, but for poetry it sells real well'.[2]

Thus, this market is not 'dead' for the future. The fact that the overall performance has been disappointing may have slowed things down, but there are still signs of life. So far as the book publishers are

Figure 9.1 Panels from *Signal to Noise*, a Gollancz graphic novel originally serialised in the *Face* magazine. Art: Dave McKean. Script: Neil Gaiman. © 1989 The creators

concerned, for example, Gollancz and Penguin have no plans to axe their graphic novel lists, and there have been reports in the fan press that HarperCollins and Pan will soon join the field. Certainly, the big publishers are being more cautious than previously, but if more and more do become involved, the cumulative effect may yet be transforming for the way comics are perceived.

The newsagent market has perhaps seen the most dramatic reverses. Yet, once again, it needs to be stressed that adult comics have not disappeared. *Deadline, 2000AD, The Judge Dredd Megazine, Viz*, the various surviving *Viz* copyists, plus several adult Marvels and DCs, still add up to a substantial number of titles on the shelves, and – lest we forget – many more than a decade ago. Thus, despite the terrible attrition-rate, they are proof that it can be done.

For this reason, there are still important publishers willing to give the market a try. Those strongly rumoured to have plans to publish adult comics for the newsagents in the near future include Dark Horse International and Tundra UK. Thus, when the editor of *Blast!* signed off from the final issue with the words 'the newsagent experiment with adult comics in this country is over',[3] he was undoubtedly being premature.

Finally, it goes without saying that in all three markets, the end of the economic recession will be a crucial factor in how comics fare. When the situation will improve depends on whom one chooses to listen to. At the time of writing, government spokespersons were claiming that the country was already coming out of recession. But with unemployment continuing to rise, and the prospect of a balance of payments crisis in the very near future, the estimate of some economic analysts that the upturn will not come for at least another five years is looking more realistic.

So, to sum up, there is no question that events since 1990 have meant confidence in adult comics has taken a blow. Nobody in the comics business has any illusions any more that the pot of gold is just over the hill. But we should ask whether that is necessarily such a bad thing. There is at least now a recognition that if adult comics are to make an impact in this country it will have to be worked at over years, not months, which is perhaps a lesson well learned.

Further reading

The best source for keeping up with comics news is the fanzines. The *Comics Journal* is still the best of the crop, but for a specifically British perspective, see *Comics International, Comic World* and *Comics Forum*.

**THE
UNITED
STATES**

Strips and proto-comics

Sunday's/the One Day/that I Like to Read/The Funnies!
(Lyrics to popular song, Paul Whiteman and his
Orchestra, 1934)

Today, Britain has a 'special relationship' with America with regard to comics, as in much else. However, as we have seen, American comics were not imported on a regular basis until 1959, and the two markets were very much separate until this point. In fact, the origins of the American industry were entirely different to those of its British counterpart, and were rooted not in satirical magazines but in newspaper strips. Because the strips were orientated towards a mixed-age readership, in America, as in Britain, the first examples of comic books (as they became known) did not exclude an older readership.

Although a tributary to the mainstream in America, there did exist towards the end of the nineteenth century a range of humorous cartoon-based magazines. These included most famously *Puck* (1877), *Judge* (1881) and *Life* (1883). They generally took their cue from the European satirical magazines, and were critical of the establishment to varying degrees; they were therefore aimed at an educated, politically-aware, adult audience. They often employed a photo-engraving process (including colour lithography on covers and centre-spreads) that allowed the cartoonist an unprecedented creative freedom, and facilitated important advances in cartoon art, and the refinement of the mechanics of the sequential panel narrative.

However, it was not until newspaper publishers started to take an interest in strips and cartoons, in the late 1880s, that the form began to reach out towards a mass audience. At this time there was a fierce struggle for the attention of readers between the two legendary magnates of the New York press – William Randolph Hearst and Joseph Pulitzer. Both were eager to tap into new markets among the immigrant populations in the big cities, for whom English was not a first-language, and cartoons and strips were an obvious entrée.[1]

In 1896, Hearst's *New York Journal* ran the 'Yellow Kid', a cartoon-cum-strip by Richard Outcault, who had previously worked for *Life* and *Judge*. This is generally acknowledged to have been the first newspaper strip. It also marked a breakthrough in printing techniques because of its use of the colour yellow (which, added to red and blue, made full-colour reproduction possible in newspapers for the first time). In terms of content, vulgarity was the keynote. The 'Yellow Kid' chronicled the adventures of a slum-urchin who wore a bright yellow smock, and was a sharp satire on city poverty (with the Kid playing the role of idiot savant). Although the Kid was not an altogether sympathetic character (the uncouthness of some of his humour was considered very risqué at the time), he became a major success with the audience Hearst was trying to reach. Outcault's invention thus had the required effect, and pushed up circulation figures quite considerably.

This crucial advance having been made, Hearst and Pulitzer began competing as hard for strips as they did for stories (the tussle for ownership of the 'Yellow Kid' is generally agreed to have given rise to the term 'yellow journalism'). More and more space was made available for visual matter, and creators were poached from the satirical magazines. The first great age of the strip was underway.

Other early examples followed in the same lightweight vein as the 'Yellow Kid', but were rarely as satirical. They included 'Buster Brown' (1902), Outcault's follow-up, about a bob-haired scamp; 'Little Nemo in Slumberland' (1905), by Winsor McCay, a beautifully-rendered fantasy about the dreams of a young boy, today recognised as a masterpiece of the form; 'The Katzenjammer Kids' (1897), by Rudolph Dirks, concerning the anarchic experiences of a pair of German-American twins;[2] 'The Kinder-Kids' (1906), by Lyonel Feininger, narratively similar to the Katzenjammers, but artistically an expressionist *tour de force*; 'Polly and Her Pals' (1912), by Cliff Sterrett, about a 'new woman' and her relationship with her family; and 'Mutt and Jeff' (1908), by Bud Fisher, about the race-track shenanigans of two friends, one tall and one short (which in its earliest days offered authentic racing tips).

Gradually, Sunday became the main day for the inclusion of the strips, which were now being popularly referred to as 'the comics'. By 1900, they were typically being printed in colour, with four entire pages to themselves (out of fifty) – essentially constituting a Sunday pull-out supplement.[3] Because of their exclusively humorous content, these supplements came to be known as the 'Sunday funnies', and thus in America the term 'the comics' came to mean an integral part of a newspaper (a significantly different association than in Britain). Later, the word would encompass the whole range of graphic narrative expression, from newspaper strips to comic books.

The crucial characteristic of the funnies was that they were not orientated solely towards juveniles. Indeed, most went for a mixed-age readership, and were intended for all the family. Within this, some were simplistic, knockabout fun without any real intellectual content, while others included sophisticated elements. A few strips, however, had a specifically mature audience in mind, and it is to these that we must briefly digress.

Two early examples in particular stand out as being especially adult-orientated: Winsor McCay's 'Dreams of the Rarebit Fiend' and George Herriman's 'Krazy Kat'. Today, both creators are recognised as giants in the field, and both strips debuted within eight years of each other (1905 and 1913 respectively).

'Dreams of the Rarebit Fiend', written and drawn by McCay under the pseudonym 'Silas', was an extraordinary exploration of adult anxieties and neuroses told in terms of the nightmares a character experienced when he or she ate welsh rarebit before going to bed. The swooping changes in perspective, and in size, served to conjure up a world where stories about cannibalism, deformity and death are related in an amusing and often satirical fashion. (Typically, society

Figure 10.1 'Dreams of the Rarebit Fiend', syndicated to various newspapers in 1905. Art/script: Winsor McCay. © 1905 James Gordon Bennett

gradually mutated and disintegrated until, in the last panel, the pro-
tagonist woke up.) The strip has often been overlooked by historians in
favour of McCay's later classic 'Little Nemo', which echoed 'Rarebit
Fiend' in many respects, but which was much lighter in tone and
intended, in McCay's words, 'to please the little folk'.[4] Yet in retrospect 'Rarebit Fiend' is an equally impressive work, with added
intellectual depth, and deserving of much greater critical attention.

'Krazy Kat', by George Herriman, had little in common with
McCay's work, save for an exhilarating sense of experimentation, and
has never suffered from a similar lack of critical appreciation. In it,
Officer Pupp, a dog – a symbol of law and order, and straightforward
and honourable – is deeply in love with an androgynous cat called
Krazy, who is innocent, open and romantic. Krazy is ambivalent about
Pupp, but head-over-heels in love with a mouse called Ignatz, who is a
wild, anarchistic symbol of chaos and disorder. Ignatz despises Krazy,
and 'beans' him/her with a brick when the opportunity arises – which
Krazy perceives as a sign of affection. Officer Pupp then steps in and
jails Ignatz. It was a plot that would be repeated by Herriman every
week for over thirty years. Although the strip could be enjoyed by children, its underlying intellectual complexity, coupled with Dadaist artwork and Joycean language, made it a favourite with the American
intelligentsia: poet e.e. cummings was known to be a fan, and President
Woodrow Wilson was reported to have read it every morning before
cabinet meetings. It was even made into a ballet in 1922.

The reason these two strips are important from our point of
view is because they showed the perimeters, artistic and cerebral, to
which the strip medium could aspire. Although other strips were read
by adults, these showed that the medium did not have to be obvious or
dumb. Later, both creators would be 'rediscovered' by the 1960s–70s
underground, and again in the 1980s–90s comics boom; and both

Figure 10.2 Panel from
'Krazy Kat', syndicated in
1926. Art/script: George
Herriman. © 1926 King
Features Syndicate

strips (though especially 'Krazy Kat') would be an enormous influence upon future adult comics creators.[5]

But in the context of their day, neither 'Krazy Kat' or 'Rarebit Fiend' were typical of American strips, and neither was especially popular. Although there was always space for the more 'highbrow' material, in general it was straightforward knockabout buffoonery that continued to draw the biggest readership (and, indeed, 'Krazy Kat' only lasted as long as it did because it was a personal favourite of Hearst).

In fact, it was largely because of the flippant tone of most of the strips that criticism of them grew. As in Britain, where middle-class objections were raised to early comics, so in America similar complaints were now applied to the funnies. Typically, they were accused of being crass, ephemeral and detrimental to reading: that they were often more popular than the actual news-pages in the papers was considered by some a national outrage.

There was also an underlying class prejudice, which again echoed the British experience. Because Hearst, Pulitzer and other tycoons were using the strips to reach an ever-wider audience (often an immigrant audience), they were branded as 'low class' and accused of 'dragging the press down'. This was closely tied to a religious objection: for many critics it was a point of principle that the sabbath was not meant for enjoying the Sunday funnies (the fact that many immigrants happened to be non-Christians was not entirely unconnected). These complaints, inaudible at first but growing much louder by the First World War, constituted the beginnings of articulated opposition to the strip medium in America, and left an unfortunate legacy for the future comic book industry.

The next phase of strip development, in the 1920s and 1930s, saw two themes develop: the gradual standardisation of humorous strips into situation comedies, and the emergence of a new genre – adventure. These were to become the staples of American newspaper strips, and were responsible for taking the form to new levels of popularity. They did not stem complaints against the medium, however, which intensified over the period.

As the big strip syndicates consolidated their control over the form, it was realised that bigger profits could be made if the funnies were less locally-orientated, and standardised in order to appeal to a wider audience. Thus, they began to speak much less to the fringes of American society, and more to 'middle America'. In the words of one historian:

> Somewhere, somehow, it was decided that what the people needed was reassurance – perhaps the people themselves decided it – that what should be going into millions of homes

all over the United States was a comforting and conformist version of the lives that were lived in those homes.[6]

The result was that time and again strips were toned down to meet a lowest common-denominator 'national norm', typically involving domestic situation comedy. Increasingly smug and self-satisfied, they reflected and reaffirmed the roles and goals of the middle class rather than their original constituency, the working class. The best-known examples of this kind of strip were 'Bringing Up Father' (1913) by George McManus, about a *nouveau riche* Irishman from lowly origins who was a constant embarrassment to his socially ambitious wife and daughter; 'Abie the Agent' (1914) by Harry Hershfield, concerning a Jewish businessman and his circle of friends; 'The Gumps' (1917) by Sidney Smith, about a household dominated by the unrepentant braggart Andy Gump; and 'Gasoline Alley' (1918) by Frank King, about everyday life in small-town America (a strip notable for the fact that the characters aged). Later these would be joined by others in the same basically middle-class mould, such as 'Little Orphan Annie' (1924) by Harold Gray, a pointedly right-wing strip about a young girl who embodied 'true American values'; and 'Blondie' (1930) by Chic Young, which developed into a bland husband and wife comedy-drama.

This trend can be over-stressed, however. These sit-coms were invariably backed up by more simplistic knockabout comedy, reminiscent of the beginnings of the form. New favourites in the old tradition included 'The Bungle Family' (1918) by Harry Tuthill, concerning a misanthropic household; 'Thimble Theatre' (1919) by E. C. Segar, which starred a spinach-eating sailor by the name of Popeye; 'Barney Google' (1919) by Billy De Beck, about an inveterate gambler's relationship with a racehorse named Spark Plug; 'Felix the Cat' (1923) by Otto Messmer, about a fearless feline (later the star of many animated films); 'Joe Palooka' (1930) by Ham Fisher, about a gormless boxer; 'L'il Abner' by Al Capp, a satirical hill-billy romp; and 'Fritzi Ritz' (1933) by Ernie Bushmiller, which starred an overweight little girl called Nancy (later to be given her own strip).

But despite the continuing popularity of humour, in the 1930s the content of strips began to change, and a completely new element crept in – adventure. The new action strips often drew on the 'pulps' – sensationalised, bit-part magazines – for inspiration, and were frequently commissioned by the syndicates themselves for a mass audience. Classics appeared in the fields of science fiction – notably, 'Buck Rogers' (1929) by Philip Nowlan and Dick Calkins, about a man who wakes up 500 years in the future and finds himself in a post-apocalyptic world of ray-guns and robots; and 'Flash Gordon' (1934) by Alex Raymond, concerning another dashing hero and his battle with intergalactic despot Ming the Merciless; jungle adventure – notably

UNARMED, AND NOT DARING TO LEAVE DALE UNPROTECTED, FLASH AND RONAL FIGHT DOWN THEIR DESIRE TO AID THE SLAVE GIRLS, AND MAKE A DASH FOR FREEDOM.

BUT RONAL DROPS SLOWLY BEHIND, AND, WATCHING HIS CHANCE, DODGES BEHIND A STALAGMITE--A DARING AND HEROIC PLAN FORMING IN HIS MIND. 7-9-38.

AS A MAGNIFICENT GESTURE TO SPEED DALE--THE GIRL HE SILENTLY AND HOPE-LESSLY LOVES--ON HER WAY TO FREE-DOM, RONAL HURLS HIMSELF ON THE PURSUING GIANT CHIEFTAIN!

Figure 10.3 Panels from
'Flash Gordon', syndicated
in 1939. Art/script: Alex
Raymond. © 1939 King
Features Syndicate

'Tarzan' (1929) by Hal Foster and later Burne Hogarth, an imaginative version of the Edgar Rice Burroughs story; detective thrillers – notably 'Dick Tracy' (1931) by Chester Gould, a hard-boiled morality play set in gangster-beseiged Chicago; historical fiction – for example, 'Prince Valiant' (1937) by Harold Foster, about a royal family 'in the days of Arthur'; and military and flight tales – notably, 'Terry and the Pirates' (1934) by Milton Caniff, about a wide-eyed youth and his adventures in China.

All these strips garnered large adult followings, and it is clear in retrospect that they represented a much-needed source of escapism for large portions of the population from the devastating effects of the Great Depression. Revealingly, most tended to transport the reader elsewhere – to outer space, the jungle, distant history, the Far East or some other exotic location where nothing had any real bearing on the problems of the day.[7]

Indeed, the Depression years became the period of peak popularity of strips generally in America. Some indication of their importance can be gleaned from an episode involving a newspaper strike in New York in 1935, when the mayor himself read the strips over the radio so his constituents could keep up to date. They were nothing less than a national institution, and nowhere else in the world had anything like them.

Yet this is also the historical point at which we must leave the discussion of strips *per se* to concentrate on their new offspring – the comic book. It was no accident that the one should emerge at the zenith of the other, at a time when the public was ready for actual comics periodicals. It should be noted, however, that newspaper strips have continued to be massively popular in America up until the present day. Heirs to the tradition have included, in the humour genre, 'Peanuts', 'Beetle Bailey', 'Bloom County' and 'Calvin and Hobbes'; and in the adventure genre, 'Rip Kirby' and 'Buz Sawyer'.

The development of comic books from the newspaper funnies

was a gradual process with numerous false starts. It is true, for example, that individual strips had been collected into volumes since the beginning of the form: 'Yellow Kid', 'Little Nemo' and 'The Katzenjammer Kids' were among the first to appear as hardback albums. Before them, collections of cartoons from the satirical magazines had been fairly common – exemplified by *The Good Things of 'Life'* series which had debuted in 1883.

In 1922, the first monthly reprint volume appeared. *Comic Monthly* featured a different strip in each issue (including 'Barney Google' and 'Polly and Her Pals'), was 10 inches by 10 inches square, had four panels per page and sold for 10 cents. Though a pioneering publication in the sense that it was regular and cheap, it did not find a viable readership, and folded after seven issues.

In 1929, another attempt was made. *The Funnies* was the first all-original strip publication with recurring characters, and was published weekly in a tabloid format (rather like a Sunday supplement without the accompanying newspapers). It was reportedly based on British comics, though with the added aim of showcasing strips for later syndication to newspapers (they included 'Frosty Ayers' about two friends on an Arctic expedition, and 'Bunk Buford' about a baseball hero). But despite keeping to the 10 cents price established by *Comic Monthly*, it soon ran into problems because, unlike British comics, it could not support a weekly turnover, and was eventually cancelled after thirteen issues. It should be noted that according to our definition of a comic, as delineated in the Introduction, this was the first American example of the form. However, *The Funnies* was not the first comic book, which as we shall see below was a category defined by format.[8]

Having learned the lesson that the public was not yet ready for original material, by the mid-1930s publishers were keen to try the market again with reprints. *Funnies on Parade* (1933) was published in full colour in what we now recognise as the modern comic book format, which was achieved by folding a Sunday supplement in half, and in half again. It was the innovation of two salesmen, Harry Wildenberg and Max Gaines, who acquired reprint rights to a variety of top strips (including 'Joe Palooka' and 'The Bungle Family'), and sold the resulting booklet to Proctor and Gamble to use as a promotional give-away. It was so successful that further examples were immediately commissioned.

It was a short step to sticking on a price-tag and selling the books commercially. *Famous Funnies* (1934), masterminded once again by Max Gaines, stuck carefully to the *Funnies on Parade* formula, and was priced the same as *Comic Monthly* and *The Funnies* – 10 cents. Once more it consisted of many of the top strips of the day (for example, 'Mutt and Jeff' and 'The Bungle Family') and proved to be an immediate hit. The news-stand comic book as we know it had finally arrived.

Several imitators followed, including *Tip Top Comics*, *Popular Comics*, *Super Comics* and *Crackerjack Funnies* – all were anthologies, and some mixed humour strips with adventure, sophisticated material with juvenilia. Indeed, such was the rush by publishers to get into the new field that it soon became clear that the syndicates would run out of strips to supply them with. Thus, original strips had to be introduced among the reprints.

The first all-original comic book with recurring characters in the new format was published in 1935 – *New Comics* no. 1. Like its predecessors, it was an anthology, and like them sold for 10 cents. How it was able to keep to the low cost while using original strips can

Figure 10.4 Cover to *Famous Funnies*, no. 1 (1934), the first American comic book to be sold via news-stands. Art: unknown. © 1933 Eastern Color Press

be explained by the meagre rates of pay for creators: as had happened in Britain, the origin of comics in cheap reprints set the tone for future staff exploitation.

It was still a risk to put out a comic that was completely new, but where *The Funnies* had failed commercially, *New Comics* was able to succeed: evidently the time was right, and the format was more to the public's taste. It finally lit the green light for other all-original comics. Eventually, these would evolve and split into constituent genres, thus establishing the kinds of comic we are familiar with today – a story we shall be taking up in chapter 11.

By now, 'comic books' was the phrase generally used to describe the new form, in contra-distinction to 'the comics' – though, inevitably, the former term was often abbreviated to 'comics' in everyday speech. It is important to re-state that the concept originally had no age connotations: the readership was a mixed-age one from the start, and continued to reflect the form's origins in the newspapers right up until the boom in superheroes in the early 1940s.

But before leaving the subject of these first American comics, there is one kind that is often overlooked, but which is important to identify for our purposes. These were the so-called 'Dirty Comics' a.k.a. Tijuana Bibles a.k.a. 8-Pagers – illegal pornographic titles that made their debut in the 1920s and came into vogue in the 1930s. Produced anonymously, what they lacked in drawing quality they made up for in explicitness. They began by putting then-famous comic characters into compromising situations,[9] but soon progressed to doing the same with film stars and media personalities. Some even starred gangsters (for example, Pretty Boy Floyd, John Dillinger), who were portrayed in a flattering light and always got the girls. According to one historian, 'it is possible that these hot items have been thought to represent the depths of depravity not only because of their concentration on sex, but because of their sociological and revolutionary

Figure 10.5 Page-panel from *Sexy Sadie in: Sadie Steps Out* (c.1935), one of the early 'Dirty Comics', featuring Popeye. Art: anon.

implications'.[10] They could not be sold from news-stands for obvious reasons, so were sold 'under the counter' or through the post. In one sense they can therefore be seen as the first American underground comics, and it should come as no surprise that they were later rediscovered by 1960s and 1970s comix publishers, and then again during the 1990s sex comics boom.

Further reading

On the early comic strips, a solid background is provided by Rick Marschall's *America's Great Comic Strip Artists* (New York: Cross River Press 1989); and Thomas Inge's *Comics as Culture* (Jackson, Mississippi: University Press of Mississippi 1990). On the transformation of strips to comic books see Chris Wooley's *Wooley's History of the Comic Book* (Lake Buena Vista, Florida: self-published 1986). There are also some useful biographies of pioneering creators, notably John Canemaker's *Winsor McCay* (Berkeley, Calif.: University of California Press 1981); and Graham McDonnell *et al. Krazy Kat: The Comic Art of George Herriman* (New York: Abrams 1982).

Comic books for everyone

What we were doing was writing up to our readers. I was aware, having come out of the [Armed] Service that there was a great readership out there among adults — not just teenagers.

(Al Feldstein, ex-chief writer EC Comics)[1]

The period 1935 to 1955 is generally recognised as the 'Golden Age' of American comic books. Sales during this period were higher than at any other time in the country's history, making the USA the undisputed comics capital of the world. Though the majority were juvenile in orientation, there were a surprising number aimed at a mixed-age readership, and also at a specifically adult audience. It was thus truly the era of comic books for everyone, and divides naturally into three periods.

The first period saw the establishment of the 'genre' comic book at the end of the 1930s, when subject-matter was heavily linked to newspaper strips and designed predominantly for a general readership. The second was the early and mid-1940s, when superheroes ruled: this constituted the first major boom in American comics history, and set the definition of a comic thereafter as quintessentially juvenile. The third period was the end of the 1940s to the mid-1950s, when superheroes were waning, and when a wider range of themes brought in significant numbers of adult readers once again, resulting in all-time record sales of approaching 60 million comics per month. The backlash against this latter phase came to a head in 1954 with the institution of the Comics Code – the subject for chapter 12.[2]

By 1936, comics were an established, if very marginal, part of American publishing. As we have seen, the industry consisted of exclusively anthology comics, sometimes packaging humorous strips with adventure fare, and adult material with juvenilia. But as time went on, it became clear that there was a more specialised demand for certain types of subject-matter – detective thrillers, western adventure, slapstick humour and so on. Thus, 'genre titles' emerged, catering to specific tastes. The original genre comics were reprint-based, and merely collected together newspaper strips of a particular orientation. But as more original material was added, so new publishers jumped on the bandwagon.

In particular, comics now attracted publishers from the pulps, who were already geared to formula-writing, and who brought with them the knowledge of how to produce stripped-down, entertaining stories on a tight budget. They were primarily interested in making quick money from the new craze, and often used their existing writers for comics scripts. The first comic devoted to a single theme reflected one of the most popular pulp genres, *Detective Picture Stories* (1936), and was followed by westerns, science fiction and numerous others.[3]

As with previous comics, the genre titles were originally orientated towards a mixed-age readership, though naturally different genres appealed to different age-groups. The funny animal comics, for example, were bought mainly by youngsters, while the more cerebral detective 'whodunnits' attracted a more adult following.

It was also at this point historically that the production process of comics in America became formalised. The splitting of comics into genres marked the genesis of 'studios' or 'shops' which produced comics rather in the same way as Ford produced cars – by assembly-line. This split production into writing, drawing, inking, colouring and lettering, with a different person (sometimes persons) responsible for each stage in the process. For publishers this was a cheap and effective way to feed the growing market; for creators it typically meant low per-page rates, with no royalties and little or no acknowledgement (see also pp. 33–4). The first studio for mass-produced comics is generally agreed to have opened in 1937.

But the system was remarkably flexible, and this together with the cheap cost of paper meant that shifts in public taste could be responded to almost immediately. A studio might concentrate on two or three genres, but could switch energies to whichever happened to be the most popular at any particular time. In other words, publishers could try out different kinds of comics, and by a process of elimination kill off those that did not sell. This had been the process that had sustained the pulps; and now became the economic imperative behind the consolidation of the genre-comics. In this way, the stage was set for a new phase in comics development, as a surge in demand developed among younger readers for one genre in particular – the superheroes.

The superhero boom initiated the second phase in the development of American comics and established the form as a mass medium. Essentially crime-fighters, these colourful costumed characters were influenced by two basic sources – the newspaper strips and the pulps. The archetype, Superman, was originally intended by Siegel and Shuster as a newspaper strip, to cash in on the 1930s vogue for adventure, and therefore contained elements that would appeal to a mixed-age readership: at his inception, the character was a kind of 'New Deal' figure, who helped striking miners against pit-owners, and took army generals to the battle-front to show them the carnage. When National Periodicals decided to use him in a comic book, however, they dropped the more political elements and turned him into an all-powerful mytho-logical hero for children. Superman now embodied 'Truth, Justice and the American Way!', and his enemies were no longer real, but imaginary monsters. It was a formula that would prove extremely popular, and Superman's first appearance in *Action* no. 1 (1938) provided a template that the vast majority of superhero comics would follow.[4]

Batman, the second major superhero, was both part of the Superman tradition, and a contrast to it. The character was much closer to the pulp tradition (especially to the pulp vogue for masked crime-fighters such as The Shadow) and, having no supernatural powers, was more of a sleuth than Superman. He therefore developed through the detective genre comics, and first appeared in *Detective Comics 27* in 1939. Other heroes would later follow this path, thus establishing a kind of subcategory within the superhero genre. (This should not be exaggerated, however: the crucial difference between the Batman-style superheroes and the detective comics was that the former replaced the cerebral-ness of the latter with a greater degree of action, and thereby appealed to a much younger readership.)

By the early 1940s, *Superman* and *Batman* were comic books in their own right, and their enormous success had precipitated a rapid fall in age-range for the comics readership generally, as now virtually every studio in the country turned their attention to superheroes. It was true that money could be made from other genres aimed at the growing children's market: for example, funny animal comics expanded dramatically, and titles starring gormless teenagers also made an impact (notably, *Archie*). But it was the men in tights that really made the money.

As *Captain America, Hawkman, Captain Marvel* and hundreds of others joined the roster, the genre came into its own. During the war years patriotic superheroes were sent off to fight for their country, and the conflict was polarised into one between supermen and super-villains: Tojo, Hitler and Mussolini stood no chance. These comics were unashamed morale-boosters, and retailed in unprecedented numbers: by 1943 it is estimated they were selling nearly 15 million copies a month, thereby totally dominating the industry.

But not everybody was convinced the new comics boom was a good thing. The early 1940s saw criticism of the medium grow, with objections to the Sunday funnies now carried over and applied to children's superhero comics. In 1943, the Children's Book Committee of the Child Study Association objected to comics because of their 'violence of subject matter, the crudity and cheapness of format, the strain of young eyes and the spoiling of taste for better reading' ('better reading', of course, meaning proper books).[5] Even when comics were 'doing their bit' in the war, it seemed, they could not win on the home front.

Despite the criticism, it was the end of the war and the changing demands of the market that brought about a reorientation of the industry. The superheroes were unable to sustain their popularity for long after 1945, and phase three in the development of American comics was characterised by the industry reaching out once again for an adult audience. From the late 1940s, comics became 'socially relevant' in a way that had not been seen before – albeit within broadly pulp narrative traditions – as genres such as crime, romance and horror came to the fore. This was to prove an extremely popular move that heralded the biggest sales boom in history. To give just one estimate of the size of the adult readership: a government sponsored survey of an Ohio town in 1950 found that 54 per cent of all comic book readers were adults over 20 years of age, and that the average reader read about eleven comics a month. If those figures were extended nationally, it was certainly true that more adults were reading comics than at any other time.

But, in entering the 'real world', comics now had to face up to real problems. They would naturally have to address a much-changed America. Indeed, with the benefit of hindsight, it is possible to say that the country was experiencing a great deal of stress due to postwar readjustment. Put very briefly, America's role in the world had changed drastically: by virtue of the country's economic strength, it had become 'the world's policeman', up against the new enemies of communist USSR, on one hand, and communist China, on the other. The existence of 'the bomb' meant that either side had the power to wipe out the other at the push of a button. At home, international tensions were reflected politically by a swing to the right, as the neo-liberalism of Roosevelt was replaced by the increasingly reactionary governments of Truman and Eisenhower. There were fears about communists at home stabbing America in the back, and this led to the infamous witch-hunts led by Wisconsin's Senator McCarthy. There were also worries about spiralling divorce rates and the perceived rise of juvenile delinquency, which sometimes made it seem as if 'the family', that cornerstone of American life, was under threat. In other words, paranoia was in the air, and culture was under pressure to conform.

Comics were not exempt from these pressures and, as we shall see in chapter 12, fell foul of them in the long run. But in order to understand the roots of the 'new realism' in the medium, we must return to the war-years and look at the readership of comics – particularly superhero comics – among servicemen.

The American armed forces were unique in that comics were sent out to the troops in much the same way as other supplies. They were considered lightweight entertainment for men with other things on their minds. In particular, comics were found to be the ideal reading matter in transit (a striking echo of the popularity of early British comics as 'railway literature').[7] They sold like wildfire, and it was reported that on the military bases comics outsold magazines like *Life* and *Readers Digest* by something like ten to one.[8]

An odd situation then developed whereby superhero stories were progressively given adult elements (mirroring the experience of the 1980s very closely). The publishers realised what was happening on the military bases, and gradually added more sophisticated elements to appeal to this audience: 'knowing humour', for example – gags that would go above a child's head, and also what would come to be known as 'Good Girl Art' (drawings of sexy women in scanty clothing, including in some cases stories involving bondage – see p 223). Some comics were now even published in a mini-format that would fit more easily into a tunic pocket.

Following this trend, the domestic readership for comics among adults grew. Since the earliest days of the form, comics derived from newspaper reprints had continued to sell well to this market – for example, *Prince Valiant, Dick Tracy* and *Terry and the Pirates* all notched up impressive sales, while throughout the 1940s *Joe Palooka* was selling over 1 million. Now they were joined by titles aimed specifically at homecoming troops. Perhaps the most popular was *Sad Sack*, by George Baker, an uproarious satire on military life (the name being an abbreviation of 'sad sack o' shit', American slang for a worthless soldier) which had begun as a strip in an army newspaper, but now became a bestseller in comic form. There were several others.

Meanwhile, the vogue for 'superheroes-plus-adult-elements' was reflected in one creation in particular, *The Spirit*, by Will Eisner. This character, too, began life in a newspaper strip (eventually being given a Sunday supplement to himself) and was given his own title in 1944. He looked and sometimes behaved like a superhero, and wore the obligatory identity-concealing mask, but there was a sophistication about the strip that had never been seen before. Eisner was strongly influenced by the pulps and film *noir*, and included in his stories *femmes fatales,* a great deal of adult humour and settings involving beautifully-rendered shadowy cityscapes. He was also a master at conveying moods through the ingenious use of 'camera angles': 'I always saw comics as an artform', he later said, 'and I knew that there was a literate audience out there who would appreciate what I was doing.'[9] Although never a bestseller, *The Spirit* soon became the standard against which other comics would be measured, and would later be 'rediscovered' by the underground, and later still by key creators in the 1980s. It is now recognised as one of the classics of the medium.

We should not exaggerate the adult audience for comics in the early-mid 1940s: titles like *Sad Sack* and *The Spirit* were exceptions. Yet the growing popularity of such comics meant that by the end of the decade publishers were confident enough to devote more resources to

Figure 11.1 Title page from 'The Elevator', *The Spirit* (1949). Elaborate openings such as this were the strip's trademark. Art/script: Will Eisner. © 1949 The creator

the market. Moreover, the paper rationing of the war years had ended, and it was economically viable to experiment. As a result, there were five major genres that boomed in the late 1940s and early 1950s that were orientated, to a greater or lesser degree, towards adults, and we must now look at each in turn.

Crime

Crime comics were chronologically the first to boom. They were a variant on the then-popular true crime magazines – typically involving factual (if sensationalised) stories about gang warfare and criminal activity told in lurid detail, often with graphic violence and erotic overtones. (Like *The Spirit* they drew from *film noir* and the pulps.) The first title to make an impact was *Crime Does Not Pay* (1942), published by Lev Gleason and featuring the gritty, distinctive artwork of Charles Biro. By 1948 it was selling an estimated 1.5 million copies an issue. Others soon cashed in – *Crime Must Pay the Penalty, Criminals on the Run, True Crime Comics* and many more – usually inferior in quality and much more explicitly violent (torture, acid-baths, 'swimming with concrete shoes' and other clichés of hard-boiled fiction were staples). By 1948, the peak year for the genre, there were thirty-eight crime titles in existence, constituting a remarkable 15 per cent of the total comic book market.[10]

Their ostensible message was that 'crime does not pay'. But, of course, their appeal was that they showed the exact opposite. It was true that, typically, the baddies would get mown down or sent to the electric chair in the end; but before that, it was they and not the police who were the centre of attention. Like the gangster 'Dirty Comics' of the 1930s, therefore, the crime comics could be interpreted as being subversive.

Of course, the genre had an appeal for younger readers (boys) on the level of rip-roaring adventure. But it is clear that the readership for many was intended expressly to be adult. For example, the pioneering *Crime Does Not Pay* briefly called itself 'illu-stories' to get away from the juvenile connotations of the word 'comic' (much in the same way that 'graphic novel' would be used in the 1980s): a readership survey undertaken in 1948 revealed that 57 per cent of its readers were over 21. Other titles took similar measures: *Murder Incorporated* carried an 'Adults Only' warning, while *Tops* styled itself 'The Adult Magazine of Dramatic Picture Stories' and even took the same format

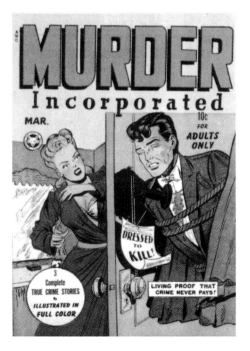

Figure 11.2 Cover to *Murder Incorporated*, no. 2 (1948). Art: unknown. © 1948 Fox Features Syndicate

as *Life* magazine in order to distance itself still further from the other comics on the shelves.

But adult or not, the crime titles were undeniably more violent than any comics that had appeared before, and it was this that provoked the most sustained assault the medium had yet faced. The anti-comics lobby was kicked into life by the first salvoes from a campaigner who would later become much more famous – Dr Fredric Wertham, Senior Psychiatrist for the New York Department of Hospitals. He claimed that crime comics glorified gangsterism (true) and led to child delinquency (false), and he used his professional position to lend intellectual credibility to his cause. At the same time he popularised his views in news-stand magazines (he was published in *Readers Digest, Colliers* and *Ladies Home Journal* among others), and worked hard to help parents' movements and church groups to start up.[11] Under his influence, isolated complaints about comics were moulded into a fully-fledged campaign: by the end of the 1940s, there were already several reported cases of comic-burnings on school grounds. Indeed, it is often overlooked that the fires were burning long before the horror comics came along. Unquestionably, after this first backlash, the comics medium was operating in a highly sensitised environment.[12]

Romance

The crime boom was followed, much less controversially, by a boom in romance comics in 1949. One was partly a commercial response to the other: crime had shown there was a large audience for comics

Figure 11.3 Cover to
Young Romance, no. 2
(1947). Art: Jack Kirby.
© 1947 Prize Comics Group

among adult males, now romance would do the same for females. Although it is possible to locate precedents for the genre in newspaper strips, it is generally agreed that the first and most influential title was *Young Romance* (1947) by Joe Simon and Jack Kirby, which was remarkable for its intelligent storytelling and finely-wrought art. 'There was a need for adult-oriented comics', Joe Simon later recalled, 'I remembered back to my childhood to the love magazines, like *True Confessions* that my parents used to read. That stuck with me; how popular this type of material was. That's what led to realistic romance comics.'[13]

Young Romance was followed by a wave of others, few of which were in the same class. They compensated for their lack of sophistication by being much more steamy: typical subject-matter included betrayal, adultery and revenge – often dealing frankly with sex (talk of 'tongues lashing the backs of throats' and 'heaving bosoms' was not uncommon). By 1949 there were 120 romance titles on the market, thus constituting a major genre, and a meteoric rise.

Like the crime comics, many romance comics made efforts to distance themselves from a younger readership. *Young Romance*, for example, carried a bright orange label 'For the more ADULT Reader of Comics'. Indeed, according to one source, in 1947 nearly half the readers of the the genre were over 18 years old,[14] and there is evidence that many publishers intended the primary audience to be 'young marrieds'. Although they were not attacked by the anti-comics lobby to anything like the same degree as the crime titles, they were still criticised for being 'overtly sexual', 'un-Christian' and 'setting a bad example'.

War

War comics boomed as a result of the Korean War in 1950 – or the 'Korean police action' as it was officially referred to. The majority were gung-ho, racist, poorly written and above all violent. Titles like *GI Joe* and *Soldier Comics* built on the level of violence established by the crime comics by depicting the enemy as 'easily slaughterable', usually by characterising them as subhuman, monkey-like sadists. (It should be noted that such racism was not new in comics – these titles mimicked the depiction of the Japanese in superhero comics during the Second World War.)

There were also one or two less bloodthirsty examples of the genre. In particular, EC, a relatively small publisher managed by William Gaines (son of Max, of *Famous Funnies* fame), published *Frontline Combat* and *Two Fisted Tales*, both edited by Harvey Kurtzman, which dealt realistically with wars past and present, and sometimes even contained anti-war strips (Kurtzman's own 'Corpse on the Imjin' being an acclaimed example). As well as being unusual for

tackling the subject from a different angle, they were also some of the best-produced comics ever seen, and featured work by artists who are now recognised as masters of the form – among them Jack Davis, Wally Wood, Will Elder and Johnny Severin.

The war genre, too, attracted a sizeable adult following, mainly among servicemen and would-be servicemen. Some titles were more orientated towards older readers than others; of these, many contained 'pin-up' pages of 'Good Girl Art'. Significantly, hostile reaction to the genre was very muted. It was true that Wertham disliked it intensely, but generally there was no backlash because the comics toed the establishment line: to put it simply, as they were only killing the enemy, nobody really took much notice. Only the EC titles came in for criticism – for being too left-wing.[15]

Horror

Horror comics boomed in the early 1950s. There had been horror comics in the 1940s, mainly based on monsters from movies – Frankenstein, the Mummy and so on – and many of the superhero comics had macabre overtones – for example, *Batman*. But the 1950s versions were new, and, as we saw briefly in chapter, 2, took blood-letting to extremes. They reflected the anxieties of the age symbolically, much in the manner of contemporary cinema (there were more horror and SF movies made in this period than at any time before or since): as one historian has explained, 'such yarns conveyed the notion that the truly demented were plentiful in American society, and that, like Communists, they could be anybody'.[16]

EC set the pace, and released three titles in 1950 that revolutionised the genre – *Tales from the Crypt, Vault of Horror* and *Haunt of Fear*. These have been briefly discussed on p. 29. They featured the work of many of the team responsible for the war comics, and were again of a very high standard, albeit in an extremely gory sense. They were enormously influential, and were followed by a plethora of imitators, few of which were of comparable quality. They had the excess, but not the talent: one title, *Mysterious Adventures* no. 15 (1953) for example, contained a decapitation, two incidences of acid being thrown in someone's face, several strangulations and a vicious knife attack. Even so, the readers could not get enough: by 1953 there were an estimated 130 horror comics on the shelves.[17]

The main market for horror was adolescents (particularly boys, but also a surprising number of girls) but there was also a significant adult readership. Some publishers deliberately targeted the over-16s, and this was especially true of EC, who often included social commentary in their stories (the blood-letting, though copious, was never for its own sake). As such, there was also a significant crossover readership with the crime comics.

Once again, it was the violence that upset people, and the horror comics raised the temperature of the anti-comics campaign to boiling point. Wertham's outbursts became more frequent, and were given more publicity, while comics-burnings now became commonplace. Under pressure, many news-stands boycotted comics altogether. By now, various shades of political opinion had thrown their weight behind the campaign, including far-right groups, and American leftists (though they were not as influential as in Britain). There were even statutes passed in some states: in parts of California, for example, the penalty for selling crime or horror comics could be a $700 fine or forty days in jail, or both. It would not be long before the US Government itself would become involved.

Satire

Satire comics were the last major boom before the final clampdown. Satirical humour had always been popular in newspaper strips, but this was the first time it had taken off in comics. The pivotal title was *Mad* (1952), again an EC comic, under the contributing-editorship of Harvey Kurtzman (he of the war comics). Subtitled 'Humor in a Jugular Vein', it patented a new style of off-the-wall zaniness illustrated by some of the best artists from the EC stable – notably Jack Davis, Wally Wood and Bill Elder. *Mad*'s impact was immediate and

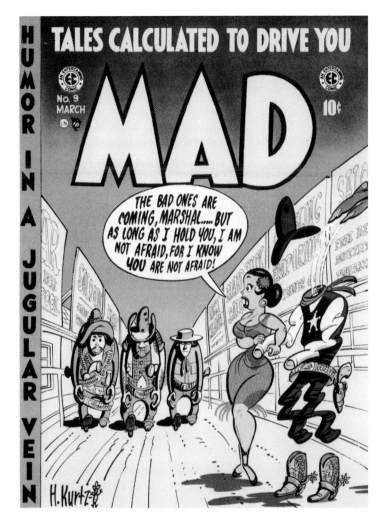

Figure 11.5 Cover to *Mad*, no. 9 (1954). Art: Harvey Kurtzman. © 1954 EC Comics

profound; it has been described as being like that of the Marx Brothers in the 1930s. By its sixth issue, it was selling 500,000 copies.[18]

Inevitably *Mad* spawned a host of other satirical comic books – including (pre-Code) *Eh!*, *Whack*, *Crazy* (all 1953), *Wild*, *Riot*, *Unsane* (all 1954) and finally *Panic* (1954), a sister title from EC, edited by Al Feldstein. Although some featured inspired artwork and gags, none were quite as mad as their progenitor.

The satire genre had adolescents as its core readership, but did attract adults. Indeed, *Mad* got 'older' with time, as it moved on from parodying other comics (early strips included 'Superduperman' and 'Bat Boy and Rubin'), to the media and then finally to politics. Of course, the nearer to the wind the comics sailed, the more likely they were to be criticised. Even though crime and horror comics were the focus for the growing backlash, satire comics were still not safe and, as we shall see in chapter 13, *Mad* was eventually forced to take a magazine format to avoid censorship.[19]

Finally, by way of a postscript, there was one other genre of comic that attracted an adult readership, and which therefore requires a mention, but which was not part of the censorship campaign because it was generally clandestine – namely, 'fetish' comics. These were a particular kind of sex comic that had precedents in the 'Dirty Comics' of the 1930s, but which appealed to a much more specialised taste. Typically they featured women in bondage, and occasionally involved flagellation, leather clothing and sado-masochism. Drawn by creators with pseudonyms like 'Stanton,' 'Eneg' and 'Willie', they reached their peak popularity in the early to mid-1950s, with titles like *Sweet Gwendoline* and *Princess Elaine* garnering sizeable cult followings. They tended to be sold either through the post, 'under the counter' or from the growing network of sex shops.[20] Like the 'Dirty Comics', they were rediscovered by the underground, and again during the erotica boom of the early 1990s.[21]

Further reading

The best general overview is Les Daniels's *Comix: A History of Comic Books in America* (New York: Bonanza Books, 1971). William Savage's *Comic Books and America 1945–1954* (Oklahoma: University of Oklahoma Press 1990) is extremely useful for a socio-cultural perspective. For detailed information on individual titles, see Mike Benton's compendium *The Comic Book in America* (Dallas, Texas: Taylor Publishing 1989). Harvey Kurtzman and Will Eisner are interviewed in G. Groth and R. Fiore (eds) *The New Comics* (New York: Berkley 1988). There are also one or two notable biographies of prominent figures: for example, Catherine Yronwode, *The Art of Will Eisner* (Princeton, Wisconsin: Kitchen Sink 1982, rev. edn 1988); and F. Jacobs, *The Mad World of William Gaines* (Columbus, Ohio: Ohio State University Press 1972).

1954 – seduction of the experienced?

Comics are supposed to be like fairy tales
(Fredric Wertham, *Seduction of the Innocent*)[1]

Our magazines are written for adults – it isn't our fault if the kids read 'em too.
(Will Gaines, publisher EC Comics)[2]

The year 1954 saw the crusade against comics come to a head in America, and the institution of a restrictive Code. Any consideration of the final stages of the backlash must centre on Fredric Wertham's book *Seduction of the Innocent*, which argued that comics led to child delinquency, and which was much more important in the whole affair in America than it was in Britain. However, there were other, political, reasons why the Code was enforced, and there was certainly more at stake than 'the good of the children'. Indeed, when the peculiar circumstances of the creation of the Code are taken into account, it is arguable whether the book's ultimate significance was more symbolic than anything else.

In retrospect, the backlash was perhaps to be expected. The breakneck pace of the rise of the comics industry in the late 1940s and early 1950s was bound to create alarm, and we can see the hostile reaction to it as part of a cyclical phenomenon affecting popular culture. Rapid media booms are periodically met with animosity – British panics included those involving the penny dreadfuls in the nineteenth century, rock 'n' roll in the 1950s and video nasties in the 1980s; similar American examples included protest against 'dime novels' in the nineteenth century, against cinema in the 1920s and 1930s, rock 'n' roll in the 1950s and video games in the 1970s. As one historian has pointed out: 'Each reaction proceeds from a new technology or a new application thereof, and technology suggests change, as do social disorders. Juxtapose the two, and it is simple enough to blame the technology for the disorder.'[3]

It was against this background that *Seduction of the Innocent* made its appearance. This was Wertham's *magnum opus*, the *Mein Kampf* of comics. It drew together all the threads of his campaigning over the years, and took in every kind of comic, raising objections to them all. He used the term 'crime comic books' to designate any kind of comic in which crime was depicted – thus extending the negative implications of the 'crime' label until it encompassed almost the whole industry. Specific comics had specific dangers: superhero comics were essentially fascist, 'übermensch' fantasies, often with homo-erotic undercurrents (especially in the case of Batman's relationship with Robin); the romance comics were lasciviously sexual and morally bankrupt. Worst of all, of course, were the ersatz crime and horror comics. These were so pernicious they could actually lead to delinquency, a 'fact' that Wertham attempted to prove by recounting true case histories of juvenile murders and sex crimes.

But Wertham's methodology, and the use of case histories in particular, was highly suspect. His logic was that because delinquents read comics, comics led to delinquency. The histories were thus juxtaposed with isolated panels and quotations from offending comics which were taken completely out of context and presented as 'evidence' of a comic's overall content. (Although the EC comics were focused upon to a large degree, the reader would never guess from Wertham's account that they were well written.) The cumulative effect was to damn all comics by association.

Thus, though *Seduction* was presented as scientific research, it was in fact blatantly sensationalist. Wertham had long ago learned the value of over-dramatisation in hyping his case, and chapter titles like 'Homicide at Home', 'I Want to be a Sex Maniac!' and 'Bumps and Bulges' give a more accurate indication of the book's tone. The cod-Freudianism of much of the analysis was, of course, another selling point – in a society as repressed as 1950s America it had the effect of exploiting in titillating fashion the same material it was ostensibly attacking.

Ultimately, there was no evidence in the book that comics were a corrupting influence. Other psychiatrists attacked the central thesis at the time, and research since has shown it to be empirically and theoretically unsupportable. (Wertham claimed his opponents were either incompetent to judge, or being paid off by the comics publishers.)[4]

However, Wertham was not pressing for a total comics ban. The aim of *Seduction* was rather to re-establish the line between what was acceptable for children, and for adults. Hence, Wertham concludes with a call for legislation: 'I'm not a lawyer, but from a medico-legal point of view I would suggest that the sale and display of crime comic books to children under 15 be forbidden.'[5] Wertham wanted a system rather like the one in operation in the 1990s (see p. 3): in other words, *Seduction* may have been his *Mein Kampf*, but his 'final solution' for comics was definitely not blanket censorship.[6]

The book was an instant best seller. Its commercial success took the anti-comics campaign into a new phase – one which saw the government enter the fray, or rather, re-enter the fray. For it is important to note that between 1945 and 1950 the Senate Judiciary Committee on Juvenile Delinquency had been assembling information and data on 'the possible influence of so-called crime comic books' on juvenile delinquency. (Indeed, some of the figures quoted in the previous chapter are from Senate reports.) Now, with the publication of *Seduction*, the issue was revived, and Estes Kefauver, one of the senators on the Committee, called for special hearings.

Why the government chose to enter publicly into the controversy at this juncture is debatable. Certainly they must have shared Wertham's fears. But it is also arguable that they had fears of their own, brought about by the statistics highlighted by their research reports. To be specific, the rapid boom in comics, and in particular the rise in the number of adults reading comics, may have been alarming from a political viewpoint. We have seen how comics were becoming socially relevant, and it must have been a short step to think of them as potentially subversive, a conduit for anti-establishment ideas. Comics for adults must therefore have been doubly suspect: delinquency among children was one thing – but children do not vote or make revolutions.

Most of the new comics were obviously not a threat in this sense. But some, like many of the EC line, had forthright political themes, and were even sometimes anti-McCarthyite: they were also read by large numbers of adults. It is not difficult to imagine that to a paranoid establishment, such aspects of the comics industry must have seemed 'out of control' and in need of containment. Was it possible, in other words, that the government saw *Seduction*, and the controversy it created, as a convenient way to get the issue into court? A great deal more research needs to be undertaken before this theory can even remotely be said to be substantiated, but subsequent events can be interpeted as lending it at least some credence.

The 'Kefauver Hearings' began in spring 1954, and were televised nationally. The only expressed aim was 'to protect children from the effects of violence', yet, throughout, the comics focused upon were not necessarily the most violent examples. Various witnesses were called, including, first on the stand, Wertham himself: he ended his statement with the words 'I think Hitler was a beginner compared to the comic book industry.'[7] Next, William Gaines, publisher of the EC line, appeared as a voluntary witness. Despite a spirited justification of his and other comics, he was backed into the absurd corner of having to defend the amount of blood that could be shown dripping from a severed head before a comic would be unsuitable for a child to read.

That the main comics focused upon should be from the EC line can be explained by the fact that they had a high profile on the newsstands, and were indeed very gory. What is not so easy to explain is the particular comics that were targeted. The one that was mentioned more than any other was *Shock Suspenstories*, a title remarkable for the fact that it contained very little overt violence at all. What it did

Figure 12.1 Cover to *Shock Suspenstories*, no. 6 (1954). Art: Jack Davis. © 1954 EC Comics

contain, however, was social commentary: an EC 'sampler' that contained both crime and horror stories, it specialised in plots which, intentially or not, laid waste to family values. They depicted wives who killed their domineering husbands, husbands who killed their nagging wives and, most notoriously, a child who engineered the deaths of her parents.[8] At the same time, more gory comics – horror titles by other publishers, the Korean War comics and so on – were conveniently ignored.

Despite the semblance of 'a fair trial', therefore, it was always clear which way the verdict would go. The hearings had all the appearances of the communist witch-hunts in microcosm, and with TV and other coverage had all the trappings of a show trial. In the summing up, it was made clear that that the government would act to censor comics if the publishers themselves did not.[9]

In the face of this intimidation, and faced with falling sales as more and more news-stands and shops refused to carry comics, a majority of publishers got together to form a self-censoring group – the Comics Magazine Association of America (CMAA). This added yet another dimension to the clampdown, for the Association provided the opportunity some publishers had been waiting for to destroy Gaines. Suffice to say they had a vested interest in forcing comics into line: if they could eliminate Gaines as a market leader, they could move

Figure 12.2 The Code
stamp of the Comics Code
Authority

into the void.[10] Whether the Senate had taken these vested interests into account before offering its ultimatum is, again, debatable.

The Association's purpose was to regulate the content of comics, and to this end it instituted the Comics Code, to be administered by a review body called the Comics Code Authority (CCA). Hereafter, publishers were obliged to submit their comics to the CCA to be evaluated before publication: if they met the standards of the Code, they were given a stamp of approval. If not (and if, subsequently, appropriate changes were not made), the comic would be denied access to the distribution network. It was proudly touted as 'the most stringent code in existence for any communications media',[11] and outlawed content involving sex, violence and, revealingly, attacks on authority. It embodied, in other words, a rigorously conservative political manifesto, and made no concessions whatsoever to the age of comics readers. (The Code is reproduced in full in Appendix 1.)

In this way, the American comics industry was radically censored. We shall see in chapter 13 the slump that this produced. Wertham, for his part, was left out in the cold. In various articles, often published in similar magazines to those in which he had started the comics controversy, he protested against the Code – about how it was arbitrary, about how it only served to draw attention to violence in comics, how it created more problems than it solved and how America would be better off without it. But by then, nobody was listening.

Further reading

Any examination of the controversy must begin with *Seduction of the Innocent* itself (New York: Rinehart 1954; London: Museum Press 1955). The best analytical text is Martin Barker's *A Haunt of Fears* (London: Pluto Press 1984), which although concentrating on the campaign in Britain has much to say about the American experience. Also, Les Daniels, *Comix: A History of Comic Books in America* (New York: Bonanza Books 1971) contains a thoughtful chapter. On Wertham himself, see James Gilbert, *A Cycle of Outrage: America's Reaction to the Juvenile Delinquent in the 1950s* (New York: Oxford University Press 1986), especially chapter 6. For a transcript of the 'Kefauver Hearings', see *Hearings Before the Subcommittee to Investigate Juvenile Delinquency of the Committee on the Judiciary, US Senate, 83rd Congress, 2nd Session, 1954* (Washington, US Govt Printing Office 1954). Finally, the video *Comic Book Confidential* (Canada: Castle Hendring 1989) includes priceless archive footage of the hearings.

The years of collapse: survivors and adaptors

A comic was a comic, but 'a magazine' was somehow more adult.

(Archie Goodwin, ex-contributing editor Warren Magazines)[1]

Most comics histories take the institution of the Code as a departure point. Thereafter, it is said, the industry went into a steep decline from which it only began to recover in the 1980s: comics content was sanitised, homogenised and essentially juvenilised. Although there is much truth in this, it is nevertheless an exaggeration, and we can identify a fairly wide range of subject matter being produced by the – admittedly much-reduced – industry post-1954. In particular, there was a big adult market post-1954, and still a considerable number of comics catering for it.

It is unquestionable that the institution of the Code was a commercial disaster for American comics. Genres were virtually destroyed, particularly crime and horror, creators left the field to work elsewhere and entire companies were forced out of business (Lev Gleason, Fiction House and Quality were annihilated, while EC only just survived, having been forced to jettison its horror and crime lines).[2] The number of titles dropped from around 630 in 1952 to 250 in 1956, while the readership plummeted from around 60 million to below 35 million over the same period.

Some historians have recently pointed to the rise of TV in the 1950s as a factor in this decline. There were around 8,000 TV sets in the USA in 1946, but by 1960 that figure had grown to nearly 57 million.[3] It would obviously be unwise to discount these figures as merely coincidental with comics' decline. But bearing in mind the evidence outlined above for the immediate post-Code collapse, perhaps we should see the rise of TV not so much as a cause, but as something that made it more difficult for comics to recover.

In terms of the content of comics, the Code left the way open for juvenile and teen-orientated material to flourish. The years following 1954 were notable for the resurgence of superheroes (especially the Marvel line), and the continued popularity of the 'goofy teenager' (*Archie*) and funny animals (primarily published by Dell, whose main line was the Disney comics, described by one historian as 'the epitome of clean').[4]

And yet, there were ways round the Code. The first and most obvious was not to produce any material that might contravene its provisions. This was especially the case for humour titles. *Sad Sack*, for example, continued to sell in its millions after the Code, and spawned a parade of offshoots (including *Sad Sack and the Sarge*, *Sad Sack's Funny Friends*, *Sad Sack's Muttsy the Talking Dog* and *Little Sad Sack*). Ironically, television, too, could be a spur to sales. TV was a novelty in the 1950s, and people of all ages liked to relive their favourite shows. Hence, titles like *Look Out For Beaver*, *Bilko*, and *I Love Lucy* now became big sellers. Dell and Gold Key were the main publishers of this kind of material.[5]

Connected with this was the trick of giving material aimed at children sophisticated elements so that it could also be enjoyed

Figure 13.1 Cover to *Sad Sack*, no. 78 (1958). Art: George Baker. © 1958 Harvey Comics

by adults. As we have seen in chapter 11 (pp. 147–8), this had happened for different reasons in the war years, primarily due to the readership among GIs. Now, this process re-emerged with regard to the Marvel superhero titles – though more by accident than design.

Marvel had been hit hard by the Code mainly because it had been heavily committed to horror and war comics. One of the company's chief writers, Stan Lee, was on the point of resigning when his wife persuaded him to have one last try at producing some self-motivated titles. The result was a new wave of superhero comics – *Thor*, *The Hulk*, the *Fantastic Four* (all illustrated by Jack Kirby) and, above all, *Spider-Man* (with art by Steve Ditko).[6] Although Lee had intended his creations for a children's audience, he was very surprised to learn that students were reading them too. Soon, on campuses throughout the country, the Marvel superheroes were being canonised as 'an American mythology'. Some had special followings: Spider-Man was liked because his *alter ego* Peter Parker was a sympathetic character, who went through crises of confidence, had trouble paying the rent and distrusted the press.[7] Dr Strange and Nick Fury were favourites for their 'psychedelic' artwork (by Steve Ditko and Jim Steranko respectively).

Having discovered this unlikely older readership, Lee, with his characteristic talent for self-promotion, played up to it. He went on lecture tours of campuses, while on the comics' letters pages he published missives from both students and university professors. The stories themselves went through subtle changes: in *Spider-Man*, Peter Parker's room was depicted with bookshelves containing existentialist texts.[8] (Later, this trend towards sophistication was taken to the point where one of Parker's friends was shown to be a drug addict – the issue went out without Code approval.) This strategy continued to be very successful into the late 1960s, and often it was the case that the older Marvel readers became the core of the 1970s fan culture.

It was also possible for publishers of other genres to get around the Code by being ingenious about the subject-matter. As we have seen, certain genres were virtually proscribed: yet, it was feasible to re-invent them in a less 'targetable' guise. Take horror, for instance. This had been the number one quarry for the Code, yet in the years after 1954 we can identify a still significant horror industry, based not on blood-letting but on suspense. *House of Secrets*, *Mystical Tales*, *Tales of the Mysterious Traveler* and *Tales of Suspense* were early examples passed by the Code, and which relied on the use of atmosphere, and creepy stories about the supernatural, for their effect. This new direction brought into focus certain creators who proved especially adept at this kind of work (just as previously some of the EC creators had been 'kings of gore'): one such was Steve Ditko, coincidentally the co-creator of Spider-Man.

It is also interesting to note that two of the companies that were left exempt from the Code because they were thought to be 'harmless' now exploited their advantage and produced horror comics. Dell, exempted because their main line was the Disney comics, published *Tales From the Tomb* (1962), described by one historian as 'full of some of the scariest horror stories ever written',[9] and *Ghost Stories* (1962), while Gilberton, exempted for their Classics Illustrated line, republished their version of the Mary Shelley masterpiece, *Frankenstein*.

Ingenuity was also the key to keeping other genres alive. Canny publishers of crime comics, for example, now shifted either to detective mysteries, or to 'cop comics' in the vein of TV serials (for example, *87th Precinct*). Similarly, the romance comics were no longer allowed to deal with adultery or sex, but were still able to attract an audience with other kinds of more subtle story: it is often overlooked that there were still over sixty romance titles on the shelves in 1960.

The third way around the Code was more audacious, and involved taking a magazine format. If a publisher did not want to compromise on questions of content, there was always the option of adding more text features, going to a bigger format, using black and white printing and calling the publication a 'magazine'. In this way, the comic was automatically considered to be for a mature readership and did not have to be submitted to the CCA.

Satire was the principal genre to benefit from this, following *Mad*'s adoption of the new format. This was a bold move at the time, and there was no guarantee of success. The *Mad* team were understandably fearful of losing their old comics audience, but there was no alternative: they had come in for increasing criticism from conservatives for 'going too far' (the comic had been attacked during the Kefauver Hearings, and the staff had been branded as 'pinkoes' in sections of the press) and it was clear that the comic could not continue in its established satirical manner under the new conditions of the Code.[10]

'We didn't have any idea what the slick magazine business was all about or where we would end up', Harvey Kurtzman later recalled, 'and Gaines was in big trouble because of his failing comic book business so he didn't have many shots in his pistol'.[11] They need not have worried. *Mad* became a magazine in 1955, and was equally as successful as its comic predecessor, even gaining in circulation. The new confidence this engendered was expressed in the hiring of new creators – including Don Martin, 'Mad's Maddest Artist', and the adoption of a new figurehead in the person of Alfred Neuman, a gap-toothed nerd who henceforward appeared on every cover (and who bore a striking resemblance to the Yellow Kid). *Mad* had been selling 500,000 copies an issue before 1954, and rose to a peak of

2.5 million in the early 1970s. By showing it could be done, *Mad* in turn inspired a whole plethora of satirical comics-magazines.

Wacko, *Trash*, *Nuts*, *Blast* and a hundred others soon had newsagents' shelves groaning – and customers groaning with the generally feeble quality of the gags. Some were genuinely amusing: *Cracked* (1958) and *Sick* (1960) were serious rivals to *Mad*. But the best of the competing magazines were edited by Kurtzman himself, after he left *Mad* in 1956. His first attempt was *Trump* (1957), funded by Hugh Hefner of *Playboy*, a glossy full-colour production featuring the work of ex-*Mad* stalwarts Jack Davis, Wally Wood and Will Elder. It lasted only two issues. Kurtzman returned to a more comic feel for *Humbug* (1957), which also featured the *Mad* triumvirate, but only survived for eleven issues. Finally, two years later, Kurtzman had what was perhaps his finest post-*Mad* hour in the form of *Help!* (1960). This magazine was different to the others in several important respects: old *Mad* contributors were still in evidence, but there was also new blood in the form of Terry Gilliam, later the animator for the *Monty Python* TV shows and a Hollywood film director, and the stars of the 'amateur pages', among them Robert Crumb, Gilbert Shelton, Jay Lynch and Skip Williamson (if it had lasted one more issue the list would have included Art Spiegelman). Unsurprisingly, *Help!*'s humour was sharper, with more risqué jokes and sexual innuendo, and there was more experimentation, with photo-strips starring famous comedians (Woody Allen and John Cleese among them). After five years,

Figure 13.2 Panels from 'The Hold Up', *Help!*, no. 2 (1961), featuring Woody Allen. Script: Harvey Kurtzman. © 1961 Warren Publications

Kurtzman had had enough, however, and *Help!* folded: but by then his future reputation as 'the godfather of the underground' was assured.[12]

In time, other genres followed satire's lead into the magazine format. Horror, for example, now had an excuse to revert to its old ways, and the early 1960s saw a new wave of horror titles put out by the Warren company specifically intended to 'take up where EC left off'. Indeed, the line used many of the original EC creators – among them Al Williamson, Joe Orlando, Jack Davis and Frank Frazetta (who came into his own as the creator of a string of stunning fully-painted covers). *Creepy* (1964), which set the ball rolling, was edited by Archie Goodwin, who wrote most of the text, and featured stories that were variations on the then-popular Hammer movies – often period-pieces with vampires, werewolves and the like ('we were very respectful of the EC tradition', as Goodwin later recalled, 'but we also wanted to bring things up to date with what was happening in cinema').[13] *Eerie* (1965) was designed as *Creepy's* 'Graveside Companion', and basically

Figure 13.3 Cover to *Eerie*, no. 8 (1966). Art: Frank Frazetta. © 1966 Warren Publications

repeated the formula. Finally, *Vampirella* (1969), edited by Bill Parente, brought a new level of eroticism to horror, the heroine being a beautiful vampire from outer space who came from a planet where evidently few clothes were worn.

Other horror titles followed, but were almost always of a lesser standard than the Warrens, echoing the pattern of the 1950s by disguising the lack of narrative content with ever-more bloody set-pieces. However, some did rise above the rest: the three Skywald titles *Psycho*, *Nightmare* and *Scream*, under the editorship of Al Hewetson, were touted as having a 'Horror Mood', and were notable for their Lovecraftian, psychological direction. By 1975, there were twenty-three horror comic magazines on the shelves.

Even war comics were reinvented. The leader was again a Warren publication, entitled *Blazing Combat* (1965). Once more the inspiration was the 'glory days' of EC and, like *Frontline Combat* and *Two-Fisted Tales*, it included realistic stories about war which were pointedly not gung-ho. The fourth issue of *Blazing Combat* was remarkable for dealing with the burgeoning war in Vietnam in the same way as the earlier titles had dealt with Korea: in some parts of the country, it was refused by distributors for being 'too political', and this was undoubtedly a factor in the title's cancellation after this issue.[14] Clearly, there were still limits to how far it was possible to go in a comic, even disregarding the Code.

There was also a new genre that was ideally suited to the more adult format – sword and sorcery. The trail-blazing title here was *The Savage Sword of Conan* (1974), based on the Robert E. Howard novels and illustrated by British artist Barry Smith. That the publisher was Marvel is not altogether surprising: after all, what was Conan except one more superhero? The magazine came with an 'M' label and the warning 'For the More Adult Reader'.

The fourth and final way to circumvent the Code was in many ways the simplest: to stay clandestine. This only applied to a tiny number of comics, of course, but their existence after 1954 is worth noting nevertheless. Specifically, the 'fetish' comics continued into the 1960s. It is often suggested that they were put out of business by the growth of the sex content in the mainstream publications. But this seems unlikely because of their specialised nature. What does seem to have happened, however, was that they got more extreme with time (as the title to the 1961 *Concentration Camp Women's Torture Ordeals* bears witness). In other words, as the mainstream got sexier, the sleaze got sleazier.

Thus, the story of comics aimed wholly or partly at an adult readership after 1954 is one primarily of hedging around the Code. Such comics existed in numbers, even if sometimes they had to disguise themselves (indeed, it could be argued that the resurgence of adult comics in the 1980s and 1990s might not seem so striking if magazine sales in the 1960s and 1970s are taken into account). Because these publications constantly undermined the Code, it became increasingly irrelevant with time. The CCA were forced to liberalise its provisions in 1971 and again in 1974. But by then a new kind of comic was appealing to adults in America – the underground.

Further reading

Les Daniels's *Comix: A History of Comic Books in America* (New York: Bonanza Books 1971) is still the best general history; the same author tells the story of Marvel in the predictably much less critical *Marvel: Five Fabulous Decades of the World's Greatest Comics* (London: Virgin 1991). The compendia by Mike Benton, *The Comic Book in America* (Dallas, Texas: Taylor Publishing 1989) and *Horror Comics* (Dallas, Texas: Taylor Publishing 1991a), are also very useful for information. Finally, the best history of *Mad* is Maria Reidelbach's *Completely Mad* (New York: Little, Brown and Co., 1991).

The modern era

**Comics were originally intended for adults, not kids, and
we're slowly getting back to that again.**
(Tom De Falco, editor-in-chief, Marvel Comics)[1]

It is possible to date the modern era in the evolution of adult comics in
America from the emergence of the underground in the 1960s. The
period thereafter has witnessed a great deal of crossover with Britain,
and therefore events have already been covered in some detail in part I.
Nevertheless, there were important variations in experience, and it is to
these we must briefly turn.

The underground 'shattered the tradition of comics as decisively
as American jazz shattered the classical European musical idiom',
according to the *Comics Journal*.[2] That is undoubtedly true. As in
Britain, the comix were an expression of the counter-culture of the
1960s and 1970s, which, in America, must be seen as in large part a
reaction to the extremely repressive atmosphere of the 1950s (discussed
briefly on p. 147). Indeed, it seemed to some observers at the time that
American society was swinging like a pendulum from one extreme to
another (though in reality, there was more continuity from the postwar
era to the Nixon years than might at first have been imagined).

The 1950s had left their mark on the mainstream comics
industry as well, of course, in the form of the Code. Thus from an
American perspective, the underground can be seen as almost as much
a revolt against the Code as an expression of the counter-culture in
general. It was, in a sense, an outpouring of all the 'unsound' ideas
bottled-up since 1954. The Code stipulated 'no sex', so the comix
revelled in every kind of sex imaginable; the Code stipulated 'no violence', so the underground took bloodshed to extremes; above all, the
Code stipulated 'no social relevance', yet here were comics that were
positively revolutionary. Some creators even made direct reference to
the Code: Crumb and Spain, for example, gleefully parodied the Code
stamp of approval on the covers of their comix (see Figure 3.1 on
p. 38).

Yet at the same time it is clear that in the USA, the comix were
part of a continuum of adult material in a way that they were not in
Britain. The creators were well aware of this tradition, and references
to (among others) 'Krazy Kat', the 'Dirty Comics', *The Spirit*, the ECs

and, above all, *Mad*, pepper their work by way of acknowledgement. (Indeed, it has been suggested that *Mad* gave rise to the term 'underground comics' in the first place, with a headline in the October 1954 edition which ran 'Comics Go Underground!'. However, this seems unlikely, and the term is more probably an extension of 'underground press'.[3]) Examples of creators acknowledging the continuing tradition include Robert Crumb, who produced his infamous sex comics *Jiz* and *Snatch* in a smaller format as a homage to the 'Dirty Comics'; the undergrounds *Snarf* and *Bogeyman* which were openly inspired by the EC horror line; Will Eisner, who was 'rediscovered' by underground publisher Denis Kitchen, and persuaded to revive *The Spirit* for an underground readership; Bobby London, who produced *Dirty Duck* in homage to 'Krazy Kat'; Harvey Kurtzman was invited to produce a cover for a *Mad*-tribute issue of *Bijou Funnies*. Some of the earlier comics and strips were also reprinted by underground presses, particularly 'Krazy Kat', the 1930s 'Dirty Comics' and the 1950s fetish comics.

There were other features of the American underground that were not so obvious in Britain. Not all the comix were exported by any means, and inevitably some creators became much better-known in their home country than internationally. This was especially true of Bill Griffith and Jack 'Jaxon' Jackson, both of whom dealt with subject-matter that was not immediately resonant with British audiences; a skewed view of Americana, on one hand, and nineteeth-century American history, on the other.

Bill Griffith was originally one of the *Bijou Funnies* set, whose most famous character 'Zippy the Pinhead', a free-associating idiot-savant for whom 'Fred Astaire is the co-pilot, and Fred Flintstone is God', was developed in a number of subsequent comix and finally syndicated as a strip in newspapers across America. Due to the popularity of this character, Griffith has been described by one historian as 'some

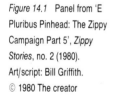

Figure 14.1 Panel from 'E Pluribus Pinhead: The Zippy Campaign Part 5', *Zippy Stories*, no. 2 (1980). Art/script: Bill Griffith. © 1980 The creator

thing of a superstar' within the underground community.[4] Griffith later explained the peculiar appeal of his work: 'my comics are not "Dada" at all. Absurd, yes, but not flippant. I think of Dada as a somewhat amusing, but shallow, art-joke. The recognition that everything is absurd, on the other hand, can be touching as well as funny'.[5]

Jack Jackson, too, had roots in the original underground, his *God Nose* (1964) being an important pre-category title, and also became better-known in the late-and post-underground period. His superbly-rendered historical trilogy depicting the story of Comanche leader Quanah Parker (*White Comanche*, *Red Raider* and *Blood on the Moon*) was a *tour de force* of comics realism that movingly

Figure 14.2 A page from *Blood on the Moon* (1978). The selective use of contemporary language was one of the comic's hallmarks. Art/script: Jack Jackson. © 1978 The creator

personalised the tragedy of native American displacement. The three comics were collected into an album as *Comanche Moon* in 1978, which included maps, archival photos and a bibliography of sources. Jackson went on to produce other equally impressive historical works, including a graphic novel on the birth of the state of Texas (*Los Tejanos*).

Finally, the causes of the American underground's decline were somewhat different to those in Britain. Certainly, hippie society went through the same changes, and despite the First Amendment there were similar confrontations with the law. The two most famous trials were those of *Zap* no. 4, declared obscene in the City of New York and prosecuted in 1972, and the Disney lawsuit of a year later, when an underground (*Air Pirate Funnies*) was taken to court for portraying Mickey Mouse smoking a joint and engaging in various sexual acts.[6] The high court ruling of 1973 that allowed individual states to determine their own obscenity laws attracted less publicity, but was more damaging to the underground in the long run. But to these factors must also be added sky-rocketing paper costs from the mid-1970s and the promulgation of 'anti-paraphernalia laws' in 1973, which shut down the headshops in many states. Without a retail network, the culture could not survive for long.

Indeed, the closure of the headshops led to a last-ditch period of experimentation for the underground in the mainstream (if that is not a contradiction in terms). Most notably, *Arcade* (1975), edited by Bill Griffith and Art Spiegelman, provided a 'life-raft' for many top creators. An outstanding comic in many respects (and in some ways a fore-runner to *Raw*), it featured work by Crumb, Shelton, Spain and others from the old guard, plus newer faces like Rory Hayes and a number of upcoming women creators (notably Aline Kominsky and Diane Noomin). But, in the stormy seas of above-ground commercialism, the life-raft had trouble staying afloat and the comic ceased publication after seven issues. Even Marvel tried its hand at mainstream under-grounds: *Comix Book* (1974) attracted the talents of Trina Robbins, Howard Cruse, Skip Williamson and others, but only lasted for five issues. More successful for Marvel was *Howard the Duck* (1976) by Steve Gerber, a kind of superhero parody crossed with underground anthropomorphics, about a cigar-chewing 'sentient duck from another dimension', which became increasingly satirical with time and garnered a sizeable cult following.

Like the underground, the emergence of fandom and the specialist shop network in America predated the British experience. Again, the spur was the appearance of the Marvel superhero titles of the early 1960s, which quickly became the focus for a collecting sub-culture (see p. 63). The first regular American fanzine, the *Comic Reader*, debuted in 1961, and the earliest proper fan convention took place in New York in 1964. The first specialist shops began to emerge in the San Francisco Bay area in the late 1960s, and by the end of the 1970s there were approximately 400 of them in the country as a whole.

It should be noted that there had been a short-lived attempt to organise a fan following for comics in America in the 1950s, based on the EC titles. A number of fanzines appeared, concerning especially the horror line and *Mad*, but, although the publishers were adult, the readers tended to be aged 8–12, and they soon ceased publication. Isolated shops specialising in comics can also be identified in the 1950s.

The next step in fandom, direct sales, marked a switch from a news-stand based comics culture to one based on the collector dollar. Specialist distribution was pioneered by one New York convention organiser, Phil Seuling and his Seagate Enterprises in the mid-1970s, and the relative success of this system contrasted sharply with the declining fortunes of the traditional news-stand market, then experiencing its worst-ever downturn. Thus, it is possible to see direct sales as 'rescuing' American comics from what was predicted by many commentators to be a lingering death.

Naturally, within this new culture there were also comics that never became quite so popular in Britain. For example, *Elfquest*, the fantasy epic by Wendy and Richard Pini, was a major early success, and appealed to an unusually wide-ranging readership both in terms of age (adult and adolescent) and sex. There were also a whole swathe of small press comics that were never exported across the Atlantic (of those comics so far mentioned in the text, the following all began in the small press: *Flaming Carrot*, *Yummy Fur*, *Love and Rockets*, *Melody*, *Tales of the Beanworld*).[7] (The reverse situation could also occur. As we have seen in chapter 5, *Love and Rockets* was never as popular in America as in Britain, leading *Rolling Stone* magazine to later describe it as 'an undiscovered classic of American fiction'.[8])

It is also true that the impact of British creators on direct sales in America was not quite as dramatic from an American perspective as British fans were led to believe. In Britain, the PR line had been that creators from *2000AD* were so talented that they were poached by American companies, and subsequently became solely responsible for reinventing American comics (an obvious attempt to sell more of their comics – new and old – in the UK market). The truth was a little less dramatic: for example, how the contributions of Americans Frank Miller, Bill Sienkiewicz and Art Spiegelman fitted into this scenario was never made clear.

Similarly, British comics characters were sometimes not interpreted by American fans in the same way as they were by the home audience. Judge Dredd, for example, became well-known in America in the early to mid-1980s through Titan album reprints of the *2000AD* strips, although the humour tended to be missed. 'Because American audiences are used to superheroes who are done dead straight, without any irony', as Dredd co-creator Alan Grant later explained, 'I think they missed the point when Dredd came along, and saw him simply as a shoot-em-up fascist – which is a little worrying, really.'[9]

Finally, within the various sub-groups of comics that piggy-backed on the fan culture, punk had a much more visible manifestation in America than it did in Britain.[10] A group of creators emerged who consciously attempted to inject a punk sensibility into their work. They were tagged 'New Wave' and included, most visibly, Peter Bagge and Gary Panter. *Weirdo* became a central title for the group, especially under the editorship of Bagge, subsequently provoking the hostility of some older members of the underground: 'Crumb told me there was an awful lot of paranoia from other *Zap* artists about the quote unquote "New Wave",' Bagge later explained. 'They would say "they're no good" or "they don't have any technique" – exactly what the old-timers had said about them. I don't think they realised that to us the biggest thing was to be in the same comic book as S. Clay Wilson.'[11]

The much-heralded 'adult comics revolution' occurred in America at the same time as in Britain, and also represented a move away from fandom and into the mainstream. The Big 3 – *Maus*, *Dark Knight* and *Watchmen* – made a similar impact, and received coverage in all the major periodicals, including *Time*, *Newsweek*, and even the *Wall Street Journal*. *Dark Knight* featured on the *New York Times* best-seller list for thirty-two weeks, while *Maus* won the American National Book Award for biography. All the major press publications reported the 'Comics Grow Up' story, and there was also significant radio and TV coverage. As in Britain, PR and advertising played a major role: a DC advertisement featured in many magazines proclaimed 'You outgrew comics – now they've caught up with you!'.

However, in America, there was a fourth major hit to add to the list – *American Splendor* by Harvey Pekar. This was a comic that had been published since 1976, but which was now repackaged into album form by Doubleday, and hence made media-friendly. In it, Pekar recounted various autobiographical stories of everyday life in Cleveland where he worked as a hospital porter. It was drawn by a variety of artists, including his old friend Robert Crumb, and the hallmarks were a strong left-wing sensibility and a delicious dry wit. 'My work deals with everyday events, which writers throughout history have ignored, but which ultimately influence human behaviour far more than seldom occurring "big" or landmark events', the author later explained, 'there are acts of heroism and great comedy happening around us every day.'[12] Pekar's fame was subsequently boosted by several controversial guest appearances on David Letterman's TV chat-show – which he then related in subsequent issues of the comic.

Events following the explosion of the (now) Big 4 pretty much

Figure 14.3 Cover to *American Splendor*, no. 14 (1984), depicting the aftermath of one of the creator's infamous showdowns with TV talk-show host David Letterman. Art: Joe Zabel and Gary Dumm. © 1984 The creator

mirrored those in Britain. The number of specialist shops leapt up to around 4,000, while the 'graphic novel' was likewise hailed as a ground-breaking step forward. In the process, comics were taken up by bookshops (Waldenbooks and Dalton's being the major chains in America to do so) and by public libraries. They also increasingly attracted the attentions of mainstream book publishers (notably Doubleday, Pantheon and Warner Books).

In general terms, as we have seen, comics boomed in America, with Marvel and DC producing the lion's share, supplemented by a greatly increased number of independents. (The only significant variation with the British experience was a greater emphasis on Japanese comics – largely because of the historically much closer ties between the two countries.) Thus, the medium saw a major renaissance, with adult fare becoming established in the mainstream in a way it had not been since before 1954.

Yet, as in Britain, there were marked limits to how far the boom could go. Despite America's much more tolerant tradition of adults reading comics, the majority of the public were not yet prepared to accept comics as a valid art form. Most people still did not read comics, and the perception of the medium remained rooted in traditional notions of it as children's entertainment. The rapid – if relative – decline of adult comics in the mainstream post-1990 was precipitated by a large degree of failure in the bookshops, and a concurrent cooling of media interest. [13]

At the same time, and partly as a consequence, opposition to adult comics was able to gain ground. The backlash was more serious in America than in Britain owing to the strength of the conservative and religious lobbies there (as typified by the 'Moral Majority', a far-right Christian fundamentalist organisation based in the midwest). From the mid-1980s onwards, this lobby had been vocally critical of popular culture, pressurising department stores not to carry records by certain artists, cinemas not to screen certain movies and so on. The new adult comics were an obvious target, and the industry duly came under attack for promoting 'sexual deviance', 'sexual promiscuity' and 'unbridled violence'.

The first reaction to this new onslaught was a debate within the American industry itself on whether or not to introduce a ratings system, along the lines of that in cinema, to replace the now widely-ignored Code. Most keen to do so were DC Comics, publishers of many of the most successful adult titles. However, some of the creators working for the company viewed this as censorship, and several big names resigned in protest – among them Alan Moore, Frank Miller and Howard Chaykin. The idea was modified to a simple labelling policy whereby the tag 'For Mature Readers' would be applied 'if deemed necessary', a system that was adopted by most of the industry. [14]

This did not satisfy the conservatives, however, and the pressure against comics became more overt, with the appearance of numerous hostile press articles and the initiation of court actions. Unlike in Britain, there were several successful prosecutions of specialist shops in America, while the Canadian situation was even worse. As if to bring things full-circle, a book entitled *Seduction of the Innocent Revisited*, funded by a Christian group, was published in 1990, though, thankfully, it did not have anything like the impact of the original. Clearly in America, Dr Wertham's ghost had not yet been laid to rest.

Yet, as in Britain, the backlash needs to be seen for what it is – a backlash, and not a complete reversal in the adult comics trend. Despite the decline in publishing, there is still enough activity to be able to speak of a continuing adult comics boom. The opposition is still formidable, and there remains a real possibility of censorship. As we have seen, however, publishers will invariably find a way around it.

Further reading

Mark Estren's *A History of Underground Comics* (San Francisco, Calif.: Straight Arrow 1974, rev. edn 1987); and Gary Groth and Robert Fiore (eds) *The New Comics* (New York: Berkley 1988) are invaluable, as ever. Joseph Witek's superb *Comic Books as History* (Jackson, Mississippi: University of Mississippi Press 1989) focuses on the work of Art Spiegelman, Jack Jackson and Harvey Pekar. For up-to-date news, see the monthly fanzine the *Comics Journal*.

part

III

ASPECTS

Worldcomics

I often see a look of surprise on people's faces when I say there are comics outside Britain and the United States. . . . The fact is, there are whole continents of comics to discover.

(Paul Gravett, publisher and comics historian)[1]

One of the most remarkable features of the recent comics boom has been the impact made by titles from other parts of the globe – 'world-comics', as they have become known. Adult comics have been a major feature of this new material, and the reason for this is the relative sophistication of the comics industries in some other countries. When Britain and America 'discovered' adult comics in the late 1980s, publishers found for the first time it was possible to launch foreign comics into a mainstream domestic market: at last they were 'talking the same language'.

It is sometimes not recognised how widespread comics reading is internationally (indeed, until recently there was a marked reluctance to admit that comics existed at all outside the anglophone world). Yet in Mexico, it has been estimated 80 per cent of all periodical publishing is comics – much of it for a mature audience. In India, the centre of the country's film industry, Bombay, is also its comics' centre, producing many thousands of religious and other titles for a variety of age- ranges. Filipino publishers claim sales of well over 1 million copies a week. In the CIS, usually thought barren of such 'western' media, it is possible to find comics telling the entire histories of individual states. Additionally, in South America, China, South-East Asia, parts of Africa and in many other parts of the world, comics play a role (sometimes an important one) in cultural life.

Yet when the term 'worldcomics' is used in Britain and America, what it invariably means is comics from Europe and Japan. This is because these are the two most advanced comics cultures in the world, and represent a fertile hunting-ground for the kind of stories that anglophone audiences prefer.[2] (In contrast to many of the countries listed above, literacy levels are not the determining factor in what kind of material is published.) For this reason it is necessary to look briefly at the history of adult comics in Europe and Japan in order to understand the context for the current boom. For the sake of simplicity, comics titles will be given in their Anglicized form, where possible.

Europe

The evolution of comics in western Europe has many parallels with that in Britain, and to a lesser extent the USA – echoing the pattern of an initial period of an industry orientated towards all ages, transmuting into a predominantly juvenile culture, followed by a boom in specifically adult comics. The main difference, however, is in the timing. In Europe, adult comics re-entered the mainstream long before Britain and the USA, due to a much more tolerant attitude towards the medium, which was rooted in an early recognition of it as an art form.

Pictorial panel-narratives developed in Europe along much the same lines as in Britain – via broadsheets and satirical magazines. These were a feature of every European country. Comic strip pioneers included the Swiss Rudolph Topffer, whose illustrated stories from the mid-1840s were the first to use a panel sequence which linked pictures and text, and the German Wilhelm Busch, credited with creating perhaps the most seminal strip of all time, 'Max und Moritz' (1865), about two young malevolent pranksters (which was later republished in *Comic Cuts*, and became the inspiration for the classic early American newspaper strip 'The Katzenjammer Kids'). However, the main centres for the early production of comics *per se* were France and Belgium. Here, they became known as *bandes dessinées* (literally 'drawn strips' – a term which encompassed all kinds of strip art), or 'BDs' for short, and were published in two forms – periodically (usually weekly or monthly) and in albums of collected strips.

In terms of content, like their British counterparts, many of the earliest titles were not aimed exclusively at children, but were designated 'Pour la Famille', with strips of specific interest to adults. Louis Forton's celebrated strip 'La Bande des Pieds Nickeles' (1908), for example, was about a group of ruffians who were clearly meant to be anarchists and who went around mocking government institutions and officials (this at a time of peak anarchist activity in France, which contributed to a nationwide wave of strikes in 1913). Similarly, material aimed at a younger audience often had adult overtones. For instance, George 'Christophe' Colomb's 'Famille Fenouillard' (1893), a pioneering strip about a gormless family, mocked bourgeois manners in a fashion a child could never be expected to understand. Forton, Colomb and their like were thus essentially working in the satirical tradition.

But gradually, in the now familiar way, the comics medium became associated more and more with children. The emergence of one character in particular cemented this drift, and, at the same time, heralded a shift in the centre of production of comics from France to Belgium –Tintin. The squeaky-clean boy-adventurer was created by 'Hergé', the pen-name of Georges Rémi, and made his debut in 1929 in

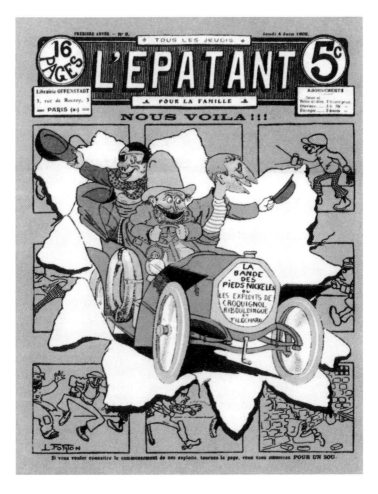

a children's supplement to a newspaper entitled *Le petit vingtième*. His first solo reprint album, the now-famous *Tintin in the Land of the Soviets*, appeared in 1930, and was published by Casterman. The character became so popular that he was given his own weekly magazine in 1946, an anthology which featured a number of other strips including, most famously, Edgar Pierre Jacobs' 'Blake and Mortimer' about two Englishmen, one an agent from M15, one a scientist.

The Tintin comics were remarkable for a number of reasons. Artistically they were revolutionary: Hergé introduced a 'clear line' technique – shadow-free, definite and the opposite of the bombastic style that often characterised British and American comics (it is often commented that just as American comics evolved artistically in the shadow of Jack Kirby, so the same was true of Europe and Hergé). The stories themselves were ostensibly straightforward adventures, but often contained politically right-wing undercurrents (the *Land of the Soviets* album upset Communists for its unflattering portrayal of that nation, while later Hergé was accused of collaborating with the Nazis during the occupation).[3] Europe's juvenile population did not seem to mind, however, and the comics sold in their millions all over the continent and then all over the world – with Tintin himself becoming arguably more famous than the Disney characters. Up until the end of 1991 it was estimated that over 100 million Tintin books have been sold.

Following in *Tintin*'s wake, the 'little papers' (as comics for youngsters were called) flourished. But from the start the economic basis of the industry was quite different to Britain and the USA. Because of the method of reprinting stories in album-form, comics were considered to be something to keep and not simply to throw away after one read. (Indeed, popular albums were often kept continuously in print.) This had important consequences for creators. First, they received two royalties for their work, and so it was financially worthwhile for them to consider comics as a 'proper' career. Second, there was no question of anonymity because a law in France enshrined 'the inalienable rights of the creator' and forbade companies to own characters (the law did not apply in Belgium, but was generally followed in spirit).[4] Third, consequently, the prestige of comics creators was much higher in Europe than in Britain or the USA.

Inevitably, there were emulators of the *Tintin* formula. The most important copyist was undoubtedly *Spirou*, another Belgian comic, which although it predated *Tintin* was moulded very much in the same style after 1946. Its most famous characters were the eponymous 'Spirou' (by Robert Velter), a hotel page-boy who behaved very much like Tintin, and 'Lucky Luke' (by Maurice 'Morris' de Bevère), a 'poor, lonesome cowboy' who was quicker on the draw than his shadow. Like *Tintin* magazine, *Spirou* became an adventure-and-humour title, and provided a platform for two major creators – 'Jigé' (Joseph Gillain) who specialised in adventure strips in a style reminiscent of Milton Caniff, and André Franquin, who edited the magazine between 1946 and 1968, and whose forte was Disneyesque humour, as exemplified in his enormously popular character Marsupilami, a lovable marsupial with a 25-foot tail. They became the two biggest names in creative terms since Hergé, and along with him are acknowledged as having established 'the Franco-Belgian School'. Again, individual stories from *Spirou* were collected into albums, although none attained the popularity of the Tintin adventures.

Spirou and *Tintin* dominated European comics into the 1950s and beyond. Undoubtedly, adults did form a percentage of the readership – rather in the same way that some humour titles garnered a following among older readers in the USA – and for many years *Tintin* magazine was labelled 'Le journal pour jeunes de 7 a 77 ans' ('the magazine for youngsters aged 7 to 77'). Nevertheless, the majority of their readers, and that of their many imitators, were children.[5]

Children were also the main readers of other kinds of comics popular at the time, including some from America. Comic books like *Superman* and *Batman* made an impact (as they did in Britain), while individual American strips (for example, 'Prince Valiant' and 'Flash Gordon') made their way into European-produced comics via international syndication: they were cheaper to publish than home-made product, and neither *Tintin* magazine nor *Spirou* were averse to making use of them.

But increasingly, an anti-American prejudice developed in parts of Europe, which was of a similar nature to that described in the case of Britain (see pp. 27–31). This reached a peak in France in 1949, when a law was passed embodying a strict moral code to clamp down on material deemed harmful to children, and which set the level for imported strips at no more than 25 per cent of any particular title. Although it was not made explicit, the target of the law was American strips and comics (the government that passed it was Communist, and many of the motivations that led the British Communist Party to become involved in the British anti-American comics campaign of the 1950s were also present here). Thereafter, the French industry was compelled to develop along its own path, largely isolated from American influence.[6]

European comics remained juvenile in the 1950s, and did not really begin to 'grow up' again, and purposefully to reach out to an adult audience, until the next decade. It was during this period that the focus for production shifted away from Belgium to France once more, and the subject-matter edged once again towards satire.

The title central to this transformation was *Pilote*, a humour/adventure weekly founded in 1959. Although originally a children's publication in the traditional sense, it featured a strip by Rene Goscinny and Albert Uderzo (both former *Tintin* magazine contributors) entitled 'Asterix the Gaul', which from the mid-1960s attracted a significant adult readership. This new comic hero was the diminutive leader of a band of Gallic warriors in 50 BC whose headquarters was an isolated village that had not yet fallen to the Romans. The strip's stock-in-trade was knockabout comedy, but it also incorporated much more knowing humour (for example, analogies with the Gauls' position and that of the French Resistance during the occupation were played on to maximum effect). In short, it appealed to children for slapstick and adults for the satire, and in the process became a major hit in both markets.

The role of reprint albums was crucial in establishing Asterix's reputation. Indeed, one in particular, *Asterix in Britain* (1966), was arguably the primary factor in creating Asterix-mania (and was even featured on the front page of *L'Express* magazine, under the headline 'Le phenomène d'Astérix'). Commercially, the growing sales of these albums legitimised comics first in France and then in the rest of Europe, and were responsible for forcing bookshops to provide shelf-space for albums. Hereafter, comics were an established literary category.

Pilote was quick to build on the older readership 'Asterix' opened up, and in time other more sophisticated strips were added. In terms of adventure, these included most famously the gritty spaghetti-western story 'Lieutenant Blueberry' (1963) by Jean-Michel Charlier and Jean Giraud, which was originally a straightforward adventure, but after 1966 became a much darker tale incorporating anti-militarist and anarchist themes (with the hero becoming an anti-hero); and the two outstanding SF strips, 'Valerian' (1967) by Pierre Christin and Jean-Claude Mézières and 'Lone Sloane' by Philippe Druillet (1970). In terms of humour, these included 'Cellulite' (1969) by Claire Bretécher,

Figure 15.2 Cover to *Pilote*, no. 628 (1972), featuring Claire Bretécher's 'Cellulite' (the tiny figure of Asterix is just visible below the letter 'p'). Art: Claire Bretécher. © 1972 The creator/Dargaud

designed as the antithesis of traditional fairy-princess fantasies and starring a sex-starved harridan (who inevitably became an icon for the emerging feminist movement); and the hugely influential strips of Marcel Gotlib, perhaps best remembered for 'Rubrique-à-Brac', his regular two-page feature in which he expressed his debt to *Mad* magazine by satirising everything from other comic strips and movies to politics, and which extended the limits of the kind of humour that was permissible in a comic. By 1968, it is estimated two-thirds of *Pilote*'s readers were aged 16–24.

Other comics followed *Pilote*'s lead and added more adult material. *Tintin* magazine, for example, featured the work of Belgian artist Herman 'Hermann' Huppen, best exemplified by the moodily-rendered 'Bernard Prince', a strip about a globe-trotting ex-Interpol inspector, and the realistic western 'Commanche', which together with 'Blueberry' was responsible for re-inventing the genre.

Meanwhile, more dramatic changes were occurring. The 1990s also saw the emergence of comics that were orientated exclusively towards the over-16s (as opposed to 'crossover' titles that appealed to a general readership). The subject-matter was erotica, and, once again, the centre of production was France. The title that set the tone was Jean-Claude Forest's *Barbarella*, which was launched in 1962 and collected into an album in 1964. Intended as 'a cross between Flash Gordon and a Brigitte Bardot movie', it concerned the space-travelling adventures of a wide-eyed blonde and her struggles to retain her clothing in different parts of the galaxy. The comic was initially confiscated by the police under the terms of the 1949 law – a move which inevitably assured its notoriety and helped turn it into a bestseller. *Barbarella* became equally well-known throughout the continent, and in 1967 was made into a successful Franco-Italian produced movie starring Jane Fonda.[7]

Although *Barbarella* was a landmark comic, its interchange with traditional comics was very limited. Rather, its resonance was with science fiction fandom, where Forest was already well-known as an SF book-cover illustrator. It was therefore an anomaly in some respects, and its influence should not be overrated.

Nevertheless, it did inspire a number of similarly non-mainstream comics in a comparably erotic vein, and other sexy females sprung up all over Europe – 'Jodelle', 'Valentina', 'Pravda', and 'Epoxy' to name the best-known.[8] They outraged many, both for their explicitness on one hand, and sexism on the other. Yet they often exhibited high standards of draughtsmanship, something which led them to be championed by some intellectuals as artistically meritorious. In the atmosphere of the 'permissive 60s' they thus attained a certain respectability in cult circles.[9]

'Respectable', however, was never a word that was applied to the erotica wave simultaneously emerging in Italy. This took the form of 'fumetti neri', or 'black comics': cheap, black and white, mass-market titles that introduced new levels of sexual content. The trend was set in motion by *Diabolik* (1962), depicting a catsuit-clad criminal and his steamy adventures, which was soon selling over 160,000 copies an issue. It was followed by more explicit titles – notably *Isabella, Jacula* and *Lucrezia* – all of which carried the 'per adulti' label and did very well commercially. Among the most popular tended to be issues in which the protagonists were drawn to look like famous film stars (notably Jean-Paul Belmondo and Ursula Andress) – a striking echo of the American 'Dirty Comics' of the 1930s.

With *Pilote* breaking new ground and erotica gaining critical credibility in France and commercial credibility in Italy, the comics medium in Europe was thus moving away from its juvenile origins in an unprecedented fashion. Now, new adult comics appreciation societies began to emerge. Again, France led the way, and in 1962 the 'Club des amis de la bande dessinée' ('Club for Friends of the Comic') was inaugurated. This later became the 'Centre d'Etudes des Littératures d'Expression' (comics study centre) or CELEG for short, and it was here that comics came to be known as 'the ninth art'. The societies spread across Europe (to Italy, Belgium and the Netherlands especially), and were invariably the province of the intelligentsia – academics, writers and most famously film-makers (the founders of CELEG included the movie-directors Alain Resnais and Federico Fellini).

In the societies' wake came serious critical magazines (*Giff-Wiff* and *Phénix* in France, *Ran Tan Plan* in Belgium and *Stripschrift* in the Netherlands); the first proper conventions (Bordighera 1965 and Lucca 1966 – both in Italy); and exhibitions focusing on comics – the most famous example being that at the Louvre in 1967 (these exhibitions featured comics in their own right – unlike the roughly contemporaneous pop-art exhibitions in Britain and the USA in which comics played no role other than as a half-acknowledged inspiration).

These were undoubtedly major steps forward for the credibility of the medium. Comics were being taken seriously in Europe and treated with intellectual respect, just as previously cinema had been, and their place within the culture was confirmed in a manner that was unthinkable in any other part of the world, with the arguable exception of Japan. Though adult comics *per se* were still very much a minority interest, the medium was being accepted as a valid means of expression for mature subject-matter, and once this groundwork was done, the scene was set for adult comics to take on a mass appeal in the 1970s.

The coming of the counter-culture in Europe had a profound effect on the arts, as it had elsewhere in the west. Politically, it developed a more violent complexion: the student riots in Paris in May

1968 led to a three-week nationwide strike that brought the government to its knees. Although the 'May Events' eventually petered out, they were unquestionably an inspiration to the youth and artistic communities of Europe, and revolutionary Situationist slogans like 'Take Your Dreams for Reality!' and 'Be Realistic: Demand the Impossible!' became the rallying cries for a new era of creative freedom in the arts.

Some established satirical magazines now pursued a more radical direction. The best known of these, *Hara Kiri* (1964), had started as a *Mad*-style review, but increasingly pushed political humour to unexplored limits. Although it was eventually banned by the authorities for a particularly outrageous gag on the cover concerning the death of De Gaulle, the magazine later reappeared as *Charlie Hebdo*. It was significant that such magazines, although not 'comics' *per se*, often included a great deal of strip art: *Hara Kiri*, for example, featured work by Jean Giraud.

In comics, this new sense of artistic liberation was reinforced and seemingly given expression by the American underground comics, which were imported and translated on a regular basis from 1968. The work of Crumb, Shelton, Spain and the others made as big an impression among the European hippie and student populace as it did in Britain: there was bound to be an indigenous follow-up. [10]

The first European comics to respond to these new stimuli were French, with the two most important titles coming out of splits from

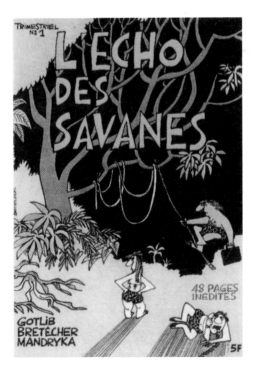

Figure 15.3 Cover to
L'Écho Del savanes, no. 1
(1972). Art: Nikita Mandryka.
© 1972 The creator

Pilote.[11] In 1972, Claire Bretécher, Marcel Gotlib and Nikita Mandryka broke away to produce *L'Écho des savanes*, a satirical, gleefully profane monthly anthology very much influenced by the iconoclastic style of the comix. Along with reprints of American strips such as 'Mr Natural', it boasted radical feminist work by Bretécher, and a bizarre strip by Mandryka, 'Le Concombre masqué' about a philosophical cucumber.

Similarly, the revolutionary SF magazine *Métal Hurlant* was first published in 1975 by the ex-*Pilote* team of Philippe Druillet, Jean-Pierre Dionnet and Jean Giraud, who worked for the magazine under the pseudonym 'Moebius',[12] together with Bernard Farkas (who had not previously contributed to *Pilote*). With its daring mix of sex, pseudo-cerebral storylines and superb artwork it became the most influential title of the post-1968 era.

There were many other adult anthologies: *Le Canard sauvage* (1973); *Mormoil* (1974); *Tousse bourin* (1975); *Circus* (1975); and *Ah Nana!* (a predominantly-female, feminist quarterly) (1976). Even Casterman, the publisher of *Tintin*, got in on the act in 1978 with (*A Suivre*). Above all, there was *Fluide glacial* (1975), the brainchild of the indefatigable and ever-popular Marcel Gotlib (*L'Écho des savanes* was temporarily bankrupt at the time), which featured perhaps the most popular humorous strip of modern times, 'Les Bidochon' by Christian Binet, an uproarious sit-com about an obstreperous working-class family who were constantly in trouble with the social security (today albums featuring their adventures sell in the region of 80,000 copies a time). By the end of the 1970s, the label 'interdit aux mineurs' had truly become the motif for a French revolution in comics.

Although these new titles were sometimes referred to as the 'French underground', in most respects they were not comparable to the American paradigm: they were invariably of a much higher production standard – making use of colour, magazine-quality paper and so on. Also, the attitude of retailers was not so hostile. The advances made for adult comics in the 1960s by *Pilote, Barbarella* and so on meant that they were more acceptable, and the new titles made it on to the news-stands without difficulty. This was facilitated by a law governing distribution which forbade distributors to refuse distribution to any legal magazine with a print-run above a certain figure. Thus there was no way that they could be marginalised in the way their American and British counterparts were.[13]

Similarly, the spin-off albums of individual stories went straight into regular bookshops. As had been the practice with children's comics, individual stories were filleted out and collected as hardback albums, typically in full-colour with around forty-eight pages. And because audiences had grown up reading the children's comics in this form, there was a natural continuity, and certainly no cultural stigma attached to reading the adult ones.

Indeed, because of the ease of distribution, and greater public tolerance, the adult industry grew remarkably quickly. In time the album side of production became more emphasised than magazine production. Because of the established economics of the industry, the focus was on the quality of the product rather than quantity and creators were often free to spend up to a year on an album (which is not to say this eradicated the possibility of mediocrity). Albums tended to be sold on the basis of a creator's reputation rather than the contents as such, and a 'star-system' developed. Top creators rapidly became as esteemed as film directors or novelists: having invented the *auteur* system with regard to cinema, the French now did it again with comics.

This *auteur* system had profound knock-on effects for the rest of Europe. The big-selling magazines were translated into several languages, thus providing a magnet for talent from all over the continent. There was also a system whereby albums would be published simultaneously in different countries. It became perfectly normal, for example, for an Italian creator to be published first in France and then resold to Italy. Thus, a 'European Comics Community' was established, with a definite market unity. Stars became stars all over the continent, and sales could be enormous: 50,000 for a single album was 'respectable', while a quarter of a million was not uncommon.

By far the most important *auteur* was Moebius or 'le grand Moebius' as the French press took to calling him, who, after Jigé and Franquin, was the most important creator to have emerged since Hergé. He continued to produce 'Lieutenant Blueberry' as Jean Giraud ('Gir'), while producing SF as Moebius. Stylistically, his western work remained fairly conventional, while his SF work became ever-more experimental and sophisticated: 'I had grown up with American westerns, and Blueberry was my homage, designed mainly for teenagers', he said later, 'but my science fiction work came from the heart, and was definitely for adults.'[14] His most famous SF story, 'Arzach' was wordless, and starred a pterodactyl-flying adventurer in a strange, beautifully-rendered alien world. In 1984–5 he collaborated with Chilean film-maker Alexandro Jodorowsky on the more obscure *Incal* series (six volumes), which reflected his new-found interest in new age philosophy. Again, spontaneity was the key: 'I am not aware from one panel to the next how the narrative will end', Moebius commented later, 'I think there's more creative danger that way.'[15] Although his western work is still much better known in Europe than his SF (the reverse is true elsewhere), sales for each have been outstanding, and he remains the central figure in European adult comics.

But there were other creators who garnered large adult followings. From France: Philippe Druillet, second only to Moebius as a

Figure 15.4 Panels from 'Adele Blanc-Sec: Le secret de la Salamandre', (A Suivre), no. 30 (1980). Art/script: Jacques Tardi. © 1980 The creator/Casterman

master of SF fantasy, whose best-known albums include various *Lone Sloane* adventures, *The Night*, a poetic SF meditation on death, *Salammbo*, a version of Gustave Flaubert's novel set in outer space, and *Nosferatu*, a claustrophic take on F.W. Murnau's vampire movie; Jacques Tardi, who produced atmospheric melodramas, most popularly *The Extraordinary Adventures of Adele Blanc-Sec* (six volumes) about a female thriller-writer in *belle époque* Paris, and less commercial personal work such as *The War of the Trenches*, a pacifist look at the First World War based partly on his grandfather's experiences; Enki Bilal, who ranged from mercurial SF (*The Woman Trap, Gods in Chaos*) to grim political allegory (*The Town That Didn't Exist, Ranks of the Black Order* – both written by Pierre Christin); François Bourgeon, whose *Passagers du vent* was an exhaustively researched tale of a slave ship and the fate of its passengers; Yves Chaland, who 'reinvented' the clear line for an adult audience, and was best known for his irascible character Freddy Lombard, an out of work detective who starred in numerous popular albums (*Testament, Le Cimetière des éléphants*, *La comète de Carthage*, *Vacances à Budapest*, *F. 52*); Max Cabanes, whose *Heart Throbs* was an unsentimental reminiscence of a childhood spent in the south of France rendered in watercolour; François Boucq, whose *The Magicians Wife* and *Billy Budd KGB* were vivid interpretations of stories by American thriller-writer Jerome Charyn; and Frank Margerin, whose series of humorous albums about a group of rocker-friends (*Rickie Banlieue*, *Votez Rocky*, *Bananes Métalliques*, *Radio Lucien*, *Rickie VII*, *Chez Lucien*) became a cult among college youth.

From Italy, the 'second nation' of adult comics, there was: Hugo Pratt, one of the most respected of European creators, best known for his *Corto Maltese* albums about a seafaring adventurer in the 1910s; Milo Manara, a master of exquisitely-drawn sex-erotica albums (*Butterscotch, Click!*) and also more serious historical fiction (*Indian Summer*, co-created with Hugo Pratt, about the conflict between settlers and native Americans in Puritan New England); Guido Crepax, another erotica/porn artist who also had a very sophisticated drawing style, with a penchant for subject-matter involving women in pain (*The Story of O*, *Emmanuelle*), but who also exhibited a more thoughtful side (*The Man From Harlem*, about jazz and racism in New York); Lorenzo Mattotti, a doyen of fully-painted artwork and a leading figure in the European avant-garde – his classic *Fires* is an expressionist symphony in greens and reds about 'fire spirits' on a deserted island; and finally, artist Gaetano Libatore, whose collaboration with writer Stefano Tamburini involving the character 'Ranxerox' (*Ranxerox in New York*, *Happy Birthday Lubna*) bought new levels of violence to European comics.

From elsewhere, too, there were talented creators. From the Netherlands, Joost Swarte, whose whimsical clear line cartoons were a staple of innumerable European magazines (some of which were collected in *Swarte: Hors Serie*). From Germany, Matthias Schultheiss,

Figure 15.5 Panels from *Corto Maltese in Irelande* (1980). Art/script: Hugo Pratt. © 1980 The creator/Casterman

who was best known for his SF (*Bell's Theorem*), but who also adapted Charles Bukowski's lowlife stories (*Tales of Ordinary Madness*). And from Belgium, Hermann, who produced mediaeval thrillers on an epic scale (*The Towers of Bois Maury*), and the pairing of artist François Schuiten and writer Benoit Peeters, whose sweeping McCay-like architectural vistas became a trademark (*Les Cités obscurés*). Creators from Spain, where the situation was anomalous, will be discussed below.

Thus, the albums covered a vast range of subject-matter. Of course, the ones mentioned above represent the best of the crop, and some critical comment is required. Faced with the full gamut, good and bad, some visiting commentators from Britain and the USA have come away with two impressions. First, that European comics are dominated by sex-erotica ('Europe's trashy equivalent to the American superhero', in the words of the *Comics Journal*)[16] and, second, that the vast majority are formulaic and of pulp quality, with the admittedly strong artwork often disguising a lack of narrative content. These observations are correct to a degree, but need qualification. European

Figure 15.6 Cartoon by Joost Swarte, *Pilote*, no. 65 (1982), demonstrating his Hergé-derived 'clear line' art style. © 1982 The creator

comics do contain a great deal of sex, and some are sold primarily on their prurient interest (particularly those by Manara and Crepax), but attitudes to sex are more liberated on the continent, and it is much more acceptable in all media. Therefore what might be perceived as prurient content by outsiders is often an integral part of genre stories. And while there is no doubt that the majority of albums are pulp writing, it has to be said that the quality of pulp in Europe is infinitely higher than in Britain and America, with more variety within standard formulas – if only because the readership has come to expect more from the medium.

From the mid-1970s, therefore, adult comics were respectable in Europe, and available from mainstream bookshops and newsagents across the continent. With this shift to mass acceptance of adult material, children's comics were eclipsed. In parts of Europe sales of post-adolescent comics actually exceeded those of comics for youngsters (one estimate put the split at 60/40 in the case of France). With this more serious treatment, comics entered a new phase, and became 'institutionalised'.

Conventions expanded and became cultural festivals focusing on the top creators of adult comics and their latest albums. The biggest by far became that at Angoulême in France (founded in 1975), which by the late 1980s was reputedly attracting a staggering 300,000 people from all over Europe (which is to say, 100 times as many as UKCAC, and twenty times as many as San Diego). A truly remarkable event, every January the entire town becomes a shrine to comics, with every available space given over to exhibitions, talks and guest appearances from fashionable *auteurs*. With the attendant media razzamatazz (the event is covered by nationwide TV), Angoulême's reputation as 'The Cannes of comics' is not far of the mark. [17]

Similarly, comics were progressively co-opted on to university courses as valid subjects for study. Well-known academics and writers associated with comics research included Alain Robbe-Grillet and Roland Barthes in France, and Umberto Eco in Italy. Journals emerged which built on the original critical magazines of the 1960s, and reflected the new seriousness of the 1970s and 1980s – notably the *Cahiers de la bande dessinée* in France and *Fumo di China* in Italy. The level of discourse in such publications was unknown in Britain and America outside the pages of the *Comics Journal*.

Finally, even governments became involved, and in many countries subsidising comics became as natural as subsidising opera or ballet. The ultimate expression of this was the partial funding by the French government of the construction of the National Centre for the Comic Strip and Image (CNBDI), an £8 million museum and study-centre in Angoulême (where else?). It was officially opened in 1990 by the French Minister of Culture, Jack Lang, with the words 'When I was appointed Minister of Culture, I thought that one of my first tasks should be to make easy public acceptance of the comic strip.'[18] Needless to say, the notion of a British or American Minister for the Arts making a similar pledge remains inconceivable.

But if the 1970s and 1980s had seen a swing away from Belgium to France with the flowering of the adult market, the late-1980s and 1990s have seen the dramatic rise of comics from areas outside these traditional powerhouses. Whether this was due to a slump in the French industry, or the relative merits of competitors is a subject for fierce debate.[19] Certainly there has been a tendency for other nations to build up their own comics industries, and to publish home-grown talent themselves. Nowhere has this been more evident than in Spain.

The reason why Spain in particular should have flourished has to do with the internal politics of the country. The development of comics ('tebeos' or simply 'los comics') was retarded by the suffocating censorship of the Franco regime.[20] However, the years following the death of the dictator in 1975 have witnessed a renaissance in the arts, including the emergence of 'El neo tebeos' ('new comics') which are aimed at adults and include previously proscribed subject-matter. The most important new titles were the anthologies *Cimoc*, *Cairo* and above all *El Víbora* ('the viper') – a bawdy, satirical monthly much influenced by the underground (it published the work of Crumb and Shelton, previously banned in Spain, among its regular Spanish fare).

In the established fashion, these periodicals spawned albums, and established numerous popular native creators and *auteurs*. They included: Daniel Torres, a stylish clear-line artist best known for his

Figure 15.7 Cover to *El Víbora*, no. 10 (1988). Art: Javier Mariscal. © 1988 The creator

Opium, about a monocled oriental villain; Javier Mariscal, whose stunning 1950s design-influenced style brought colour and vitality to the pages of *El Vibora*; Nazario, creator of the bizarre *Anarcoma*, the eponymous star of which was a transvestite gay detective; and Max, creator of *Peter Pank*, a 'punk' reworking of the J. M. Barrie fairy-tale with added sex. Jordi Bernet and Sanchez Abuli should also be mentioned. They were not strictly connected with this 'new wave', but were responsible for creating the most popular adult Spanish strip of recent times, *Torpedo*, about the brutal adventures of a hired killer in 1930s Chicago. With this explosion of new comics and talent, Spain in the 1980s can in many ways be said to have inherited the dynamism of France in the 1970s.

Finally, there was also a challenge to France's hegemony from outside Europe – from America, and to a lesser extent from Britain. The prejudice against American comics was very slow to die in some areas of Europe – they had traditionally been perceived as gauche, poorly-produced children's fodder, and infinitely inferior to the classily-produced home-made article. Indeed, in 1988 the major French publishers Glenat were slammed by critics for 'going American' when they announced plans to target a more teen-orientated audience.[21]

But, with the coming of 'graphic novels' and more adult-orientated material in the late 1980s, the Europeans found that the American and British product was more to their taste. Several successes were notched up in quick succession – notably, *Watchmen*, *V for Vendetta*, *Dark Knight* and *Maus* (which, as in America and Britain, was marketed as a book rather than a comic). Even Thierry Groensteen, editor of the *Cahiers de la bande dessinée*, was moved to declare: 'Comics in Europe developed first under the influence of Belgium, and then of France. The future, in my opinion, belongs to America.'[22] Whether American and British publishers, in the recessionary 1990s, can live up to this remains to be seen.

Japan

In 1992, the Japanese comics industry was by far the largest in the world. Its pre-eminence is recent, only superseding the American industry in the late 1970s. As in America and Britain, but unlike parts of Europe, the culture is a predominantly juvenile one, although adult comics have played an increasingly significant role since the early 1960s. Unlike Britain and America, but like Europe, the status of the medium as a valid art form has long been established.

Many histories trace the beginnings of Japanese comics to medieval religious scrolls, or to seventh-century caricatures, or sometimes even to the origins of Japanese writing, which is derived from pictographs. But in many ways, to establish such a lineage is just as problematic as tracing western comics to the Bayeux Tapestry and cave-paintings, and similarly implies historical connections that are not necessarily valid.

Instead, the story can be said properly to begin with Japan's rapid westernisation in the mid-nineteenth century, when traditional notions of artistic style began to be challenged by new ones from Europe. Previously, the predominant indigenous graphic mode of expression had been a 'wispy' watercolour brush technique, developed primarily in the production of scrolls on themes typically involving religion or nature. Pen and ink were not common tools, and social commentary was strictly controlled by the authorities.

But as trading links with Europe were established a demand grew among the expatriate European community for satirical publications on the European model. In 1862, an Englishman, Charles Wirgman (a correspondent from the *Illustrated London News*) published *Japan Punch*, an English-language version of the British magazine concerning Japanese themes. In it he drew cartoons which to the Japanese involved completely alien ideas about shading, perspective and word-balloons – not to mention a new form of satirical wit. As other European cartoonists followed in his footsteps (notably Frenchman George Bigot), this kind of western cartoon became established.

The real transformation came when Japanese artists started to imitate the fashionable new style. For the first time, artists made widespread use of pens instead of brushes, and began to break long-standing taboos about ridiculing the establishment. A translated version of *Japan Punch* was published, followed by numerous home-produced satirical magazines. Soon all the big cities of Japan had them, the foremost example being Yokohama's *Marumaru Chimbun* (1877).

The more obvious legacies of this first flowering of Japanese cartooning for the comics industry of the late twentieth century include the fact that most comics contain an English word in the title, and the ubiquitous technique of portraying characters with large, round, eyes – evidently adopted in this era as an ideal of beauty. Charles Wirgman, for his part, is regarded as the father of the Japanese cartoon, and a ceremony continues to be held every year in his honour.

Yet comic strips *per se* had yet to make a significant impact. Indeed, they did not become popular until the early twentieth century, under the influence not so much of European cartoons, but of the American funnies. By the turn of the century, economic links with America had become as important as those with Europe, and there was a similar cultural cross-fertilisation. In 1902, Rakuten Kitazawa created the first serialised Japanese strip with recurring characters, 'Tagosaku To Mokubei No Tokyo Kembutsu', about a pair of bumbling country-folk on a visit to Tokyo, which appeared in the paper *Jiji Shinpo* in the form of a Sunday supplement. It spawned several other examples, mostly on humorous themes, while the growing demand for this kind of entertainment was supplemented with translations of strips from America – for example, 'Mutt and Jeff' and 'Polly and her Pals'. Soon virtually every Japanese newspaper had discovered the value of strips as a method of raising circulation.

By the 1920s strips were also being introduced into children's magazines, where they became even more popular. They were first serialised in monthly magazines like *Shonen Club*, and were later collected into albums. The classic children's strip from this early period was *Norakaru*, by Suiho Tagawa, about a mischievous dog. These magazines were the first publications to fit our basic definition of 'a comic' and can thus be considered the first Japanese examples of the form.

By the mid-1930s the medium was almost exclusively a juvenile one. By now the word 'manga', which had its origins in the early nineteenth century[23] had become the generic term for cartoons, narrative strips and animated films. Henceforward, it would be the name most commonly used to describe comics in Japan.

The Second World War meant the total devastation of the country, and also a temporary end to comics due to paper shortages. Nevertheless, after 1945 there was renewed demand, spurred partly by the influence of American comics (which entered the country with the occupying GIs), and partly by the simple fact of a need for cheap escapism. New boys' magazines like *Shonen* and *Manga Shonen* emerged, with strips mainly about funny animals and cute robots, and proved so popular that they inspired an unprecedented boom. While sales multiplied, one by-product was that by the 1950s 'pay-libraries' were being established all over the country, where children could borrow manga for a few yen.

The pivotal figure in this postwar manga explosion was Osamu Tezuka. He occupies a position in Japanese comics history analogous to Hergé in Europe or Jack Kirby in America, and he is known in his homeland as 'the god of comics'. Much influenced by the animation of Walt Disney, he introduced new cinematic effects into strip art – for example, camera-angles, exploded layouts and imaginative 'cutting' – and allowed his comics to last much longer than had previously been the custom, in order to attain greater depth of characterisation and plot complexity. These innovations revolutionised the medium, and garnered an ever-increasing audience. His first major work, *New Treasure Island*, was 200 pages long, and sold over 300,000 copies. He followed it up with other bestsellers including *Lost World*, *Metropolis* and *Tetsuwan Atomu*, which was later made into an animated cartoon series known to westerners as *Astro Boy*.

However, the pay-libraries left the way open for a new kind of comic. Gradually, in the late 1950s, other creators took Tezuka's innovations and applied them to more mature themes. New subject-matter involving adult romance and adventure was explored – robots and funny animals were out; sex and violence were in. At the same time, although Tezuka's ideas involving long stories and cinematic composition were retained, creators set themselves up in opposition to what was by now the 'Tezuka school', and dropped the Disney-style artwork in favour of more realistic rendering. They aimed their work specifically at an older readership – typically male and working class (factory workers and high-school students) – although there was never a bar against youngsters, and the intended outlet was often exclusively the pay-libraries, which by the early 1960s numbered over 30,000 nationally. Because these new adult manga were so distinctive, they soon acquired a new name – 'gekiga' or 'drama-pictures'.

The samurai story became particularly popular among older readers. The pioneering work in this genre was *Ninja Bugeicho* by Sampei Shirato, published in seventeen separate volumes between 1959 and 1962. Set in the wars of the late sixteenth century, it was a deceptively simple adventure story, with plenty of gory sword-fights, which could simultaneously be read on the level of a political struggle by the oppressed against their feudal masters. Shirato also attempted to capture a sense of the strict samurai code, to give the story a philosophical dimension, and used a realistic (if still cartoony) art style to emphasise the seriousness of his intentions. The comic was a major step forward, inspiring a plethora of other samurai manga, and setting the tone generally for future gekiga on adventure themes.

Perhaps the second biggest genre in the wake of the samurai manga was sport – a not unconnected subject as Japanese society has historically tended to view sport as a 'testing of the spirit', with much in common with the samurai ethic. These came to prominence in the wake of General MacArthur's lifting of the ban on competitive sports, and usually involved a variant on the themes of honour and endurance: the standard story-line follows an individual's rise from obscurity to winning a championship. It was a genre greatly boosted by the appear-ance of real-life Japanese sporting heroes in successive Olympics in the 1960s; by the end of that decade sumo, baseball, soccer, judo and just about every other sport had been featured in comic form.

But, despite the new vogue for adult manga, it remained typi-cally the case that creators working in gegika for the pay-libraries were under-paid and little known. Even though there was less prejudice in Japan than in Britain or the USA against comics as an inherently juvenile medium, they were still considered as cheap entertainment for the masses, and except in very few cases (for example, the work of Tezuka) had little artistic credibility. However, gradually individual talents associated with the pay-libraries rose above the rest, among them Takao Saito, Yoshihiro Tatsumi and Yoshiharu Tsuge. They constituted the so-called 'new wave', and were among the first to be acclaimed as masters of the adult form. Manga would increasingly be borrowed, and sold, on the strength of their reputations.

But, by the mid-1960s it was clear that the pay-libraries were just a phase in manga development. The 1960s was the decade in which Japan's economy took off: suddenly, people had a much greater disposable income – and proved themselves more than willing to spend it on comics. In terms of the industry generally, in the words of one historian, 'the phoenix became a Godzilla'.[24] Tokyo became the centre of manga production, with hundreds of studios turning out myriad titles for an exponentially growing market. Manga magazines went from monthly schedules to weekly, and in 1966 *Shonen* became the first to break the 1 million circulation barrier. In the process, the pay-libraries gradually became obsolete, as the economies of scale of comics publishing meant people could now afford to buy rather than to borrow.

With the shift to buying manga, a commercial comics culture was formalised. In terms of the actual product on sale in newsagents, a typical manga would be of a size analogous to British telephone directories (1 to 2 inches thick) at 150–200 pages long, printed on low-quality paper in one colour and priced very cheaply. It would be intended to be speed-read and then thrown away. (It is because of this tradition of speed-reading that Japanese comics have a tendency to be much more visual than western comics, with more silent panels.) Additionally, if individual stories proved to be popular, they might be collected into book form, sometimes in hardback, for bookshop sale.

Simultaneously, pay and working conditions within the industry were put on a more sound footing. In contrast to the old days of the pay-libraries, creators now retained control of copyright and received royalties (the size of which depended on their reputation). They would also collect another royalty from the book version, if and when it appeared. This laid the foundations for the emergence of super-rich and super-famous creators: in short, the creation of comics now became a profession to aspire to.

There were some dissenting voices to be heard on this new manga explosion. Fears were expressed that mirrored those in the west – that Japanese society would become illiterate, that comics were an inherently sensationalist form and so on. But, in general, there was not the same stigma attached to comics as was the case in the west, and from the 1960s onwards, it is fair to say that the economic and cultural status of creators was considered comparable to that of anybody involved in any other kind of art form.

But the 1960s were only a start; the 1970s saw the greatest advances for adult comics yet. The traditional genres remained popular and generated new bestsellers: *Lone Wolf and Cub* (1970–6), by

Kazuo Koike and Gōseki Kojima, for example, was another samurai
epic and another artistic triumph. The story concerned a discredited
warrior who becomes a paid assassin and travels across medieval Japan
in search of his prey with his baby son in tow. It was very bloody, and
very long (a single sword-fight lasted thirty pages), but retained an
intensity throughout that was unparalleled. It proved to be very influential both in Japan and, later, in the west. [25]

The traditional genres were joined by new ones, which took old
themes and remolded them. The classic samurai theme of a warrior
working alone, for example (as seen in *Lone Wolf*), reappeared in
another bestseller, *Golgo 13*, by Takao Saito, about a suave modern-

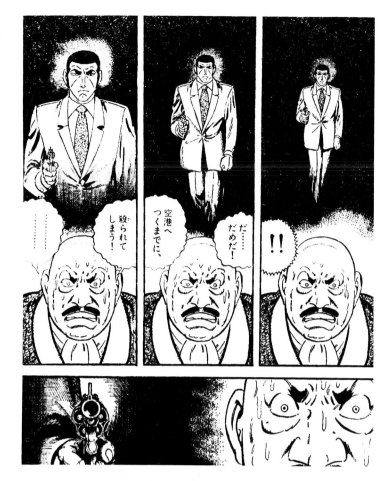

day hitman. The character resembled James Bond, had no scruples and
spent his time flying to exotic locations to fulfil contracts. The story
began in 1969 and remained a major hit right through the 1970s: in
1992 there were estimated to be a staggering 60 million copies in print.

Similarly, 'Yakuza manga' developed. These mythologised life
in the Japanese version of the mafia, and again frequently referred to
the samurai ethic (perhaps the best-known example was *Evil in the
Showa Period* by Kazuhiko Murakami). In the same vein, 'Teen-gang
manga' were fantasies about gang-fights that emphasised loyalty to the
group and traditional notions of honour (and which, unlike the
Yakuza comics, were totally imaginary – delinquency on the American
or British model being almost non-existent in Japan at the time).

Humorous manga for adults also came to the fore. So-called
'salaryman' titles satirised the Japanese 'economic miracle' and were
aimed at white-collar workers, focusing on the absurdities of office life

(the nearest equivalent in Britain is probably the Bristow strip in the *London Evening Standard*). They were shorter than regular manga, were drawn in a minimalist style and proved an enormously popular way of letting off steam for this section of the population.[26]

There was more non-fiction. Manga emerged on everything from gourmet cookery, to the stock market, to 'how-to' comics on car-maintenance. Even political parties put out manifestos in comic form. Sometimes, reality would be made palatable by the addition of fictional scenes. One acclaimed masterpiece of 'fact-ion', *Japan Inc* (1976) by Shotaro Ishinomori, provided a witty and remarkably attention-retaining history of the US–Japanese trade war, complete with sex-fantasy scenes, and sold over 1 million copies. 'People do not read economics books because they are too difficult', the creator later explained, 'but in a comic such subject-matter is accessible.'[27]

In particular, biography and autobiography were growth areas. *Barefoot Gen* (1972–3), by Keiji Nakazawa, was a harrowing eyewitness account of the bombing of Hiroshima and its aftermath: during its course, the reader came to 'know' Nakazawa's family, and so empathised all the more with their terrible fate. It was indicative of the status of manga in Japanese culture that he chose this medium to tell his story: as he later explained: 'I named my main character Gen [meaning "source"] in the hope that he would become a source of strength for a new generation of mankind – one that can . . . have the strength to say "no" to nuclear weapons.'[28] *Banzai Charge* (1973) by Shigeru Mizuki was another acclaimed autobiography, this time questioning the suicide tactics of the Imperial army at the end of the Second World War. There was even a thriving trade in the vanity-publishing of the autobiographies of the rich and famous.

These trends continued in the 1980s, and were amplified. Action comics were once more updated, with a particular vogue for high-tech SF, reflecting the country's technological 'superpower' status. The key title here was *Akira* (1986) by Katsuhiro Otomo, an apocalyptic thriller about a motor cycle gang in a dystopian Tokyo that cleverly mixed cyberpunk themes with the old teen-gang genre. It was adapted into a spectacular animated movie by Otomo himself, which became the biggest Japanese box-office hit of 1988.[29] The comic spawned many copyists.

Sports comics, too, were given a contemporary twist, with the growth of gambling comics – about horse-racing, pachinko (a kind of Japanese pinball) and especially mah-jongg, in which tense games were played for big stakes in smoky back rooms (readers typically followed the exact plays in a game as it progressed through the story).

The 1980s did see two major departures in terms of genre. The first was manga for women. There had long been an industry aimed at girls, but now sophisticated romance titles for women rivalled sales of

Figure 15.10 A page from *Akira* (1988). Art/script: Katsuhiro Otomo. © 1988 The creator/Kodansha

men's comics. The groundwork had been laid in the 1970s by the first major female comics creator, Riyoko Ikeda, whose *The Rose of Versailles* (1972–4), a fictionalised account of the life of Marie Antoinette, had been a top seller. It inspired several other costume dramas with European settings, and a plethora of titles which were more slushy than historical. Later in the 1980s, the trend for women's comics expanded to include subject-matter involving career women climbing the corporate ladder and women sports heroes. In the early 1990s the best-known creator working in the field, and one of the richest women in Japan, is Rumiko Takahashi – dubbed 'the manga princess' by fans.

The second new genre, and the biggest growth area in recent years has been pornography, or so-called 'juicy manga'. This has coincided with a 'sexual revolution' in Japanese society comparable to that in Britain and America in the 1960s, and in 1992 it was estimated that a quarter of all comics in Japan contain sexual content, with a significant proportion dedicated specifically to the subject. But although there is a great deal of it, it is not explicit, contrary to the belief of many western commentators, since laws[30] prohibit the graphic depiction of genitalia or the sex-act.[31]

The official policy on this matter may seem strange to westerners given the appalling level of sexual violence that is permissible in manga. Sado-masochism and rape-fantasies, for instance, are very common: *The Rapeman*, for example, concerns the exploits of a priapic superhero who trusses up his victims (male and female) and violates them in various ways. It is considered to be 'mild' for its genre.

Yet, such themes are tolerated because Japanese officialdom sees fictional violence, sexual or otherwise, as a safety valve. In a country where so much importance is placed on social order and conformity, the establishment seems to tacitly condone the idea that such material is a harmless way to keep people under control. Supporters of the policy point to the fact that street-crime is very low in Japan, and suggest that this is a reversal of the situation Fredric Wertham might have predicted.[32]

Some Japanese groups do not agree. The first major campaign against the sex comics was launched in 1990, involving everybody from left-wing feminists to right-wing conservatives (like the campaigns against comics in Britain and the USA, there were numerous underlying political motives, including one attempt to actually change the constitution). This backlash constituted the most serious challenge to the manga industry in its history. One result has been that, for the first time, publishers have put 'adults only' labels on their covers.[33]

But despite the new porn comics and the accompanying controversy, in general manga have continued to gain cultural respectability in the 1980s and 1990s. The most striking manifestation of this is the way in which they have been incorporated onto all kinds of college courses, and have become the subject for numerous learned academic journals. Yoshiya Soeda, a lecturer at the University of Tsu Kuba, summed up their educational importance very simply: 'manga are the dominant force in Japanese pop culture, and are a window on Japanese society, revealing its fears and fantasies'.[34]

At the same time, and partly as a result of this increasing respectability, the stock of creators has continued to rise. They now became as revered as pop- and film-stars, with some being given the opportunity to present their own television programmes. It was even true that one or two attempted to run for political office. It should be no surprise, therefore, that in 1989 it was reported that six out of the ten most wealthy people in Japan were manga creators.[35]

It is for these reasons that the 1990s are likely to see the biggest sales of manga yet achieved. The juggernaut set in motion in the 1960s continues to gather momentum, and the latest figures for sales are quite staggering. Annually, there are 3,750 titles produced with total sales of 1.9 billion. This adds up to about thirty comics published for every household, and represents 25 per cent of all publishing. In terms of the readership-breakdown, boys' comics are the most popular, then girls', then men's, then women's – though, as ever, the crossover readership is extensive.[36]

What this means is that manga are no longer a branch of the entertainment business, but an inescapable fact of Japanese life. The citizen's day is invaded by them: board a train in the morning, and you are surrounded by businessmen reading manga on their way to work; go to a restaurant at lunchtime, and customers will be reading courtesy-manga between courses; and if you suddenly get the urge for reading matter in the middle of the night, there are manga vending machines on street corners in most cities. Ozamu Tezuka, in many ways the man who started it all, summed up the situation perfectly when he commented that we have reached the point of 'manga as air'.[37]

Further reading

Comics histories that take the world outside Britain and the USA into account are few and far between: Paul Gravett's *The New Penguin Book of Comics* (Harmondsworth: Penguin, forthcoming 1993) promises to be a major exception. On Europe specifically, the best sources tend to be foreign-language – though David Kunzle's two-volume *History of the Comic Strip* (Berkeley, Calif.: University of California Press 1973 (Vol. 1); 1989 (Vol. 2)) impressively covers the very early history of the form. Useful overviews include Jacques Sadoul's *93 ans de BD* (Paris: J'ai Lu 1989); Andreas Knigge's *Comic Lexicon* (Frankfurt: Ullstein 1988); and Thierry Groensteen's *La bande dessinée depuis 1975* (Paris: MA Editions 1985). On Japan, the outstanding text is Frederik Schodt's superb *Manga! Manga!* (New York: Kodansha International 1983, rev edn 1988). For more general information, Maurice Horn (ed.), *The World Encyclopaedia of Comics* (6 vols) (New York: Chelsea House 1976) is dated but still useful, while John Lent's *Comic Art: An International Bibliography* (Drexel Hill, Penn., USA: John Lent 1986) points up some profitable avenues. Back issues of fanzines can also bear fruit, while other sources can be found in the bibliography.

Adult comics and other media

Most people don't know comics exist, so a smart [cinema] producer can go to his cellar, read these things and then use them. The film audience has no idea.
(Howard Chaykin, comics creator)[1]

Despite the characteristic narrow focus of most comics histories, it is clear that comics do not exist in a vacuum. There is inevitably a spill-over into other media, other areas of the arts, and this has been as true historically for adult comics as for children's. We have seen in previous chapters how far outside agencies have influenced comics in the past: from Dickens' influence on Ally Sloper to Frank Miller's fascination with the 'Dirty Harry' movies. The following necessarily brief (and impressionistic) survey seeks to look at the relationship from a reciprocal perspective.

Far from being a negligible area of comics history, we can say from the outset that the crossover with other media has been particu-larly rich. There are two main reasons for this. The first is that comics, because of their curious history, have been an exemplary medium to generate myth-like characters perfectly suited to media exploitation. The other is that because comics have historically been held in such low cultural regard, they have been 'borrowed from' by other media to a degree that is extraordinary compared to other areas of the arts. These were factors that were present from the start.

The first adult comics of the nineteenth century were aimed at a working-class audience, and had strong links with other modes of working-class cultural expression. The character that had the biggest impact in this respect was, inevitably, Ally Sloper. He was the subject of several popular songs and of a score composed for brass bands ('Ally Sloper's Grand Parade March' by Albert Pfennig). In the music halls, his adventures were copied in stage comedy-routines, and there were at least two ventriloquist acts with Ally Sloper dolls (which now fetch handsome prices at auction). In due course, when cinemas began to take over from music halls as the main focus for working-class enter-tainment, he made the transition to several very early movies. According to one historian, Ally Sloper's visibility in the years before the First World War was 'comparable to that of Disney half a century later'.[2]

Other early comics no doubt had similar resonances, albeit on a much lesser scale. It is likely, for example that the various tramps and misfits that followed Sloper in the comics (for example, 'Weary Willie and Tired Tim') were a similar inspiration to music hall acts and early movies. It is worth recalling that at this time Charlie Chaplin first performed on the London stage as 'the Little Tramp'.

The next phase in comics development, the boom in children's comics between the 1930s and 1960s, naturally produced its own resonance. British comics, however, did not cross-fertilise with other media to any significant degree owing to the reluctance of DC Thomson and IPC to license characters (though the Hulton Press's Dan Dare did become the subject for a short-lived radio serial). The off-shoots of American comics, on the other hand, were ubiquitous.[3] The first movies starring Batman and Superman were produced in the 1940s and 1950s, while later they and many other superheroes became animated television cartoons. Batman also featured in the classic 1966 live-action TV series (which also spawned a movie), with Adam West in the title role – a pop art Caped Crusader with a paunch and plenty of witty lines. Funny animal cartoons were also much in evidence, as the great American companies Disney and Warner Looney Tunes battled it out for juvenile audiences on both the small and big screens. Indeed, animation historians today invariably see this period as a 'golden age', the corollary being that animation was stereotyped as a children's medium much in the same way that comics were.[4]

But because of the way the economics of the comics industry developed in this period (on both sides of the Atlantic), the exchange with other media was typically not to the benefit of comics creators. Publishers were at liberty to do what they liked with the characters, and were free to license them without consultation with creators or to offer commensurate recompense. Perhaps the most galling example of this was the case of Disney and the creations of Carl Barks. Barks laboured anonymously on various comics characters (most famously the miserly duck Uncle Scrooge) for a paltry flat-page fee for most of his working life; characters which would then be made into cartoons that generated millions of dollars all over the world. In the words of one historian, Barks's 'working conditions under Disney make him look like a Donald Duck vis-à-vis Uncle Scrooge as Uncle Walt'.[5]

The underground marked the re-emergence of adult comics in the modern era, and their cross-polination with other cultural forms began with the wider manifestations of the hippie culture. Psychedelic artwork – typically LSD-inspired patterns in swirling day-glo colours – quickly defined the look of the movement, and we have seen how many of the key American comix creators emerged from the poster scene (Rick Griffin, Victor Moscoso and Robert Williams particularly). But as the comix became established, so images from them worked their way back into the posters, including the more conventional druggy strips of creators like Crumb and Shelton. From these beginnings, poster and comix art dispersed into wider areas of illustration, which could include anything from adverts for headshops and record covers to T-shirts, custom-car and -bike art and tattoo designs. (The comix creator most associated with this kind of work in Britain was Hunt Emerson.)[6]

But the underground had much wider influences. Importantly, in movies there were several attempts to revolutionise animation by taking on adult comix-inspired subject-matter. The most well-known animated feature was Ralph Bakshi's version of Robert Crumb's *Fritz the Cat* (1972), which in Britain became the first cartoon film to be awarded an X certificate. It was an eccentric interpretation of the comic that substituted outrage for political subtlety; nevertheless it received favourable reviews and was a box-office hit, although Crumb himself was not so happy with the result, and went to court to get his name removed from the credits. *Fritz* was followed by several other feature-length cartoons in an 'underground' mould, including the dismal sequel *The Nine Lives of Fritz the Cat* (1974), and two more directed by Bakshi (both incorporating live action) – *Heavy Traffic* (1973) and *Coonskin* (1975). Despite the often debatable quality of Bakshi's movies, he should nevertheless be considered a pioneer of commercial adult cartoons: he commented later that 'I've always wanted to push

Figure 16.1 Original cinema poster for *Fritz the Cat* (1972)

animation to its limits', acknowledging as an inspiration the fact that 'comic books have progressed further than screen animation has'.[7]

Even on television, the influence of the underground could be seen. The animated sequences on the comedy show *Monty Python* (1968–72), for example, can be counted as the first exposure for most of the population to the comix art style. The talent behind them was an American, Terry Gilliam, who had contributed strips to Harvey Kurtzman's *Help!* in the mid-1960s. His subject-matter changed for *Python* to incorporate the more sexually audacious orientation of the comix, and his cartoons were often the most risqué part of the show. (Gilliam later went on to become one of the world's top film directors, with movies such as *Brazil*, *Baron Munchausen* and *The Fisher King* to his credit.)

However, although the underground comics embodied a totally different economic rationale to their commercial counterparts, there was still a problem of creator exploitation when it came to exchanges with other media. In the early days of the comix, there was a generally *laissez-faire* attitude to copyrighting work, and it was assumed that images and strips would be used in other counter-cultural publications or forms. The problems arose when the 'straight' media realised that they had a potentially wider appeal, and began to co-opt them for their own ends (as had happened with the *Fritz* movie). This led creators to copyright material to a much greater degree, with some banding together to form unofficial 'unions'.[8] As one creator and publisher recalls:

> The unions were not serious – artists are a very disparate group, and it has never been feasible to organise them effectively. But at the same time there was some disillusionment and bitterness about what was happening, and they were a sincere effort to get everybody to play fair.[9]

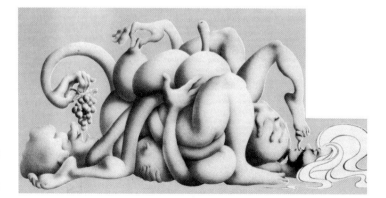

Figure 16.2 Animation-still from *Monty Python's Flying Circus*, demonstrating Terry Gilliam's underground influence. © 1976 Methuen

The development of organised fandom in the 1970s and 1980s saw the emergence of three separate categories of adult comics, each of which had a distinct relationship with other media. They were comics inspired by the science fiction renaissance; titles resulting from the direct sales revolution; and comics that originated from alternative sources, but which were sold from the fan shops. Each continued along the avenues the underground had opened up.

The SF comics were undoubtedly the most influential. The illustrative style associated with them was termed 'fantasy art', and was typically characterised by a smooth airbrush technique (as featured in *Métal Hurlant*) and subject-matter ranging from Tolkienesque or alien landscapes inhabited by grotesque creatures to the complex technologies of distant futures. This style became increasingly fashionable for posters, record-covers and so on, and to a large degree superseded underground images in these areas. Fantasy artists who were also comics creators included Richard Corben, Angus McKie, Boris Vallejo, Phillippe Druillet, Moebius and, above all, Frank Frazetta, nicknamed 'the Michelangelo of Brooklyn', who briefly became the most highly-paid commercial artist in the world.

One particularly important aspect of the fantasy art craze was

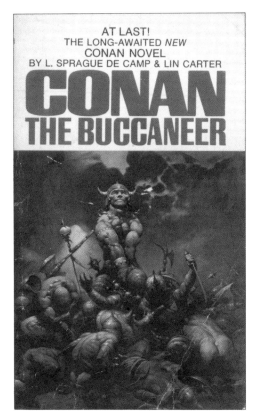

Figure 16.3 Cover to the Lancer paperback *Conan the Buccaneer* (1971), with art by Frank Frazetta (proof that you can never judge a cover by its book). © 1971 Lancer Books

the spillover into book covers. As Dez Skinn recalled:

> In a shop like Dark They Were, science fiction fans would often be knocked out by the artwork on book-covers, and subsequently got interested in the comics in the shop through this route. That was especially true of the Lancer *Conan* paperbacks – which really put Frank Frazetta on the map.[10]

Later, the same would also be true of the illustration for the packaging of games such as 'Dungeons and Dragons' and for computer games software.

In movies, too, the SF comics and fantasy art had their influence. Once again the name Ralph Bakshi was in evidence for his animated features *Wizards* (1977), *Lord of the Rings* (1978) and *Fire and Ice* (1983) (which was actually based on artwork by Frazetta). However, the big movie of the period was Gerald Potterton's *Heavy Metal* (1981), an animated epic based on the eponymous comic, which utilised designs by Howard Chaykin and Angus McKie among others. Touted as a 'rock *Fantasia*', it featured music by a variety of groups including Devo and Cheap Trick (which is to say, not necessarily heavy metal), and a dazzling array of animation styles, reportedly produced simultaneously by 5,000 animators in five countries. But despite some entertaining moments, the episodic stories tended to emphasise the chauvinist and pretentious tone of their comic-prototypes, and the movie was roundly savaged by critics: it sank like a lead weight at the box office.

On a more subtle level, SF movie-makers increasingly made use of comics creators for things like design and storyboarding.[11] Moebius was perhaps the most in demand, and his work was used (in various forms) by such cinema luminaries as Ridley Scott on *Blade Runner* and *Alien*, Steven Lisberger on *Tron*, Alexandro Jodorowsky on his aborted *Dune*, and George Lucas on *The Empire Strikes Back*.[12]

The comics produced specifically for the fan market were a less visible influence on outside media. Because fandom tended to be very insular, and the comics referential to comics traditions, there was a limit to how far ideas would translate. This period saw a number of successful screen adaptations of more traditional American comics – notably the four *Superman* movies, and the *Wonder Woman* and *Hulk* TV series. But in terms of adult comics, the few adaptations that were attempted ended in failure. The two most notable examples were the live-action film version of *Howard the Duck* (1986), based on Steve Gerber's adult Marvel comic, which turned out to be a turkey, and *Swamp Thing* (1982), a B-movie directed by horror king Wes Craven, which hearkened back to the character's original incarnation rather than the more sophisticated Alan Moore version.[13] (Indeed, the only really successful adaptation of an adult comic in the period was of the bookshop orientated *When the Wind Blows*, made into a very moving cartoon feature in 1986, directed by Jimmy Murakami, with voices by John Mills and Peggy Ashcroft.)

Finally, there were the 'alternative' comics (roughly defined as the avant-garde, small press and the continuing underground): these tended to be more experimental than the previous two categories and so had distinct resonances with other media. In particular, the punk phenomenon of the late 1970s became a focus for new kinds of artwork, in the same way that hippie had been a decade before, with new comics artists becoming popular whose style was both different to the psychedelic, drugs images of the underground period, and to the smooth, polished look of the fantasy artists. For instance, in Britain the wild, spiky artwork of Savage Pencil, né Edwin Pouncey (*Knockabout*, *Escape*, *Corpsemeat*) could be seen on posters and record-covers and became very closely associated with certain groups (notably The Lurkers). In America, creators broadly associated with punk included Gary Panter, Peter Bagge and the Hernandez Brothers.

Yet despite the gradual amelioration of pay, working conditions and status for creators during the period of the growth of fandom, there were still problems of unacknowledged 'borrowing' by other media. To the outside world, comics were still at the bottom of the cultural pyramid, and too often considered to be 'there for the raiding'. Howard Chaykin echoed many creators' frustrations when he told the *New York Post*: 'That's one reason I want to get out of comics – I'm tired of providing reference and source material for filmmakers.'[14]

The years 1986–87 marked the point at which adult comics 'went overground' once more. They entered the public eye in a way that was unprecedented since before 1914, and with publications as respected as the *Sunday Times* predicting that comics would be 'the art-form of the 90s', it was perhaps inevitable that outside agencies should take a special interest. Suddenly comics-related images and comics-style artwork were everywhere.

The disparate world of commercial art was quick to pick up on the new trend, and the new big-name comics artists were increasingly in demand for illustration work. For example, Dave McKean produced book covers for Unwin paperbacks, while Bill Sienkiewicz designed stage backcloths for rock bands, plus several movie posters. Similarly, youth subcultures continued to pick up on comics art styles. The new dance-club culture, for example, co-opted work by Chris Long (*Escape*) and Jamie Hewlett (*Deadline*) among others: their 'upbeat' style articulated perfectly the feel-good sensibility of the new scene (partly a reaction to punk), and was much in evidence on flyers, record-sleeves and the like – often in pirated form.[15] (The *Watchmen* smiley-face logo also became a dance motif.)

In the cinema, the adult comic adaptation to top them all was

Figure 16.4   The changing face of record-sleeve art: above, the Grateful Dead album *Aoxomoxoa* (1967), with art by Rick Griffin; below, the punk compilation album *Streets* (1977), with art by Savage Pencil

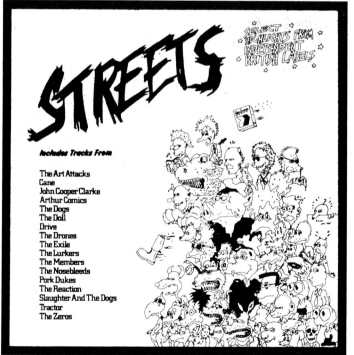

Batman (1989), a Hollywood blockbuster inspired by the success of Frank Miller's *Dark Knight* which became the fastest-grossing movie of all time. [16] With lavish production values, top stars (Michael Keaton as the lead, Jack Nicholson as the Joker), and an up-and-coming director noted for his inventiveness (Tim Burton), the film should in theory have been an intriguing new cinematic departure. Unfortunately the producers, wary of the costs and fearful of alienating the traditional Batman audience, compromised the adult elements of the Miller story in favour of a bland exercise in special effects: instead of being made an '18' or '15' certificate, the film was given a newly-instituted '12' – which was undoubtedly good for business, but disappointing for anybody expecting something a little more sophisticated.

Nevertheless, *Batman's* success ushered in a new era of movies derived from comics and newspaper strips. Notable examples included *Dick Tracy*, with Warren Beatty as Chester Gould's hard-boiled sleuth; *Teenage Mutant Ninja Turtles*, now reinvented as a children's fantasy; *The Punisher*, an ultra-violent 18-certificate thriller based on a Marvel superhero comic; and *The Rocketeer*, a romantic adventure set in the 1930s and based on a graphic novel by Dave Stevens. None had anywhere near the impact of *Batman* although this has not deterred production companies from pursuing comic adaptations: in April 1992 *Comics Scene* magazine listed over seventy movies in production or pre-production, many of which are based on adult titles (among them *American Flagg!*, *Lone Wolf and Cub*, *Watchmen* and the inevitable *Batman Returns*. [17]) Finally, some mention should be made of *Akira*, a Japanese animated feature directed by Katsuhiro Otomo from his own cyberpunk comic, which broke art-house box-office records throughout Britain in 1989: its success can be seen as in part a reflection of the growing popularity of Japanese adult comics in this Britain, and has again given rise to many copyists which will reach British and American screens in the next few years. [18]

Television, too, was not left unaffected by the comics boom. *The Simpsons* (1990) was a hilarious American animated series about an unattractive blue-collar family dominated by 10-year-old Bart (an anagram for 'brat'). Although not derived from an adult comic *per se*, it was touted as 'the first ever adult cartoon' and was created by a former alternative press cartoonist (Matt Groening). Though often extremely amusing, it was over-praised by critics, and not as innovative as its PR made out, amounting really to little more than *The Flintstones* with a dash of satire (not that there was anything wrong with that). [19] Nevertheless, its success spawned several other such American animated series, some based on direct sales comics. [20]

Meanwhile, Britain had its own home-grown adult animated TV series in the form of *Billy the Fish* (1990), and *Roger Mellie* (1991), based on strips from *Viz*. These were much less sophisticated productions, and despite featuring the vocal talents of Harry Enfield and Peter Cook, did not do justice to their source: because the originals had been parodies of children's comics, they worked perfectly in strip form, but when they were transferred to television, this reference point was one step removed, and the humour consequently diminished.

Finally, even the advertising industry picked up on comics. Images of Tank Girl were used to sell Wrangler Jeans, while the Fat Slags appeared in poster commercials for Tennents beer (the ad was swiftly banned by the Advertising Standards Authority for being sexist). In general terms, it was also true that the ad agencies were noticeably more inclined to use comics-influenced art: Barclays Bank, for example, used Marvel-style comic images on posters to entice students.

Yet even in this period of maximum comics exploitation, the problem of abuse of creators' rights did not go away. However, this was not so pronounced as before for two reasons. First, creators had a much higher profile than previously, and they tended to be in a much better bargaining position; second, because the mainstream press was more aware of their plight, journalists were more likely to expose rip-offs. A case in point happened in 1990 when *Time Out* exposed the 18-rated SF movie *Hardware* for stealing the plot from a *2000AD* story. The coverage resulted in an out-of-court financial settlement, and the accreditation of the two creators (Kevin O'Neill and Steve MacManus).

But the period from late 1980s was not just remarkable for the fact that comics were more visible in other media, but also because they were exploited in much more systematic fashion. The entertainment media had become dominated by a number of huge multinational con-glomerates, who now saw comics as a fresh area to colonise. Some-times licensing deals were struck with publishers to commercialise characters.[21] On other occasions, a conglomerate would take over completely in order to exploit the comics copyright from top to bottom. This latter course was taken by Warner Brothers with regard to DC Comics, and New World Productions with Marvel. In both cases, it opened up the possibility of a multi-level marketing exercise based on a single theme.

This was achieved most spectacularly by Warners with the *Batman* movie in 1989. The movie itself, the soundtrack (by Prince) and the merchandising (over 300 licensed product tie-ins) were all pushed in a single advertising campaign, and then reviewed in Warners-owned magazines (it was no accident that Batman was fea-tured on the cover of *Time*). There was even a comic produced with characters drawn to look like Michael Keaton, Jack Nicholson, *et al.* (the comic-of-the-movie-of-the-revisionist-comic-of-the-comic, no less!). This strategy of vertical integration was a huge success: the film alone made $240 million in a year, the Prince album went double-platinum, and revenues from merchandising ran into several millions; as we have seen, subsequent Bat-comics also sold unprecedentedly well. Not surprisingly, Warners have been in the forefront of the movie tie-in boom ever since.[22]

Despite the fact that no comics-related project of this nature has yet been as successful as *Batman*, the phenomenal success of its marketing remains an ideal for the media corporations to aim for. This trend for the systematic super-commercialisation of comics is therefore certainly one that will continue in future. It reflects the fact that, for the first time in their history, the cross-media fertilisation of comics is not just a by-product, but a calculated goal.

Further reading

Sources are unfortunately quite thin. On the connection between adult comics and youth and alternative culture there exist various illustrated books about psychedelic and underground art (for example, Suzanne White, *Psychedelic Collectables of the 1960s and 1970s* (New York: Wallace Homestead Books 1990)), fantasy art (Eckart Sackmann (ed.), *Masterpieces of Fantasy Art* (Berlin: Taschen 1991)), punk art (Brian Cannon, *Going Nowhere: The Art and Design of the Punk and New Wave Movements* (London: Omnibus 1989)) and dance culture art (Cynthia Rose, *Design After Dark*, (London: Omnibus 1992)), many of which contain references to comics artists. Individual creators' portfolio collections are another good source. On adult comics and cinema, see Ralph Bakshi, *The Animated Art of Ralph Bakshi* (Virginia Beach, Virginia: Donning 1984), and William Schoell's *Comic Book Heroes of the Screen* (London: Plexus Publishing 1991). For a consideration of vertical integration as it applied to *Batman*, see the excellent R. Pearson and W. Uricchio (eds), *The Many Lives of the Batman* (London: BFI Publishing/Routledge 1991).

Women and adult comics

I really think that as girls get older there's a 'double barrier' against reading comics . . . a) the fact that they're considered for kids, and b) the fact that they're a male domain.

(Carol Bennett, publisher, Knockabout Comics)[1]

In the survey that has formed the bulk of this book, it may have been noticed that women have rarely featured as creators, publishers or readers. When they appear as characters, they are invariably either plot devices (there to be rescued) or sex symbols (all plunging necklines and endless legs). While not the most 'politically correct' of records, it is echoed in many other areas of the arts, of course – except that in the case of comics, the negative attitudes to women are doubly pronounced.

'Why?' is a question that can only be answered by separating the subject into its constituent parts. There are three basic issues: the representation of women in the comics themselves; women working within the comics industry; and the female audience for comics. Although each is interconnected to a large degree, from a feminist perspective there are problems that are germane to each. Although here is not the place to go into this in detail, it is necessary to point out that there are many grey areas.

For example, there are differing opinions on what constitutes positive and negative images – and, moreover, such categorisations tend to change with time. Take the issue of pornography: when does an image of a woman change from being 'erotic' to being 'pornographic'? And if one is more 'acceptable' than the other, by what criteria are we to make such a judgment? Similarly, one might ask what is a 'stereotype'? Very simply, it is a shorthand image that asks us to fill in gaps from our knowledge: but does this have a useful function in a discussion, or does it create more problems than it solves? As for women working within the comics industry, clearly there is a difference between comics that happen to be created by women and 'women's comics', which purposely concern themselves with the articulation of women's experience. With this in mind, are women excluded from the industry as a policy, or is it, in the words of one creator, that they 'don't want to draw what the majority of comics readers want to see'?[2] By the same token, female readers of comics are no more the same, or look for the same things, than female readers of novels or female viewers of films. Do comics that feature 'women's issues' automatically attract more women readers? And what exactly are 'women's issues'?

Questions like these make any exploration of the subject very difficult. It is therefore unavoidable that the following survey will only attempt a superficial discussion of them, partly because they are in themselves so complex (and require much more space to explore), and partly because the historical information about women and comics is so patchy that it often precludes meaningful conclusions. As ever, the following is intended as an overview, and does not pretend to be comprehensive.

The first adult comics of the nineteenth century set the tone for the industry ever since – they were produced primarily by men, for men and were about 'male subjects'. Humorous in intention, they reflected the mores of their age, and contained as a matter of course jokes that would now be deemed 'sexist'. These varied in intensity from rather obvious gags about battleaxe wives, delectable nubiles and so on, to sometimes rather bitter comments about the 'new women' of the first feminist movement (*c*. 1860–1920). *Ally Sloper's Half Holiday*, for example, contained some scathing references to the suffrage issue. Other early comics used images of women for alternative purposes: *The Joker*, for example, contained pin-up cartoons of well-known music hall stars.

And yet, from the start women were recognised as an audience. *Half Holiday*'s subtitle was 'For Old Boys, Young Boys, Odd Boys Generally, . . . and Even Girls', while *Comic Cuts* was 'Mother's Comfort, Father's Joy'. Sometimes a special effort was made to play to this market: famously, in *Half Holiday*, a daughter was introduced for Sloper – 'Tootsie' – specifically to attract more women readers; more pointedly still, *Butterfly* was touted for several years as 'A Dainty Comic'.[3]

It is even possible to identify one or two female creators. For example, the inker for the original 'Ally Sloper' strip in *Judy* (and possibly occasionally the artist as well) was Emily de Tessier, working under the pseudonym Marie Duvall, the wife of Sloper's creator Charles Ross. Her work was regularly reprinted in *Half Holiday*. However, she was very much the exception: although much of the work in the early British comics was anonymous, it is fair to generalise that such female input was rare.

The children's comics that boomed between the 1930s and 1960s at first perpetuated this overall set-up. The workforce was also dominated by men, and the audience was primarily boys. However, it should be noted that as the industry expanded more women were drawn into it on the production side, as inkers or colourists, or sometimes even as editors.

As before, though, the female market was far from ignored.

Most of the humour titles claimed a large readership among girls, and in the case of the *Beano* that proportion is thought to have risen to as much as 50 per cent in the 1950s. (It should be noted that the *Beano* did feature several prominent female characters – most famously Minnie the Minx – though we should be careful about making the connection with the female readership's 'identification' with them.)[4]

The adventure comics were not so welcoming to girls, however, and *Eagle* was responsible for initiating a trend towards the glorification of 'manly' values – leadership, aggression, stiff-upper-lipped resolve – and the segregation of comics by sex.[5] In terms of the representation of women, they were generally relegated to secondary roles, though how often this equated with 'negative images' is debatable.

As a response, a new genre of comics sprang up specifically aimed at girls and teenage women. This was spearheaded in the 1950s by *Schoolfriend* and *Girl* (itself a companion title to *Eagle*) which, for example, featured stories about boarding-school japes and horsey adventures. They traced their lineage to the girls' story papers of the 1920s and 1930s. They were joined in the 1960s by the more cosmopolitan romance comics, of which *Jackie* was the archetype. These hailed from a different tradition, and were rather an outgrowth of the women's magazine industry – the result of an initiative to lower the age-range for women's magazines rather than to raise that for comics.

Taken together these titles notched up considerable sales, and the girls' industry was relatively well-developed in Britain compared to other parts of the world. (As we have seen, *Jackie* was selling a phenomenal 1 million-plus copies per issue at its peak in 1973–4.) It should be reiterated, however, that even in this sector of the industry the vast majority of creators were men.[6]

Finally, the American children's comics that were being imported were adding another dimension to the way women were presented.[7] The superhero titles were generally male power-fantasies, and women rarely appeared as anything other than plot-contrivances (Superman's girlfriend Lois Lane, for example, really didn't do very much). However, included among them were titles like *Wonder Woman* and *Sheena – Queen of the Jungle*, which were popular among girls. These comics also appealed to (older) boys owing to their undisguised erotic charge: the superheroines were invariably curvaceous and scantily-clad. Indeed, a new concept in comics draughtsmanship emerged – that of 'Good Girl Art', which described an artist's ability to draw sexy women.[8]

It should not be surprising that in America, too, the great proportion of creators were men, though as in Britain women were increasingly involved behind the scenes as colourists, inkers and so on. One unique aspect of American comics' history, however, was that certain American publishers had for historical reasons (such as the drafting of men during the war) employed a relatively large number of women creators. One such was Fiction House – oddly enough remembered today for its propensity for Good Girl Art.[9]

Later, in the 1970s and 1980s, all these children's comics, but particularly the girls' comics, would be criticised from a feminist perspective. The early comics in the genre (for example, *Girl*) were attacked for being unnecessarily twee and reinforcing notions of girls as inferior to boys; the romance comics for promoting the message that a woman's purpose was to make herself attractive in order to find a mate; the American female-superhero comics for merely being imitators of the male variety and so on. However, many of these objections have recently been reassessed in the light of new research.[10]

The emergence of the underground in the 1960s and 1970s was as much a turning point for women in comics as for adult comics *per se*. For the first time in the medium's history, women creators not only became visible, but were able to set their own agenda. This was the period of the emergence of the Women's Liberation movement (the second feminist wave – *c*. 1967 to the present), and the comix invariably concerned themselves with themes that were more or less defined by it.

What was peculiar about the women's comix, however, was that they did not emerge as an integral part of the regular underground, but rather as a reaction to it. The chief reason for this was that attitudes to women here were frequently as unenlightened as those in the regular comics industry. It was male-dominated, and often quite macho: 'It was like a boy's club', as one woman creator later recalled, 'where they swore and smoked grass – definitely no girls allowed!'.[11] In terms of the content of the comix themselves, this could often express itself in work that could only be described as misogynist – Robert Crumb, Spain and S. Clay Wilson were the three names most singled out for feminist criticism in this respect.[12]

Yet the underground was no more or less 'sexist' than the counter-culture as a whole. Generally speaking, however politicised hippie men may have been on subjects like Vietnam, ecology and drugs, when it came to sexual politics there was often a surprising ignorance and insensitivity. As a result of this, feminist organisations developed that were separate to, and sometimes antagonistic towards, existing counter-cultural bodies. Hence the growth of the feminist press, feminist theatre, feminist cinema and so on. In Britain, perhaps the most visible expression of this was the emergence of *Spare Rib* magazine as a direct response to what was seen as the rampant male chauvinism in *Oz*.[13]

Thus, women creators began to set up comix on their own. Although small-circulation women's comix can be traced to the mid-1960s in America, the first major anthology appeared in 1970 – *It Aint Me, Babe*, edited by Trina Robbins, and openly dedicated to 'Women's Lib' (Figure 17.1). It was quickly followed by a clutch of others: most famously *Wimmins Comix*, designed 'to give support and encouragement to aspiring women cartoonists everywhere';[14] *Tits 'n' Clits*, a more lighthearted anthology which aimed, in the words of the editors, 'to bring humour to the women's movement';[15] *Wet Satin*, about women's erotic fantasies; and several lesbian titles including *Dynamite Damsels* and *Dyke Shorts*. All were imported into Britain in small numbers – even if customs took more notice of them than the regular underground output.[16]

This first wave of women's comix was important for two reasons. First, it was effective as a cheap and cheerful way of transmitting the feminist message. On the whole, the comix were highly political, and humorous in tone: subject-matter ranged from lighthearted parodies of what were seen as sexist images in mainstream and underground comics, to more serious explorations of 'real life' feminist

Figure 17.1 Cover to *It Ain't Me Babe* (1970), depicting a range of female comics characters in a display of sisterly solidarity (from left to right Olive Oil, Wonderwoman, Mary Marvel, Little Lulu, Sheena – Queen of the Jungle, Elsie the Cow). Art: Trina Robbins. © 1970 The creator

concerns, such as abortion, menstruation, rape and male violence. A common way of dealing with these subjects was through autobiography, and this again was one of the defining characteristics of the comix. Occasionally strips would drop any pretence at being funny and concentrate on expressing anger on a particular subject: some issues of *Wimmins Comix*, for example, which concerned a different topic each issue, contained particularly sober work.

Inevitably the comix were accused of being man-hating, and of falling into the trap of female chauvinism. However, the evidence does not bear this out, and although it is possible to locate individual strips that are hostile to men (even examples depicting castration and other mutilations), it is clear that in general an effort was made to avoid this kind of subject. [17]

Second, and perhaps most importantly, the women's underground introduced a number of female creators to comics who may otherwise never have become involved in the field. Among them were Trina Robbins, whose 'glamorous' artwork contrasted strikingly with her fiery political subject-matter; Melinda Gebbie, whose dark, claustrophobic style matched her often disturbing treatment of sexual topics; [18] Aline Kominsky, an early primitive artist, and formidable wit in the Woody Allen mould, for whom no personal detail was taboo; Shary Flenniken, whose innocent-looking characters Trots and Bonnie got up to anything but innocent adventures; Lee Marrs, best known for her early satires of office work and her character Pudge, Girl Blimp, an overweight hippie who had problems with men; and Lynda Barry, whose ratty line work complemented her mischievous and deeply personal oddball humour.

Meanwhile, in Britain the indigenous underground was experiencing a similar feminist challenge. Certain British creators were also criticised for their sexism – notably Mike Matthews and Brian Bolland. Eventually, in 1978, a British women's underground title was attempted – *Heroine* (1978), a one-shot from the Birmingham Arts Lab (the home of *Street Comix*). Under the editorship of contributor Suzy Varty, the comic took on a definite punk sensibility, and included an hilarious satire on the 'pretty vacant' tone of commercial British girls' comics. The reasons for its failure to become a regular ongoing title were various, but centred on a lack of female contributors: 'it was a struggle to get the original out, let alone any others', Varty later explained. 'Today it would be easy to do a comic like *Heroine*, but at the time there were just so few women interested in the idea.' [19]

But the women's comix, like the underground itself, had a limited lifespan. By the end of the 1970s this first wave was dead. They had never sold in anything like the quantities of *Zap* or the *Cozmic Comics* and when the underground as a whole began to die out, they were the most 'expendable' and the first to go. Only *Wimmins Comix*

survived and kept to a (more or less) regular schedule. However, their influence was out of proportion to their sales, and it is no exaggeration to say that hereafter women's relationship with comics would never be quite the same.

Whatever effect the underground may or may not have had on the mainstream, in 1983 British comics got their most rounded female character yet – Halo Jones, created for *2000AD* by Alan Moore and Ian Gibson. Although she was unique within *2000AD*, with its essentially male sensibility (and we have seen how unique *2000AD* itself was compared to other mainstream comics), she still managed to become a cult success with both male and female readers. An insecure everywoman of the future caught up in an intergalactic war, her stock in trade was psychological depth: although she could throw a punch with the best of them, she was not a 'pseudo man' in the fashion of so many American heroines, but rather exhibited a complex personality (a personality, moreover, that was not defined by the men around her). She even menstruated – a taboo for most adult comics let alone a newsagent weekly that could be read by 8-year-olds. In time, her exploits were celebrated in a play and several rock songs, while reprint albums of individual stories became top sellers.[20]

But the next phase of adult comics development was only tangentially connected with the mainstream, and instead took its cue from the growth of organised fandom. Here, too, there were advances for women, though once again this was still in a very marginalised sense, and largely a reaction to predominant trends. For, on one level, the new fan culture was more of a ghetto than even the underground, being orientated primarily towards adolescent boys and older male collectors. The popular comics were superhero titles, and 'Good Girl Art' was more prevalent than ever. The new specialist shops reflected this, and had a 'locker-room' atmosphere that was unwelcoming to women; the conventions were similarly intimidating.[21] 'Women do not go to fan-shops, and it's easy to see why', Trina Robbins later protested. 'With so many comic covers with images of women with basketball breasts and high heel shoes, who'd want to?'[22]

Yet at the same time, the adult comics that were a part of this market provided a platform for female creators, and in terms of content included a growing number of positive female images. Some types of comic were more receptive in this sense than others, of course, and we must look at each of the three sub-groups identified in chapter 5 in turn: namely, comics inspired by the science fiction renaissance; comics generated by direct sales; and comics that derived from alternative creative motivations, but which were sold from the specialist shops.

Partly due to their close associations with the underground, the SF comics exhibited two conflicting characteristics with regard to women. On the one hand, most were simply macho fantasies in space: they took the nudity and sex from the comix and transferred them to SF settings. 'Adult comics' in the post-underground period could often simply mean 'more tits and bums', and creators criticised by feminists for taking comics in this direction included Richard Corben and Howard Chaykin.

On the other hand, it was possible for female creators to make an impact. Some underground stars seemed to make the crossover quite easily: for example, Trina Robbins and Lee Marrs were published in *Heavy Metal*, *Epic Illustrated*, *Star*Reach* and other SF anthologies. At the same time, newcomer Wendy Pini made her name as artist and co-writer of *Elfquest*, an adventure-drama set among a Tolkien-esque society of elves, which, although not very successful in

Britain, became the single most popular comic among women readers in America. It inspired a whole subgenre of imitators that similarly appealed to women: one reason put forward, contentiously, was that fantasy themes were closer to romantic fiction than to traditional technologically-based SF, and therefore more acceptable.

The comics that derived from direct sales similarly exhibited a variety of attitudes towards women. The subject matter of the new independent companies' output tended mainly to be macho adventure to appeal to the biggest market, and hence the tone of the adolescent fan titles was perpetuated (as we have seen, many of the new companies were simply content to compete with Marvel and DC on this level).

Yet some independents were prepared to give other kinds of subject-matter a chance, and here we can see more positive representations of women. The most acclaimed title in this regard was *Love and Rockets* by the Hernandez Brothers, published by Fantagraphics, which in each story featured women as strong characters ('Mechanics', most famously, featured without sensationalism a lesbian affair between two Los Angeles punks, while 'Heartbreak Soup' was a tale which grew naturally from the matriarchal setting in a Mexican village). 'We didn't set out deliberately to do stories about women', Jaime Hernandez later explained, 'it just happened naturally.'[23]

In terms of female creators working for the independents, the level of willingness to hire them depended largely on the type of subject-matter the company was concentrating on. Eclipse were arguably the most enlightened in this respect, a consequence no doubt of having a woman (Catherine Yronwode) as editor-in-chief – the only woman to hold such a position in the entire industry in this period. The list of women creators published by Eclipse included Shary Flenniken, Sue Cavey, Wendi Lee, Trina Robbins, Lee Marrs, Elaine Lee, Christy Marx, April Campbell and Sandy Saidak. 'I think it does matter to have a woman as editor', Yronwode later explained, 'both in terms of letting less sexist material through, and in terms of commissioning other women. There is a definite sympathy there.'[24]

Meanwhile, the two giants, Marvel and DC, were generally content to revamp existing characters for the older readership, and this generally meant (once again) perpetuating the male sensibility of their comics. That said, within this there was room for manoeuvre. Alan Moore in *Swamp Thing*, for example, managed to introduce several complex female characters, and a number of feminist subtexts, including one notorious story linking lycanthropy to menstruation. Similarly, Frank Miller elevated Elektra, a bit-player in the *Daredevil* series, to her own title (*Elektra:Assassin*, illustrated by Bill Sienkiewicz), and made the character a ninja killer at the centre of the action. Whatever the politics of the rest of the story, Elektra herself was a strong, positive image.

There were some Marvel and DC titles which were slightly more adventurous in their subject-matter, and where relatively more women creators were employed – a case in point being *Epic Illustrated* (Marvel). However, generally, the companies remained as male dominated as before – notwithstanding the promotion of Jenette Kahn to the position of editor-in-chief at DC in 1986.

Finally, there were those comics which derived from other creative sources but which were sold from the fan shops (the avant-garde, the small press and the continuing underground). As a whole they were not catering to the fan market, so were under no obligation to be self-referencing to American comics traditions: for this reason, more women worked within this sector than anywhere else, and the level of sensitivity in the portrayal of female characters was much higher.

In the avant-garde, *Raw* was responsible for showcasing the talents of, among others, the Frenchwoman Françoise Mouly (who doubled as co-editor), whose strips are best described as a kind of cubist surrealism; the Canadian Carel Moisewicz, who traded in disturbing tales of urban alienation rendered in an angular style; and American Lynda Barry, formerly an underground star, but by now better known for her syndicated newspaper strips. *Escape*, meanwhile, boasted two new British creators in the persons of Julie Hollings, who specialised in cartoon strips involving predatory and sexually assertive women, and Myra Hancock, whose thoughtful, scratchily-rendered autobiographical vignettes were a feature of all the early issues. In the small press, it was Hancock again who was the best-known female creator, primarily for her *Myra Comics*, which she sold from a stall at London's Camden Market. In the continuing underground, undoubtedly the most important title was *Weirdo*, which under the editorship of Aline Kominsky-Crumb (who had married Robert in 1978) became a focus for female creators – including Dori Seda, whose tragi-comic strips chronicled, among other things, her descent into alcoholism, and Julie Doucet, a French-Canadian with a flair for making even her darkest nightmares seem entertaining.

The events of 1986–7 promised to bring an end to the marginalisation of women in comics, and to usher in a new era of gender-balance. Above all, the success of *Dark Knight*, *Watchmen* and *Maus* moved adult comics into the mainstream, and in the process freed up vital new markets in the bookshops and newsagents. Now women need not be intimidated by the specialist shops, so the logic went, but could buy comics from the same places they bought other reading matter. 'It is marvellous news', Myra Hancock enthused at the time, 'because it means women just browsing in a bookshop can pick up a comic, when maybe they'd never thought of it before.'[25]

Suddenly, because of the potential of the changed market, the 'woman question' came to life. Within fandom, debate was generated on the subject in an unprecedented fashion, with entire issues of fanzines dedicated to it, and packed panel discussions at conventions. What did women want from comics? Were men capable of creating positive female characters? Why were there so few women creators? And of those that did get work, how many were there as a token gesture? These and other questions – questions asked long before of other areas of literature and the arts – now became the issue of the moment.

The publishers, for their part, played up to this sudden interest, and promised all manner of major changes: there would be new titles on more broad-based subject-matter, including some specifically aimed at a female readership, plus a radical overhaul of policies relating to the employment of female creators. PR was once more used as a means of getting industry propaganda across, and a variation on the theme of 'comics grow up' was expounded to the effect that the comics industry was in the process of reinventing itself in more politically correct guise.

And superficially, the hype did seem for a time to have some basis to it. The years following the Big 3 saw more positive images, with 'strong women' becoming a particular vogue (indeed, a cynic might argue that the trend set in motion by Halo Jones became a cliché in this period). The two most prominent characters were 'Eve' in *Crisis* (created by Pat Mills and Carlos Ezquerra), a black anarcho-feminist caught up in capitalist third-world exploitation,[26] and 'Tank Girl' in *Deadline* (by Jamie Hewlett and Alan Martin) – a more lighthearted creation – a shaven-headed Australian whose motto was 'if it annoys you, shoot it; if it doesn't, sleep with it!'. The latter was regularly voted 'Best Comics Character' at conventions, and became something of a youth icon, being the subject of a best-selling album of collected stories from Penguin and an advertising campaign by Wrangler Jeans. There are plans for a *Tank Girl* movie in 1993.

There were more rounded characterisations, too – albeit emanating primarily from the underground and independent publishers. The eponymous heroine of 'Jaka's Story' in Dave Sim's *Cerebus* series, for example, was not merely the subject for Cerebus's amorous attentions, but a subtly-drawn aristocrat eager to live life to the full after a cloistered upbringing. Even Robert Crumb produced a strong female character in the person of 'Mode O'Day', a symbol of the 1980s yuppy generation, in *Weirdo*.

Women creators similarly had a higher profile. Julie Hollings now produced her best-known character, 'Beryl the Bitch', a fearsome man-eater, for *Deadline*, and a similarly sex-obsessed student household in 'Dire Steets' in *Revolver*; Myra Hancock wrote 'Sticky Fingers', about the joys and perils of shoplifting, for *Crisis*, plus several stories for *2000AD*; undergrounders Trina Robbins and Melinda Gebbie appeared in *Heartbreak Hotel*; Carol Swain's superbly moody charcoal work featured in *Escape* and her own *Way Out Strips*; Rachael Ball produced her quirky 'Box City' strips for *Deadline*; Julie Doucet's solo title *Dirty Plotte* confirmed her reputation as one of the most exciting talents in comics (Figure 17.3); finally, Sylvie Rancourt was responsible for the first extended narrative by a woman in the form of *Melody*, her 'autobiography of a nude dancer', about life as a stripper in Ontario.

There was also some evidence of more women readers. Some comics claimed substantial female audiences – over 25 per cent in the

Figure 17.3 A page from 'The English Lesson', *Dirty Plotte*, no. 3 (1990). Art/script: Julie Doucet. © 1990 The creator

case of *Deadline* and *Love and Rockets*.[27] Even the specialist shops reported more custom from women, while female faces were becoming more common at conventions: as UKCAC-organiser Frank Plowright commented, 'They used to get dragged along by their boyfriends, but now they come of their own accord.'[28]

The mainstream press saw the new visibility of female creators and strip characters as proof of fundamental change, and were encouraged in this view by industry PR. 'Women in Comics' became an increasingly popular subject for articles in women's magazines and in the women's pages of national newspapers. The line taken was invariably that a 'revolution' was taking place whereby the tradition of male dominance in comics was coming to an end. As the *Sunday Express* put it: 'Out go the bimbos, in come the assertive females, rough, tough and dangerous to know . . . . And because [comics] are no longer the exclusive province of adolescent boys, they are being written, edited and drawn by women.'[29]

Yet, once again the image portrayed by the story was far from true. Certainly there had been improvements, but in actual fact, despite what they said, the major publishers were generally not inclined to reorientate the content of their output towards the market in the bookshops and newsagents, and instead continued to publish comics that were informed by fan values. This meant, of course, a similar diet of macho action to that before 1986 – and in particular more superheroes, albeit now with an 'adult' slant. In other words, the success of the Big 3 was seen not as proof of the existence of a 'general' market, but of a larger market among men. Publishers paid lip-service to the idea of more comics for women, but in reality that was all it was.

Thus we should not treat uncritically the trend for more women creators and characters in the post-Big 3 period. In the rush to cash in on these comics' success, there was certainly a great deal of cynicism on the part of publishers, and in some cases a calculated policy to 'show the media what they wanted to see'. How far the improvements involving women in comics were down to tokenism is debatable, but there is no doubt that it was a factor.[30] In terms of positive images, there is also the important caveat that some of the worst cases of negative representations of women in the history of comics can be identified in this period. Of the new sex and hardcore horror comics, many tended towards the glorification of violence against women, while in superhero comics one fanzine article concluded 'rape, sexual harassment and violence towards women are "in" with a vengeance'.[31]

By 1990, the true position had become clear. From then on, hopes of an improved situation for women in comics became focused once again on the more 'alternative' publishers – the continuing underground, the avant-garde, the small press and the more progressive independents. This was especially true in Britain, where Knockabout set up a new imprint under the aegis of co-founder Carol Bennett specifically with the aim of promoting female creators – 'Fanny'. The line was heralded with *The Seven Ages of Woman* (1990), in which seven creators explored the different stages in a woman's life, and there have been a further two releases under the Fanny imprint: *Ceasefire* (1991), an anthology protesting against the Gulf War, and *Voyeuse* (1992), which humorously explored female views of sex.[32] Commenting on the motivations behind the line, Bennett summed up the situation thus:

> Nobody else had any interest in doing it, so we decided to give it a go. It's a sad comment on the state of things that for women to stand a chance of being published they still have to get together and do it for themselves. Our comics can be seen as a form of graphic protest in that respect.[33]

In the early 1990s, at least, the laws of the market rule. Only a rise in the female readership of comics will result in women making more demands on material, and thus causing more comics of interest to women to be published. But, without such comics in the first place, the readership will not rise. Very little has changed in this respect since 1986: the mainstream still remains the 'male-stream'. It continues to be true that whoever breaks out of this circle stands a chance of taking comics into a new era of creativity, not to mention making large sums of money. But scanning the horizon, it is hard to see who might be willing to invest and take the risk.

Further reading

The best general source is Trina Robbins and Catherine Yronwode, *Women and the Comics* (Forestville, Calif.: Eclipse Books 1985), an admirably international survey. Trina Robbins, *A Century of Women Cartoonists* (Princeton, Wisconsin: Kitchen Sink 1992) promises to provide a complete compendium of American women creators. Martin Barker's *Comics: Ideology, Power and the Critics* (Manchester: Manchester University Press 1989) reassesses feminist critiques of girls' comics to revealing effect, and its conclusions are often relevant to adult comics. Maurice Horn's *Women in the Comics*, and *Sex in the Comics* (both New York: Chelsea House 1986, 1985) contain some useful information, but are basically paeans to 'Good Girl Art'.

The graphic novel in context

> If a comic is a melody, a graphic novel can be a symphony.
>
> **(Will Eisner, creater, *A Contract With God*)[1]**

> Personally, I always thought Nathanael West's *Day of the Locusts* was an extraordinarily graphic novel.
>
> **(Art Spiegelman, creator, *Maus*)[2]**

In 1986–7 the term 'graphic novel' entered common parlance with the success of the album of versions of *Dark Knight*, *Watchmen* and *Maus*. Since then, it has become emblematic of the comics renaissance generally, and the 'adult revolution' in particular. Overnight, it was claimed, comics had developed from cheap throwaway children's fare to expensive album-form 'novels' for adults to keep on bookshelves.

But, of course, the story was not that simple. On one level, as a piece of marketing hype, the idea of an evolution from 'comics' to 'graphic novels' had a specific purpose – to add prestige to the form and thus to sell more product (as Art Spiegelman pointed out: 'graphics are respectable, novels are respectable, so whammy: double respectability').[3] We have seen in chapters 6 and 7 how successful – or not – this strategy proved to be. But on another level, the graphic novel is a definable category of comic that can be said to have a history of its own. Just as comics did not 'grow up' in the 1980s, so too the graphic novel has a much longer history.

To begin, as ever, with a definition. It is fair to say that there are three kinds of graphic novel. The first is perhaps closest to what the name might be imagined to imply: a one-shot book-form publication involving a continuous comics narrative, of a scope that is longer than a normal comic. In production terms, it is published without prior serialisation: the analogy is with the majority of prose novels.

The second kind can be described as a 'pre-serialised' work, which is to say that it appears in sections in an anthology comic before being collected into a volume. (It may even be produced during the process of serialisation.) The analogy here is with bit-part novel publishing in the last century, as exemplified by the work of Charles Dickens. (This is also the most common form in Europe.)

The third and most common type involves what can be called 'a section of a comics continuity', and applies to American or American-style comics. If we think of such comics as soap-operas, then a graphic novel can be a collection of four or six or twelve or however many instalments in a single volume, with the added provision that the creator has consciously worked towards the longer framework.[4]

Thus, a graphic novel can be a complete story or a collection of linked short stories (or any variation in between) – either published as a self-contained whole, or as part of a longer continuity. The key to the concept is that it has to have a thematic unity. To put it another way, a graphic novel is a comic in book form, but not all comics in book form are graphic novels (for instance, by our definition, a collection of self-contained newspaper strips does not qualify as a graphic novel, and nor does a collection of *Superman* comics that are not part of a finite story).[5]

Creatively speaking, the expanded scope of the graphic novel opens up all sorts of possibilities. It can allow for greater character development, more complex plots, more detailed scene-setting and the generation of mood. Qualitatively, therefore, the form can have properties that a regular comic lacks, and the skills required to produce one are subtly but distinctively different. (Which is why, as we shall see below, some creators have historically been more 'at home' with a longer narrative.) Thus, in the creative sense, we can say that the graphic novel is to the comic what the prose novel is to the short story.

With this definition in mind, it is clear that graphic novels were in existence long before the term itself was coined. True, the comics industry was slow to exploit the potential of lengthier narratives, being hidebound by the idea that comics should consist of short, snappy strips and be orientated towards children – who supposedly 'by nature' did not have long attention spans. (It is also true that popular comics had been collected and reprinted in book form since the beginning of the medium – 'Ally Sloper' featured in a collected volume as early as 1873, while both the British 'annual' and American 'bumper edition' have long histories – though these, of course, were not graphic novels.)[6]

Nevertheless, the children's industry did generate occasional book-length continuous stories. The American *Classics Illustrated* series of the 1940s and 1950s, for instance, designed to introduce children to 'quality literature', frequently appeared in editions of over sixty pages. The line included, among others, hefty versions of Dickens's *Tale of Two Cities* and Hugo's *Les Misérables*.

There were other examples. Albums of Tintin stories were translated from the French from the late 1950s, and these were joined by albums starring Asterix and other European heroes in the 1960s. The 1950s and 1960s also saw several American large-scale movie adaptations, giving a twist to the *Classics Illustrated* idea, including *King Kong* and *The Magnificent Seven*. Finally, in the late 1960s, IPC

produced several war and spy stories in a pocket-size 'Super Library' format of around 130 pages.

These children's titles may not always have been particularly sophisticated, but they were graphic novels by any other name. Apart from anything else, they prove that the concept can no more be restricted to a particular age-range than can the concept of 'the comic' itself.

But the real roots of today's boom are in adult comics, and here we can identify three distinct but overlapping historical strands. They are: the influence of the European adult album 'revolution' of the 1970s and 1980s; the paradigm of 'maverick' creators working in a longer context before the idea was generally acceptable; and the generation of a 'book culture' within the direct sales market. All three aspects should be seen against the backdrop of the intellectually-liberating influence of the underground: not only did it reintroduce comics to an adult readership, but it also inspired creators to 'think bigger' in every sense.

In Europe, as we have seen, there developed from the mid-1970s an adult comics culture where works designed ultimately to be published as albums (or series of albums) were 'pre-published' (a French term) in monthly magazines, a few pages at a time. This system allowed for longer narratives, with good quality production, plus an unprecedented level of prestige for creators, who received two royalties for their work. Eventually this developed into an '*auteur* system' whereby albums would be marketed on the basis of a creator's reputation (rather in the same way as novels by certain authors, or films by particular directors). Thus, in general, in contrast to the prevailing system in Britain and America, the emphasis in the European industry was on quality rather than quantity (although it should be said that some European creators certainly seemed to crank out the albums). The fact that European albums were translated and imported on a regular basis from the 1970s meant that they were some of the first 'adult graphic novels' available in Britain and the USA.

The European paradigm was an influence in Britain and America for two reasons. First, the sales of albums could be phenomenal: albums tended to be distributed throughout the continent, and sales of 50,000 for a single album were not uncommon. This was naturally an incentive to British and American publishers to adopt a similar system, and to reach out to a similar kind of audience. Second, creators in Britain and America were inspired by the respect that their European counterparts received, in terms of cultural (and financial) status, and the creative freedom this implied.

In the light of this, there emerged several American and British creators in the post-underground period who were prepared to experiment with longer narratives. 'Mavericks' are by definition creative spirits who are impossible to categorise, following their own course regardless of the vagaries of fashion or of the market. Working against a background of an industry where short, sharp stories for children were the norm, these creators were responsible for redefining the boundaries of what the anglophone tradition could encompass. To look at the most important names in turn: [7]

Will Eisner

The veteran American creator of *The Spirit*, Eisner had worked in the context of underground since the early 1970s, and in 1978 had published the outstanding *A Contract with God*, a semi-autobiographical series of linked vignettes about life in the tenements of 1930s New York. It was published in book form, without prior serialisation, and

was the first publication of its kind to be marketed as a 'graphic novel' – thus establishing the term.[8] 'I had made a conscious decision to work on a larger scale', he later explained, 'I wanted the stories to end when they were meant to end, without regard to space or the rules of panellisation, and I wanted it to work as a whole.'[9] Eisner returned to the format frequently in his later career, notably with *A Lifeforce*, *The Dreamer*, *The Building* and *To the Heart of the Storm*.

Dave Sim

A Canadian with little experience in comics, Sim set up his own company in 1977 (Aardvark–Vanaheim) to publish himself and to retain complete creative control. He then proceeded to turn his continuing

Figure 18.3 Cover to *Church and State* (1987), a 592-page Cerebus novel. Art: Dave Sim. © 1987 The creator

series *Cerebus the Aardvark* from a straightforward parody of Conan the Barbarian into a complex satire – which subsequently divided into large-scale graphic novels. Uniquely, Sim made a lifelong commitment to complete 300 issues of the comic – a project that he estimated would last twenty-six years. 'There is a different "quality" to doing an extended story', he later explained, 'You get to know your characters, and you can set your own pace, building to a climax when the plot requires it.'[10] The *Cerebus* volumes are also notable for their rich depiction of an entire fictional world ('Estarcion') consisting of city-states with their own laws and religions. Sim's most successful volumes have included *High Society*, in which Cerebus becomes prime minister of one such city-state, 'Iest', and *Church and State* (published in two volumes) in which he becomes Pope. Other volumes include *Jaka's Story* (two volumes) and *Melmoth*.

Figure 18.4 Panels from
*The Adventures of Luther
Arkwright*, book 2 (1987).
Art/script: Bryan Talbot.
© The creator/Valkyrie
Press

Bryan Talbot

One of the stars of the British underground, Talbot was able to continue with his masterwork *The Adventures of Luther Arkwright* because he was sponsored by Frenchman Serge Boissevain (almost in the fashion of a Renaissance artist by a rich patron). The story was serialised in various publications and collected in three volumes between 1982 and 1988. An ambitious, densely-textured SF odyssey, it wove together occult themes, scenarios from British history and anarchist politics, and took place in several 'parallel universes' at once. Stylistically influenced by the films of Nicolas Roeg, the narrative featured jump-cuts, flashbacks and sudden scene-shifts that were difficult to follow in a serialised form, but which worked superbly when compiled into a graphic novel: 'It is true that I don't make many concessions to the reader', Talbot later admitted, 'because ultimately I think they are intelligent enough to work it out for themselves. Besides, they can always flick back through the pages to make sure they haven't misunderstood anything. It's all part of working on the larger scale.'[11]

Raymond Briggs

Another British creator, famous for his 1970s children's albums (including *Fungus the Bogeyman* and *Father Christmas*), who in 1982 published the adult graphic novel *When the Wind Blows*, about a pair of pensioners caught up in a nuclear attack. His motivations were purely personal: he had been incensed by the government's attitude to public defence, and wanted to do something for the anti-nuclear cause. The book was marketed to bookshops rather than to comics shops, and became a surprise best seller, later being turned into an equally successful West End play and animated movie. It can thus be counted as the first adult graphic novel to be commercially successful in Britain. Briggs returned to adult subject-matter in his 1983 album *The Iron Lady and the Tin Pot General*, a satire on the Falklands war.

Figure 18.5 Panels from
When the Wind Blows
(1982). Art/script: Raymond
Briggs. © 1982 The creator

Art Spiegelman

Best known for *Maus*, which has been covered in detail in chapter 6,
Spiegelman had been one of the leading lights of the Chicago underground scene, and began work on *Maus* in 1978. Again, it is significant
to note that his motivations were very personal: 'I think any son or
daughter of a [holocaust] survivor eventually has to come to some kind
of reckoning', he later explained. 'In my case, as I was already a cartoonist, it was very natural for me to do it in comic-book form. I knew
it was going to be a long job, and I was already past 30 in 1978, but it
had to be done.'[12] *Maus II*, which completed the story, was published
by Penguin in 1992 (too recently, unfortunately, to have been properly
assessed in the present volume).

The last of our three historical threads was the generation of a 'book
culture' in direct sales. Early collectors had a problem accumulating
runs of comics because once a title had passed its sell-by period, it was
returned to the distributor/publisher to be pulped. However, with the
emergence of specialist shops and direct sales, the basis of the market
began to change. Monthly publications were turned into items for continuous resale. There were no 'returns' for this market, and the publication of an issue marked the point at which quantities of a title could
be bought, stocked, sold and reordered for as long as they were available. It was, in other words, a book culture in miniature.

More than this, because direct sales meant more competition
between publishers, as the new 'independents' vied with Marvel and
DC for a market share, this provoked a drive towards better quality
comics packaging and design to attract readers' attention. This also
represented a recognition of the fact that within fandom comics were
being collected and stored away by a more serious (and more affluent)

clientele, and that therefore it would be sensible to publish in more durable formats.

Similar pressures caused publishers to vie for the services of creators who were favourites of the fans, and led to a situation where the names on the cover of a comic were often more important than the contents (this was a similar process to the one that had occurred in Europe some years earlier). This in turn meant that some creators had more bargaining power, and hence more creative freedom: artists could now press for the opportunity to do fully-painted strips, or work involving collage and mixed-media; writers could negotiate to produce longer, self-contained stories as well as to explore more personal (and more adult) subject-matter. It was the genesis of an indigenous *auteur* system, and once again mirrored the book-trade, with its emphasis on 'best-selling authors' and 'designer production'.

These various imperatives were formalised over time as publishing strategies were progressively directed towards tailoring comics output for future compilation. This was especially true of the introduction of 'limited series'. These were designed partly to satisfy collectors who were fed up with never-ending stories, and partly to give creators the opportunity to work on a finite, theoretically more satisfying project. Thus the old-style soap-opera plots were superseded by briefer, more tightly-structured stories in 'mini-' or 'maxi-' series of four, six, eight or twelve parts, which could then be republished as a single volume, and sold on the basis of the creators' names. [13] A number of individuals became known as *auteurs* via large-scale commercial projects produced for the fan-market. Though pioneers, they were not 'mavericks' as such, because of their position within the industry. Three in particular are worth mentioning:

Howard Chaykin

One of the first comics *auteurs*, Chaykin made his name on *Heavy Metal*, *Star*Reach* and *Epic Illustrated*. He then went on to larger ground-breaking projects in which he demonstrated with some panache the possibilities of more ambitious artwork for longer narratives. Three early 'graphic novelisations', in particular, demonstrated his talent for dynamic panel layouts and exciting colours: *Empire* (from an original Samuel Delaney story), *The Swords of Heaven the Flowers of Hell* (written by Michael Moorcock) and *The Stars my Destination* (adapted from an Alfred Bester fantasy). He moved on to produce several notable limited series, particularly in the *American Flagg!* continuity. Moorcock later wrote of Chaykin:

> He has benefited from the discipline of the standard comic-book format the same way some of us benefited from learning our trade as magazine or newspaper writers and others gained, like

Figure 18.6 A page from *Empire* (1978). Art/script: Howard Chaykin (adapted from a novel by Samuel Delany). © 1978 Byron Preiss

Once more the *Proteus* tore free of its mooring. Amid laser beams and blasters, it left the reluctantly wounded and careened into the night.

"To get that last fragment, my friends, we have to go down to Praxis herself!"

the Beatles, say, from the 'tyranny' of the old two-and-a-half minute single.[14]

Frank Miller

Best-known for his work on Marvel's *Daredevil* and DC's *Dark Knight*, which have been discussed in detail in chapters 5 and 6, Miller's stock-in-trade in the 1980s was the visceral action story, typically involving pared-down dialogue and a great deal of bloody violence. His other longer projects have included *Ronin*, about a samurai in a time-warp, *Elektra Assassin* (with Bill Sienkiewicz), a spinoff from *Daredevil*, and *Give Me Liberty* (with Dave Gibbons), a dystopian thriller with a black heroine. Miller has increasingly concentrated on his writing rather than his illustration, and has developed a parallel career scripting the SF movies *Robocop 2* and *Robocop 3*.

Alan Moore

Best-known for *Swamp Thing* and *Watchmen* (discussed in chapters 5 and 6), Moore is generally credited with introducing greater psychological depth into comics, a quality used to optimum effect in his lengthier projects. His other graphic novels have included *V for Vendetta* (with David Lloyd), a futuristic thriller, *From Hell* (with Eddie Campbell), about Jack the Ripper, and *A Small Killing* (with Oscar Zarate), about an advertising executive's crisis of conscience. Moore's career is curious in that, having started via the 'corporate route', working for IPC and then DC, he has since turned his back on the large companies, working primarily for smaller independents. He shows no sign of abandoning large-scale comics, and future works include *Big Numbers* (with Bill Sienkiewicz and Al Columbia), concerning the despoiling of a Northampton town by property developers, and *The Lost Girls* (with Melinda Gebbie), an erotic fantasy.

By the mid-1980s, the term 'graphic novel' was well and truly established, within fandom if nowhere else (other phrases like 'visual novelisation' and 'illustrated novel' had been tried, but had not taken root).[15] However, it should be noted that the percentage of actual continuous narratives was small. Most graphic novels, because of their origins as bit-part comics, tended to consist of interlocking short stories. Indeed, some bogusly used the name, and made no pretence at a unified whole,

Figure 18.7 Advertisement for Titan Books' range of graphic novels (1987)

borrowing the terminology merely as a useful way of repackaging old product – a practice that became more common with time.

In 1986–7 the graphic novel went overground. The Big 3, far from being seismic breaks with the past, were the natural outcome of the developments in fandom outlined above. *Dark Knight* and *Watchmen* were derived from limited series, while *Maus* was a collected serial. (*Watchmen* and *Maus* were continuous narratives, while *Dark Knight* was more a series of linked short stories.) By the same token, PR did not 'invent' the graphic novel, but brought it out into the open. Although the hype was extensive, the graphic novel was clearly not simply 'a reflection of the industry's yearning for unearned status ... semantic jiggery-pokery',[16] as one source put it.

Thereafter, as we have seen (pp. 96–109), there was an unprecedented boom in adult comics in general, and in graphic novels in particular (a news article in the *Comics Journal* announced the 'Graphic novel explosion for '88', and it was no exaggeration).[17] They were available in hardback or paperback, for anything between £5 and £20 (although the usual form was trade paperback of approximately fifty pages, priced at around £6). Virtually everything was published or republished in this way – sometimes reformatting was so swift that creators would be several issues into a story before being told.

Publishers had a huge reservoir of material to exploit: comics from Europe, Japan and other parts of the world, together with the best series from the direct sales of the preceding decade, newer stories commissioned after 1986, plus even some continuing newspaper strips that constituted finite stories. Now there were graphic novels on autobiographical themes (*Spiral Cage*, *Melody*, *Alec*), historical fiction (*Towers of Bois Maury*) and non-fiction (*Wilderness*), political journalism (*Brought to Light*), science fiction (*The Incal*, *Akira*), horror (*Sandman*, *Hellblazer*), war (*The Nam*) and many more. In terms of variety, it was the sort of range one might previously have expected to see only on prose novel lists.

Not every graphic novel was very good by any means. In the rush to cash in, quality was not always the highest priority. Some were hastily collected together from existing sources; others were commissioned from creators who were clearly in love with the idea of the graphic novel, but had little to say. Moreover, numerically speaking, the genre titles were swamped by revisionist superhero stories, pumped out in the wake of the success of *Dark Knight* and *Watchmen*, and by numerous albums that were not 'graphic novels' at all, but that were using the term purely as a marketing device. On a more positive note, some of the new product was genuinely outstanding: new *auteurs* included Neil Gaiman (principally for his work on the horror title *Sandman*) and Grant Morrison (whose one-off Batman story *Arkham Asylum* was the biggest-selling graphic novel of the post-Big 3 era).

But, whatever the quality of the product, retailers seemed ready to take it. W. H. Smith, Dillons, Waterstones and other bookshop chains set up graphic novel shelves, and publishers increasingly targeted this market. In this regard, Titan Books, who had published two of the Big 3, were now confirmed as the biggest graphic novel publisher in Britain, republishing not just American fare, but European albums as well.

This boom led what might loosely be called 'the literary establishment' to finally take notice. Mainstream book publishers began to publish graphic novels – Penguin and Gollancz in particular. Reports in the book-trade journal, the *Bookseller*, and elsewhere optimistically spoke of a major reorientation of publishing into this area. Penguin even instituted what was described as 'the comics Booker Prize' in the form of the Comic Awards, presented each year at the Glasgow Convention for the best graphic novels. To cap it all, graphic novels were now frequently reviewed in the literary pages of the quality press, and were even studied at some universities and polytechnics.[18]

This co-option was the final stage in the transition of part of the comics industry from a 'comics culture' to a 'book culture'. In short, it served to remake comics in prose literature's image. So far as the arts media were concerned, graphic novels were invariably reviewed in the books section rather than the general arts pages, writers were profiled rather than artists, and on the whole the quality of writing in a work was held in higher esteem than the art (a striking reversal of the traditional situation in fandom). But, as lecturer Paul Dawson, the first academic in Britain to introduce a university course on graphic novels, commented:

> We have hardly begun to sketch out an aesthetic appropriate to the [comics] form, and it is inevitable that our understanding of it will continue for some time to rest on the transference of concepts and assumptions from other, more familiar forms . . . the assimilation of comics to the novel is tempting, because it offers a way to domesticate a form which we are still struggling to understand adequately.[19]

But for all the optimism of the post-Big 3 period, graphic novels have sold disappointingly. The problems of innappropriate fan-themes, overpricing, the inexperience of the book trade, and continuing public indifference have already been discussed (pp. 110–15). Suffice to say that commercial failure has been so marked in some cases that by 1991 some bookshops were withdrawing graphic novels from the shelves, and certain publishers were disconnecting from the market altogether. Media cynicism was a inevitable result. *Time Out* magazine summed things up by including graphic novels in their annual

'Hated 100' list for 1991: 'Biff, Bang, Krapp!', ran the listing, 'If adult comics are the wave of the future, how come nobody's reading them?'.[20]

Clearly, these are substantial barriers to overcome in the future. Yet if publishers are not to give up altogether (and the majority show no signs of doing so), it is clearly imperative that they employ more inventiveness in their sales strategies. Worth mentioning in this respect is the plan conceived by the latest mainstream publisher to enter the field, HarperCollins, whose main selling point involves graphic novels written by already-established book authors. Names so far announced include Doris Lessing, Anne McCaffrey, Clive Barker and Dean Koontz. What is unusual about this idea is that the graphic novels will be specifically marketed as part of the authors' existing *oeuvre*.

So, to sum up, although graphic novels currently have their problems, they are manifestly not 'graphic novelties', as some cynics have suggested. They exist in their own right as a definable category of comic, and have a history going back to the 1940s. Since entering the public eye in the late 1980s, they have certainly had their ups and downs: the dream of emulating the huge sales achieved on the continent has remained just that – a dream. Yet they have established themselves, albeit in a marginal sense, and are now a feature of the publishing landscape in a way they were not before. Nobody today doubts that they are here to stay.

Further reading

Because the graphic novel is seen as a relatively recent form, very little has been written on the subject. Relevant sources tend to relate to individual creators. For example, Catherine Yronwode, *The Art of Will Eisner* (Princeton, Wisconsin: Kitchen Sink 1989 rev. edn) includes discussion of his graphic novel work, while Gary Groth and Robert Fiore (eds), *The New Comics* (New York: Berkley 1988) contains interviews with Howard Chaykin, Dave Sim, Will Eisner, Alan Moore, Frank Miller and Art Spiegelman. (Other references for the Big 3 have been given in chapter 6.) Additionally, the videos *Will Eisner: A Life in Sequential Art* (London: Acme Video/CA Productions 1988) and *Raymond Briggs In Conversation* (London: ICA In Conversation Series 1982) contain useful information.

Conclusion

If comics had 'grown up' in the mid-1980s, this would have been a very short book indeed. Instead, we have identified a rich and complex history of adult comics stretching back over a century. In a sense, we can say that it is not they that are the historical aberration, but the fact that the medium was ever restricted to children at all.

But if the idea of comics suddenly 'maturing' is a myth, we can go further and say it has been a convenient myth for certain interest groups. For at its centre is the concept of comics 'advancing' in a particular direction, and of adult comics as 'the new wave'. In other words, this version of events marshalls events from the past in order to give impetus to the present, and thus confers a certain spurious status on post-1986–7 adult comics as some kind of 'vanguard' of a 'new era'. As a corollary, any comics for older readers that happen to have emerged before this date – such as those of the nineteenth century, the underground and the titles that grew out of fandom – are preferably ignored. They don't fit the plan, so the less said about them the better.

Not everybody involved with comics in the 1980s (either as producers or as commentators) endorsed this view by any means, but a good many did and it is easy to see who benefited. First, the media, who propagated the myth in the first place, and by repeating it turned it into an orthodoxy: they put two and two together to make five, and came up with one of those once-in-a-decade arts stories that are guaranteed to attract the attention of readers and viewers. Second, the comics publishers, who actively encouraged the media's bad arithmetic, and reaped the rewards of the increased sales it generated. Finally, the comics' creators, the 'stars' of the story, who benefited from improved pay and status and who rarely disagreed publicly with their publishers' line. It is worth remembering, therefore, that many parties made – and in a few cases continue to make – a lot of money out of the 'adult comics revolution'.

But for such a story to have had any currency, there had to be one crucial extra element – public ignorance. A recurring theme of this book has been the way in which the general public has traditionally been profoundly unaware of the potential range of the comics medium, and has continued to see it essentially as entertainment for children. Despite the enormously rich anglophone comics heritage, who except a few enthusiasts has ever heard of Ally Sloper, Mr Natural, Luther Arkwright and the rest? This void made it easy for those with a vested interest in rewriting history: for them, other peoples' ignorance was bliss. Adult comics had no history, which is why an invented one was so powerful.

So much for the hype. We know now that adult comics are not the inexorable future of literature. They may not even be the future of comics. (It would have been tempting to write a book that perpetuated the idea that they were – but to whose benefit would that have been?) Yet, in the end, we should ask whether any of this matters. Is it really necessary to continue thinking of adult comics in these terms, and to justify them in this way? Perhaps instead it is high time that we started to enjoy them for what they are, rather than what some quarters would like us to think they are.

Appendix 1
Code of the Comics Magazine Association of America, Inc.

(Adopted on October 26, 1954, the enforcement of this Code is the basis for the comic magazine industry's program of self-regulation.)

CODE FOR EDITORIAL MATTER

General Standards   Part A

1) Crimes shall never be presented in such a way as to create sympathy for the criminal, to promote distrust of the forces of law and justice, or to inspire others with a desire to imitate criminals.

2) No comics shall explicitly present the unique details and methods of a crime.

3) Policemen, judges, government officials and respected institutions shall never be presented in such a way as to create disrespect for established authority.

4) If crime is depicted it shall be as a sordid and unpleasant activity.

5) Criminals shall not be presented so as to be rendered glamorous or to occupy a position which creates a desire for emulation.

6) In every instance good shall triumph over evil and the criminal shall be punished for his misdeeds.

7) Scenes of excessive violence shall be prohibited. Scenes of brutal torture, excessive and unnecessary knife and gun play, physical agony, gory and gruesome crime shall be eliminated.

8) No unique or unusual methods of concealing weapons shall be shown.

9) Instances of law enforcement officers dying as a result of a criminal's activities should be discouraged.

10) The crime of kidnapping shall never be portrayed in any detail, nor shall any profit accrue to the abductor or kidnapper. The criminal or the kidnapper must be punished in every case.

11) The letters of the word 'crime' on a comics magazine cover shall never be appreciably greater in dimension than the other words contained in the title. The word 'crime' shall never appear alone on a cover.

12) Restraint in the use of word 'crime' in titles or sub-titles shall be exercised.

General Standards   Part B

1) No comic magazine shall use the word horror or terror in its title.
2) All scenes of horror, excessive bloodshed, gory or gruesome crimes, depravity, lust sadism, masochism shall not be permitted.
3) All lurid, unsavory, gruesome illustrations shall be eliminated.
4) Inclusion of stories dealing with evil shall be used or shall be published only where the intent is to illustrate a moral issue and in no case shall evil be presented alluringly nor so as to injure the sensibilities of the reader.
5) Scenes dealing with, or instruments associated with walking dead, torture, vampires and vampirism, ghouls, cannibalism and were-wolfism are prohibited.

General Standards   Part C

All elements or techniques not specifically mentioned herein, but which are contrary to the spirit and intent of the Code, and are considered violations of good taste or decency, shall be prohibited.

Dialogue

1) Profanity, obscenity, smut, vulgarity, or words or symbols which have acquired undesirable meanings are forbidden.
2) Special precautions to avoid references to physical afflictions or deformities shall be taken.
3) Although slang and colloquialisms are acceptable, excessive use should be discouraged and wherever possible good grammar shall be employed.

Religion

1) Ridicule or attack on any religious or racial group is never permissible.

Costume

1) Nudity in any form is prohibited, as is indecent or undue exposure.
2) Suggestive and salacious illustration or suggestive posture is unacceptable.
3) All characters shall be depicted in dress reasonably acceptable to society.
4) Females shall be drawn realistically without exaggeration of any physical qualities.

NOTE: It should be recognized that all prohibitions dealing with costume, dialogue or artwork applies as specifically to the cover of a comic magazine as they do to the contents.

Marriage and Sex

1) Divorce shall not be treated humorously nor represented as desirable.

2) Illicit sex relations are neither to be hinted at or portrayed. Violent love scenes as well as sexual abnormalities are unacceptable.

3) Respect for parents, the moral code and for honorable behaviour shall be fostered. A sympathetic understanding of the problems of love is not a license for morbid distortion.

4) The treatment of love-romance stories shall emphasize the value of the home and the sanctity of marriage.

5) Passion or romantic interest shall never be treated in such a way as to stimulate the lower and baser emotions.

6) Seduction and rape shall never be shown or suggested.

7) Sex perversion or any inference to same is strictly forbidden.

CODE FOR ADVERTISING MATTER

These regulations are applicable to all magazines published by members of the Comics Magazine Association of America, Inc. Good taste shall be the guiding principle in the acceptance of advertising.

1) Liquor and tobacco advertising is not acceptable.

2) Advertisement of sex or sex instruction books are unacceptable.

3) The sale of picture postcards, 'pin-ups,' 'art studies,' or any other reproduction of nude or semi-nude figures is prohibited.

4) Advertising for the sale of knives, concealable weapons, or realistic gun facsimiles is prohibited.

5) Advertising for the sale of fireworks is prohibited.

6) Advertising dealing with the sale of gambling equipment or printed matter dealing with gambling shall not be accepted.

7) Nudity with meretricious purpose and salacious postures shall not be permitted in the advertising of any product; clothed figures shall never be presented in such a way as to be offensive or contrary to good taste or morals.

8) To the best of his ability, each publisher shall ascertain that all statements made in advertisements conform to fact and avoid misrepresentation.

9) Advertisement of medical, health, or toiletry products of questionable nature are to be rejected. Advertisements for medical, health or toiletry products endorsed by the American Medical Association, or the American Dental Association, shall be deemed acceptable if they conform with all other conditions of the Advertising Code.

Appendix 2 Ready reference dates for key British and American comics

Aargh! (Mad Love) 1988.

Action (IPC) Feb.–Oct. 1976: Dec. 1976–Nov.1977.

Action Comics (National Periodical Publications/Detective Comics/DC) June 1938–.

Akira (Marvel – Epic) 1988–.

Alec (Escape) 1984–6. (Acme graphic novel: 1990.)

Aliens (Dark Horse) 1988–9; 1990; 1992–.

All Atomic Comics (Educomics) 1976.

Ally Sloper (Class) 1976–7. (Semi-underground – different to below.)

Ally Sloper's Half Holiday (Gilbert Dalziel) 1884–1914. Becomes *Ally Sloper* (The Sloperies) 1914–16. Reverts to *Ally Sloper's Half Holiday* (The Sloperies) 1922–3. Becomes *Half Holiday* (The Sloperies) Apr.–Sept. 1923. Becomes *Ally Sloper* (McKensie Press, 1 issue only) 1948. Reverts to *Ally Sloper's Half Holiday* (Ally Sloper Publications, 1 issue only) 1949. (List does not include one-off specials and 'Christmas Holiday' editions.)

American Flagg! (First) 1983–8; 1989–9.

American Splendor (Harvey Pekar) 1976–, Albums: *Best of American Splendor* (Doubleday Dolphin) 1986; *More American Splendor* (Four Walls, Two Windows) 1991.

Anarcoma (Catalan) 1983.

Animal Man (DC). 1988–.

Arcade (Print Mint) 1975–6.

Asterix (Brockhampton Press/Hodder and Stoughton) 1969–.

Barefoot Gen (Britain: Penguin) 1989; (USA: New Society) 1987.

Barefoot Gen: The Day After (Britain: Penguin) 1990; (USA: New Society) 1988.

Batman (National Periodical Publications/Detective Comics/DC) 1940–.

Batman 3D Graphic Album (Britain: Titan) 1990; (USA: DC) 1990.

Batman: Arkham Asylum (Britain: Titan) 1989; (USA: DC) 1989.

Batman: Digital Justice (Britain: Titan) 1990; (USA: DC) 1990.

Batman/Judge Dredd: Judgement on Gotham (Fleetway and DC) 1991.

Batman Movie Adaptation (DC) 1989.

Batman: The Dark Knight Returns (DC) 1986. Graphic novel: (Britain: Titan) 1986; (USA: DC) 1986.

Batman: The Killing Joke (Britain: Titan) 1988; (USA: DC) 1988.

Batman vs Predator (DC) 1992.

Battle Picture Library (Fleetway/IPC) 1961–84.

Beano, The (DC Thomson) 1938–.

Big Baby (Raw) 1986.

Big Numbers (Mad Love/Tundra) 1990–.

Bijou Funnies (Bijou Publishing/Print Mint/Kitchen Sink) 1968–73. (One British reprint in the Cozmic line (see below).)

Black Kiss (Vortex) 1988–9.

Black Orchid (DC) 1988–9.

Blast! (John Brown) Jun.–Dec. 1991.

Blazing Combat (Warren) 1965–6.

Blueberry (Marvel–Epic) 1989–.

Brainstorm Comix (Alchemy) 1975–7.

Brat Pack (King Hell/Tundra)1990–.

Brought to Light (Britain: Titan) 1989; (USA: Eclipse) 1989.

Butterscotch (Catalan) 1987.

Ceasefire (Knockabout–Fanny) 1991.

Cerebus the Aardvark (Aardvark–Vanaheim) 1977–. Graphic novels/albums: *High Society* 1986; *Cerebus* 1987; *Chuch and State*, vol. 1 1987, vol. 2 1988; *Jaka's Story* 1990; *Melmoth* 1991.

Clive Barker's Tapping the Vein (Britain: Titan) 1990– ; (USA: Eclipse) 1990–.

Comanche Moon (Last Gasp) 1978.

Comic Cuts (Harmsworth/Amalgamated) 1890–1953.

Comix Book (Marvel) 1974–5.

Commando Library (DC Thomson) 1961–.

Conan, Savage Sword of (Marvel) 1974–.

Contract With God, A (Britain: Titan) 1988; (USA: Baronet) 1978.

Corto Maltese (NBH). Albums by name: *Brazilian Eagle* 1986; *Banana Conga* 1986; *Voodoo for the President* 1987; *A Midwinter Morning's Dream* 1987; *In Africa* 1988; *The Early Years* 1989; *In Siberia* 1989; *Fable of Venice* 1990.

Cozmic Comics (H. Bunch) 1972–4. Titles by name: *Cozmic Comics* 1, 2, 4, 5 1972; *Cozmic Comics* 3 (The Firm) 1972; *Edward's Heave Comics* 1973; *Half Assed Funnies* 1973; *Ogoth and Ugly Boot* 1973; *Zip Comics* 1973; *View From the Void* 1973; *Sin City* 1973; *Rock 'N' Roll Madness 1* 1973; *Animal Weirdness* 1974; *Dope Fiend Funnies* 1974; *Tales from the Fridge* 1974; *Bijou Funnies*

1974; *Cosmic Comics* 6 1974; *Rock 'N' Roll Madness* 2 1974; *It's Only Rock 'N' Roll Comix* 1975; *Serious Comics* 1975. (Also, *Trials of Nasty Tales* (H. Bunch and Bloom Publishing) 1973.)

Creepy (Warren) 1964–85 (Dark Horse) 1991–.

Crime Does Not Pay (Britain: Arnold) 1950; (Britain: Pemberton) 1951; (USA: Comic House/Lev Gleason/Golfing) 1942–55.

Crisis (Fleetway) 1987–91.

Cyclops (Innocence and Experience) Jul.–Oct. 1970.

Dandy, The (DC Thomson) 1937–.

Daredevil (Marvel) 1964–. (Frank Miller art begins issue 158.)

Dazzler, The (Marvel) 1981–6.

Deadline (Britain: Tom Astor) 1988–; (USA: First) 1991–.

Desert Storm Journal (Apple) 1991–.

Despair (Print Mint) 1969.

Detective Comics (National Periodical Publications/DC) 1937–.

Detective Picture Stories (Comics Magazine Co.) 1936–7.

Dirty Duck Book, The (Company and Sons) 1972.

Dirty Plotte (Drawn and Quarterly) 1990–.

Doc Chaos (Escape) 1984–5; '*The Chernoble Effect*' (Hooligan Press) 1988.

Doctor Strange (Marvel) 1968–9; 1974–87; 1988–. (Formerly *Strange Tales* 1951–68.)

Drawn and Quarterly (Drawn and Quarterly) 1990–.

Eagle (Hulton/Longacre/Odhams/IPC) 1950–69; (IPC/Fleetway) 1982–.

Eerie (Warren) 1965–83.

Eightball (Fantagraphics) 1990–.

Elektra: Assassin (Marvel/Epic) 1986–7.

Elfquest (Warp) 1979–85; 1990–; (Marvel–Epic) 1985–8; (Apple) 1987–8. First appeared in *Fantasy Quarterly* (IPS 1 issue only) 1978.

Empire (Byron Preiss) 1978.

Epic Illustrated (Marvel–Epic) 1980–6.

Escape (Escape/Titan) 1983–90.

Fabulous Furry Freak Brothers, *The* (Britain: Hassle Free Press) 1976–8; (Britain: Knockabout) 1980–; (USA: Rip Off) 1971–.

Famous Funnies (Eastern Color) 1934–55.

Fantastic Four (Marvel) 1961–.

Fast Fiction (Fast Fiction) 1980–.

Fast One (No Exit) 1991.

Faust (Northstar) 1989–.

Flaming Carrot (Aardvark/Renegade/Dark Horse) 1984–.

Fritz the Cat (Britain: J. J. Flash) 1972–3; (USA: Ballantine) 1969–72.

From Hell (Tundra) 1991–.

Frontline Combat (EC) 1951–4.

Funnies on Parade (Eastern Color) 1933.

Funny Wonder, The (Harmsworth) 1893–9; 1899–1901; (Amalgamated) 1914–42. Becomes *The Wonder* (Amalgamated) 1942–53.

Gay Comix (Kitchen Sink) 1980–1.

GI Joe (Ziff-Davis) 1950–7; *GI Joe, A Real American Hero* (Marvel) 1982–.

Girl (Hulton/Longacre) 1951–64; (IPC) 1989–90.

Give Me Liberty (Dark Horse) 1990–2.

Graphixus (Graphic Eye) 1977–9.

Green Arrow (DC) 1988–.

Hate (Fantagraphics) 1990–.

Haunt of Fear (Britain: Arnold) 1954; (USA: EC) 1950–4.

Heartbreak Hotel (Willyprods) Jan.–Dec. 1988.

Heavy Metal (Heavy Metal/Metal Mammoth) 1977–.

Hellblazer (DC) 1988–.

Hellraiser, Clive Barker's (Marvel–Epic) 1991–.

Help! (Warren) 1960–5.

Heroine (Birmingham Arts Lab.) 1978.

House of Secrets (DC) 1956–66; 1969–76; 1976–8.

Howard the Duck (Marvel) 1976–9; 1986; 2nd series magazine 1979–81.

Hulk, The Incredible (Marvel) 1962–3; 1968–.

Humbug (Humbug Publishing) 1957–8.

Illustrated Chips (Harmsworth/Amalgamated) July–Aug. 1980; 1890–1953.

Incal, The (Britain: Titan) 1988; (USA: Marvel–Epic) 1988.

It Ain't Me Babe (Last Gasp) 1970.

Jack Survives (Raw) 1985.

Jimbo (Raw) 1983.

Judge Dredd Megazine (Fleetway) 1990–.

Knockabout Comics (Knockabout) 1980–.

Lady Chatterley's Lover (Knockabout–Crack) 1986.

Leather and Lace (Aircel) 1989–91; 1991–92.

London's Dark (Titan–Escape) 1989.

Lone Wolf and Cub (First) 1987–.

Lord Horror (Savoy) 1989–91.

Los Tejanos (Fantagraphics) 1982.

Love and Rockets (Fantagraphics) 1982–.

Luck in the Head, The (Gollancz) 1991.

Luther Arkwright, The Adventures of (Valkyrie) 1987–9; (Dark Horse) 1990–1. Graphic novels: vol. 1 (Never Ltd) 1982; vol. 2 (Valkyrie) 1988; vol. 3 (Proutt) 1988.

Mad (Britain: Thorpe and Porter/Surron Enterprises/London Editions/Fleetway) 1959–; (USA: EC) 1952–. (Magazine format from no. 24.)

Marshal Law (Marvel–Epic) 1987–9; (Apocalypse) 1990–1.

Maus (Britain: Penguin) 1987; (USA: Pantheon) 1986.

Maus II (Britain: Penguin) 1992; (USA: Pantheon) 1991.

Melody (Kitchen Sink) 1988–90.

Mr Natural (San Francisco Comic Book Co./Kitchen Sink) 1970–7.

Moebius (Marvel–Epic) 1987–. (Series includes *Arzach*, *Upon a Star*, *Airtight Garage* and others.)

Murder Incorporated (Fox) 1948–9.

Myra Comics (Myra Hancock) 1982–.

Nam, The (Marvel) 1986–.

Nasty Tales (Bloom 1971–2); *Trials of Nasty Tales* (H. Bunch and Bloom) 1973.

Near Myths (Galaxy Media) 1978–80.

Neat Stuff (Fantagraphics) 1985–90.

New Comics (National Periodical Publications) 1935–6.

New Teen Titans (DC) 1980–4; 1984–8; 1988– (as *The New Titans*).

Nick Fury, Agent of SHIELD (Marvel) 1968–71; 1989–.

Nightbreed (Marvel–Epic) 1990–.

Nightmare (Skywald) 1970–5.

Peter Pank (Knockabout-Crack) 1990.

Predator (Dark Horse) 1989–.

Pssst! (Never–Artpool) Jan.–Oct. 1982.

Psycho (Skywald) 1971–5.

Puck (Harmsworth/Amalgamated) 1904–40.

Punisher (Marvel) 1987–.

Ranxerox (Catalan); *In New York* 1985; *Happy Birthday Lubna* 1985.

Raw (Raw/Penguin) 1980–.

Reaper of Love, The (Fantagraphics) 1991. A collection of reprints by Berni Wrightson – the illustration on p. 7 appeared originally in *Web of Horror 3* (Major) 1970.

Revolver (Feetway) 1990–1.

Rock N' Roll Comics (Revolutionary) 1989–. (Biographies of bands and artists, e.g., Sex Pistols, Alice Cooper, Prince, etc.)

Roy of the Rovers (IPC/Fleetway) 1976–.

Sabre (Eclipse) 1978. (Graphic novel followed by series, 1982–85.)

Sad Sack Comics (Harvey) 1949–82.

Sandman (National Periodical Publications) 1974–5; 1975–6; (DC) 1989–. (Neil Gaiman scripts begin 1989.)

Scream (Skywald) 1973–5.

Sergeant Bilko (DC) 1957–60.

Seven Ages of Woman (Knockabout–Crack) 1990.

Sheena, Queen of the Jungle (Fiction House) 1942–53.

Shock SuspenStories (EC) 1952–5.

Silver Surfer (Marvel) 1968–70; 1982; 1987–.

Slow Death Funnies (Last Gasp) 1970–.

Small Killing, A (Gollancz) 1991.

Sphinx (Bold) 1990–.

Spider-Man, The Amazing (Marvel) 1963–.

Spiral Cage, The (Britain: Titan) 1990; (USA: Renegade) 1989.

Spirit, The (newspaper insert) 1940–52; (Quality) 1944–50; (Harvey) 1966–7; (Kitchen Sink) Jan.–Sept. 1973; (Warren) 1974–6; 1977–83; (Kitchen Sink) 1983–92.

Starblazer (DC Thomson) 1979–91.

*Star*Reach* (Star*Reach) 1974–82.

Street Comix (Birmingham Arts Lab.) 1976–8.

Strip (Marvel UK) Feb.–Nov. 1990.

Strip AIDS (Britain: Willyprods) 1987; (USA: Last Gasp) 1987.

Superman (National Periodical Publications/DC) 1939–.

Swamp Thing (National Periodical Publications/DC) 1972–6. *Swamp Thing, Saga of the* (DC) 1982–. (Alan Moore scripts from issues 20–64.)

Taboo (Spiderbaby Grafix/Tundra) 1988–.

Tales from the Crypt (Britain: Arnold) 1952; (USA: EC) 1950–5.

Tales of the Beanworld (Beanworld/Eclipse) 1985–91.

Tank Girl (Penguin) 1990.

Teenage Mutant Ninja Turtles (Mirage) 1984–.

Thor (Marvel) 1966–.

Thrrp! (Knockabout) 1987.

Tiger (Amalgamated/Fleetway/IPC) 1954–85.

Tintin (Methuen) 1958–85.

Tits 'n' Clits (Nanny Goat/Last Gasp) 1972–.

Toxic (Apocalypse) Mar.–Oct. 1991.

Trident (Trident) 1989–90.

True Faith (Fleetway) 1990.

Trump (Hugh Hefner) Jan.–Apr. 1957.

TV Century 21 (City) 1965–9. Becomes *TV21* and *Joe 90* (City/IPC) 1969–71.

Twisted Tales (Pacific/Eclipse) 1982–4; 1987.

Two-Fisted Tales (EC) 1950–5.

2000AD (IPC/Fleetway) 1977–.

V for Vendetta (DC) 1988–9. (Reprints Warrior instalments, and completes story with new material.)

Vampirella (Warren) 1969–83; (Dark Horse) 1991–.

Vault of Horror (Britain: Arnold) 1954; (USA: EC) 1950–5.

Vietnam Journal (Apple) 1987–.

Violent Cases (Titan–Escape) 1988; (Tundra) 1991.

Viz (Viz/John Brown) 1979–.

War Picture Library (Amalgamated/Fleetway/IPC) 1958–84.

Warrior (Quality) 1982–5. Preceded by *Warrior* (Derek G. Skinn/Penwith) 1974–5 (mostly IPC reprints).

Watchmen (DC) 1986–7. Graphic novel: (Britain: Titan) 1987; (USA: DC) 1987.

Way Out Strips (Britain: Carol Swain) 1988–; (USA: Tragedy Strikes) 1992–.

Weirdo (Last Gasp) 1981–90.

When the Wind Blows (Hamish Hamilton/Penguin) 1982.

Wilderness (Four Winds) 1988.

Wimmins Comix (Last Gasp) 1972–.

Wonder Warthog (Millar) 1967; (Fawcett) 1967; (Rip off) 1973–80.

Wonder Woman (National Periodical Publications/All-American Publications/DC) 1942–.

X-Force (Marvel) 1991–.

X-Men, The Uncanny (Marvel) 1963–70; 1970–5; 1975–.

X-Presso Special (Fleetway) May and July 1991.

Young Romance Comics (Prize/Headline) 1974–63; (National Periodical Publications) 1963–75.

Yummy Fur (Vortex) 1987–.

Zap (Britain: Unknown) 1969; (USA: Apex Novelties/Print Mint/Last Gasp) 1967–.

Zippy Stories (Rip Off) 1977–8.

Notes

What is a comic?

1   In America, the word 'comic' has significantly different associations – see p. 134.

2   See D. Kunzle, *History of the Comic Strip, Vol. 2: The Nineteenth Century* (Berkeley, Calif.: University of California Press 1989) chapter 15: 'Movement Before the Movies: The Language of the Comic Strip' (pp. 348–74), which explains how cutting, perspective and so on were all established either during or before the nineteenth century.

3   The Pentagon Press Office were not able to give an exact reference for the research, but say it was undertaken by the US Army in around 1981.

1   The first adult comics

1   The link between the penny dreadfuls and comics is one that has been particularly overstressed. Certainly, they were often published by the same houses, and the penny dreadful publishers were already geared to producing cheap reading matter for a working-class audience. But, the often-cited 'crusade' against the dreadfuls by Alfred Harmsworth took off in 1892, a full two years after he had launched *Comic Cuts* and *Illustrated Chips*, and was based on boys' adventure story papers (not comics) which were designed specifically to wean younger readers away from the 'morally-corrupting' dreadfuls. These later evolved into the 'tuppenny bloods' of the 1920s and 1930s (papers like *Gem* and *Magnet*), and it was not really until the 1950s and *Eagle* that adventure comics proper emerged (see pp. 24–5). The story papers remained a separate tradition, and can be traced through to 1960s publications like *The Sexton Blake Library* and *Romance Library*.

2   The origins of the individual characteristics of comics are very difficult to trace. Various techniques appear sporadically in the chapbooks, broadsides, almanacs and religious tracts of the medieval period. See D. Kunzle, *History of the Comic Strip, Vol. 1: The Early Comic Strip* (Berkeley, Calif.: University of California Press 1973).

3   D. Kunzle, *History of the Comic Strip, Vol. 2: The Nineteenth Century* (Berkeley, Calif.: University of California Press 1989), p. 12.

4   W. P. Frith, *John Leech: His Life and Work* (London 1891), p. 5; quoted in Kunzle, *The Nineteenth Century*, op. cit., p. 13.

5   Although *Half Holiday* is generally recognised to have been the first, other contenders have been suggested. Dennis Gifford, for example, in his article 'The Evolution of the British Comic', cites *Funny Folks* on account of its relatively sophisticated layout.

6   These character modifications were not consistent, because material continued to be reprinted in large quantities from *Judy*. Hence it was possible within the same comic to find one representation of Sloper as a drunken reprobate, and another as a relatively sophisticated social commentator.

7   'Ally Sloper's Jubilee March', by Louis Mallett, free with *Ally Sloper's Half Holiday*, 18 June 1887.

8   Kunzle, *The Nineteenth Century*, op. cit., p. 10, analyses the sociological breakdown of 581 winners of a competition to win Ally Sloper watches, run between August 1887 and February 1888. Of the total, clerks represented 8 per cent; skilled artisans 18 per cent; teachers 4 per cent; rural 3.4 per cent; 'ladies' and 'gentlemen' (presumably leisured) 6 per cent.

9   Browne was the exception that proved the rule in terms of the exploitation of creators. There is evidence that he could command handsome page-rates, and that he lived comfortably from his work. (Even he, however, eventually lost creative control of 'Weary Willie and Tired Tim'.)

10   As 'railway literature' comics were also held to have anaesthetic qualities, to take the reader's mind off the possibility of an accident (of which there were a considerable number in late nineteenth-century Britain). *Half Holiday* even gave away insurance premiums against real accidents; the comic itself doubled as a free premium, with £150 guaranteed if a copy was found on the victim of a fatal accident.

11   Whether comics were frowned upon for their 'immoral' view of the world – the glorification of vagrants and petty criminals, the emphasis on the outwitting of authority and so on – is open to debate. Certainly these sorts of complaints were levelled at some penny dreadfuls, and there is some evidence for comics censorship. (For example, the name and personality of the front-page star of *Butterfly*, 'Portland Bill', originally an ex-convict, was changed to reformed character 'Butterfly Bill' in what Denis Gifford has speculated may have been the result of 'some early clean-up-the-comics campaign' (*Encyclopaedia of Comic Characters* (London: Longman 1987, p. 169)). However, ultimately the comics were not politically radical, and this goes a long way to explaining why there was no concerted backlash.

12   This can be seen as an extension of the high culture/low culture debate that had been rife since the eighteenth century, the origins of which are traced in Pat Rogers, *Literature and Popular Culture in 18th Century England* (Brighton: Harvester 1985).

13   There had been a comic for children as early as 1895 – *Jack and Jill*. However, the market was not yet ready for such a bold step, and it had to be reinvented in more adult guise.

2 Kids' stuff

1   Denis Gifford, *The International Book of Comics* (London: W. H. Smith 1984, rev. edn 1990), p. 26.

2   Accurate figures for overall comics sales are notoriously difficult to ascertain

(due, above all, to the fragmentary nature of the industry). To give two esti-
mates: Kevin Carpenter (ed.), *Penny Dreadfuls and Comics* (London: Victoria
and Albert Museum 1983) has 16 million per week in the 1950s, 8 million in the
1960s, 10.5 million in the 1970s, less than 7 million in the early 1980s. (It is not
clear what the sources are, or whether this includes American titles.) The
Observer, however, in an article 'Comics: The Battle for Survival' by Iain
Murray (21 July 1985), gives the following: over 12 million in the 1950s, 5.5
million in the mid-1970s, 3 million in 1985 (again, sources are not given). It
should be noted that sales figures are not necessarily an indication of readership,
since comics have historically tended to be 'passed around'. This is especially
true of children's comics, where the ratio of readers to sales is estimated to have
been sometimes as high as 6 to 1.

3   Alan Moore and Hunt Emerson, especially, have cited Baxendale as an
     influence. In Maurice Horn (ed.), *The World Encyclopaedia of Comics* (New
     York: Chelsea House 1976), he is listed as 'The most imitated artist in British
     comics today.'

4   It should be noted that adventure had long been a subject for continuing strips
     in newspapers.

5   For example, Reg Perrott's pioneering strip 'The Road to Rome', an epic Ben
     Hur-style adventure, appeared incongruously in the back of *Mickey Mouse
     Weekly* in 1936.

6   *Eagle* was in fact the brainchild of a proselytising Lancashire vicar, the
     Reverend Marcus Morris. Dan Dare's name was originally to have been 'Lex
     Christian', while the comic also included a strip based on the life of St Paul ('The
     Road of Courage'). Even the *Eagle* logo was based on the design of a church
     lectern.

7   M. Barker, *A Haunt of Fears: The Strange History of the British Horror Comics
     Campaign* (London: Pluto Press 1984), p. 214.

8   Source: D. McAlpine, *The Official Comic Book Price Guide for Great Britain
     1991/2* (London: Price Guide Productions), p. 30.

9   It should be noted that, in America, the horror and crime titles were often
     expected to appeal to an adult as well as juvenile audience. In Britain, however,
     because of the much more rigid stereotyping of the comics medium, they were
     sold to the traditional 8–12 age-group without warning of content (see also
     chapter 11).

10   The paradox of communist involvement was that many of the EC comics were
     themselves implicitly anti-McCarthyite. See p. 159, and also Barker op. cit.,
     esp. pp. 112–39, 170–5.

11   Wertham himself concurred with British critics of American comics: that they
     were a manifestation of a society that was over-commercialised and vulgar (see
     Seduction of the Innocent (New York: Rinehart 1954; London: Museum Press
     1955)).

12   One response to the perceived damaging effect of the American crime and
     horror comics was the emergence of *Eagle*. Marcus Morris had been prominent
     in the censorship campaign in its early days, viewing them as 'deplorable, nastily
     over-violent and obscence' (quoted in Marcus Morris (ed.), *The Best of Eagle*
     (London: Michael Joseph and Eburg Press 1977)).

13   The horror comics campaign should be seen in the context of other 'moral

panics' through history. In Britain, these have included the controversies surrounding penny dreadfuls in the 1860s, the alternative press in the 1960s and video nasties in the 1980s. Typically the subjects of the panics contained social comment and were attacked by a wide range of political opinion for a variety of reasons. On the cyclical nature of such panics, see Geoffrey Pearson, *Hooligan: A History of Respectable Fears* (London: Macmillan 1983).

14 These comics were very much in the EC style, and once again were expected to garner an adult as well as juvenile audience in their native America (see pp. 167–9).

15 For a hard-hitting exposé of working conditions at DC Thomson, see the ironically-titled (and quite definitely unofficial) *The DC Thomson Bumper Fun Book* edited by Paul Harris (Edinburgh: Paul Harris Publications 1977).

16 Some of these creators were later to become much better-known in their home countries: for example, Jesus Blasco in Spain and Hugo Pratt in Italy.

17 For a thorough investigation (and reinterpretation) of the major complaints against comics, see Martin Barker, *Comics: Power, Ideology and the Critics* (Manchester: Manchester University Press 1989).

18 Barker, *Haunt of Fears*, op. cit., p. 175.

19 There exists today a growing literature on the history of (and theories of) childhood. For a basic introduction see Steve Humphries, Joanna Mack and Robert Perks, *A Century of Childhood* (London: Sidgwick and Jackson 1988).

3   Underground comix

1 Interview with Mick Farren, 28 November 1989.

2 It should be noted that there was also a *Zap 0*, but that this was published after *Zap 1* (the artwork had been lost, and Crumb was forced to re-ink photocopies). Further, although *Zap 1* was completed in 1967, it did not become widely available until 1968.

3 Smaller sized machinery meant that modern lithographic printing became available to all. It also meant speedier, more flexible publication, less vulnerable to the censorship of compositors – in other words, a more devolved unit, which had obvious political implications.

4 Jay Kennedy, 'Introduction', *The Official Underground and Newave Price Guide* (Cambridge, Mass.: Boatner Norton Press 1982), p. 12.

5 'Fritz the Cat' had made his first appearance in the alternative press in 1965 (though Crumb had started to draw the character in prototype form long before, when he was a child, to entertain his brother). The character was finally killed off in response to the movies being made about him (see p. 212).

6 Robert Crumb, interviewed in Ron Mann's film *Comic Book Confidential* (Canada: Castle Hendring 1989).

7 Interview with Gilbert Shelton, 27 January 1990.

8 Spain Rodriguez, interviewed in Don Donahue and Susan Goodrick (eds), *The Apex Treasury of Underground Comics* (New York: Quick Fox 1974), p. 140.

9 LSD occupies a special place in the history of the underground, and indeed of the counter-culture generally. It was not used purely for recreational purposes, but was believed to be able to raise the taker to different planes of consciousness,

to 'remove the filters on reality' and thereby to promote more harmonious coexistence. As Trina Robbins later recalled 'we spoke, in all seriousness, about putting LSD in the water supply to save the world' (*Heartbreak Hotel*, 6, Nov.–Dec. 1988). For more on this see Jay Stevens's excellent *Storming Heaven: LSD and the American Dream* (London: Paladin 1990).

10   Figures from Susan Goodrick, 'Introduction', in Donahue and Goodrick (eds), op. cit., p. 9.

11   Although no published histories of the British underground exist, there is an excellent Ph.D thesis by David Huxley entitled 'The Growth and Development of British Underground and Alternative Comics 1966–86' (University of Loughborough 1990), which can be obtained through Inter-Library Loan. (Huxley was himself a contributor to the underground and subsequent 'alternative' comics.)

12   Interview with Bryan Talbot, 13 September 1990.

13   The origins of *Street Comix* are convoluted. An editorial to issue 2 explained: 'The first issue of *Street Comix* was a free supplement to *Street Poems* 3 [an Arts Lab poetry pamphlet]. The response to that modest effort was very favourable, not least from cartoonists, and so we've been able to publish *Street Comix* 2 as a complete magazine' (Hunt Emerson, editorial, 1976).

In fact, the Arts Lab had been producing comix from as early as 1972 (Emerson had founded the comics wing, and his first solo comic, *Large Cow Comix* no. 1 appeared in that year). However, early output was small-scale, and not widely distributed. By the mid-1970s, however, it was possible to produce much larger print-runs, and to attempt national distribution. Remarkably, the Arts Council (a government body) was unknowingly responsible for this, due to their funding of the Arts Lab. Hunt Emerson takes up the story:

> We had a grant from the Arts Council, which meant we had an obligation to keep the presses busy. So we produced a great many comix, because that was what we were interested in. The trouble was that we were not so good at distributing and selling them. So, print-runs could be anywhere up to 10,000 an issue, but sales were always nearer 2000.
> (interview with Hunt Emerson, 3 January 1990)

14   Interview with Hunt Emerson, 3 January 1990.

15   There was one notable exception to this rule in the person of William Rankin (who used the pseudonym 'Wyndham Raine'), who frequently referred back to British comics in his work. However, it was not until the emergence of *Viz* in 1979 that the potential for parodying this tradition was realised (see chapter 8).

16   There is some debate over whether *Ally Sloper* can strictly be considered an 'underground'. On the one hand, it featured comix creators like Bryan Talbot and Hunt Emerson, and was clearly aimed at an adult audience (its title making an explicit connection between the satire of the nineteenth-century comic of the same name and that of the new comix). Published in 1976, when the British underground was having its 'second wind', it was clearly intended – at least in part – to tap into a similar audience; duly, it was listed along with other undergrounds in Mal Burns's *Comix Index* (Brighton: John Noyce 1978). On the other hand, the comic also featured mainstream creators such as Frank Bellamy and Frank Hampson, plus various vintage strips; its founder and editor,

historian Denis Gifford, always distanced himself from underground connections, and eschewed underground networks of distribution in favour of a traditional, mainstream, newsagent-based approach.

17 On the question of control of copyright, this tended to change with time. Generally speaking, in the early days of the underground, there was a *laissez-faire* attitude to reproducing strips (there was even an Underground Press Syndicate – a sort of alternative free wire service). This was how the British underground press and comix were able to reproduce so much American material. However, later, attitudes hardened as the 'straight media' began to take advantage of the situation, and help themselves to ideas, characters and so on. For an informative account of how Robert Crumb was exploited in this respect (and thus ended up copyrighting everything he did) see M. Estren, *A History of Underground Comics* (San Francisco: Straight Arrow 1974; rev. edn 1987) pp. 242–63.

18 Some undergrounds did manage to get a measure of news-stand distribution. But this was via independent newsagents, not the big chains like W. H. Smith. The distributors Moore Harness, who dealt with *Cozmic Comics*, *Nasty Tales* and *Brainstorm*, were reasonably successful in this respect.

19 Interview with Mick Farren, 28 November 1989.

20 Robert Crumb, interviewed in *Comic Book Confidential* (dir. Ron Mann, Canada: Castle Hendring 1989).

21 See Tony Palmer's *The Trials of Oz* (London: Blond and Briggs 1971).

22 Interview with Mick Farren, 28 November 1989.

4   *2000AD*: 'The comic of tomorrow!'

1 Alan Moore, interviewed for *Ten Years of* 2000AD – *A Video Celebration* (London: Acme Video/CA Productions 1987).

2 The *Sun* 30 April 1976.

3 M. Barker, *Comics: Ideology, Power and the Critics* (Manchester: Manchester University Press 1989), esp. pp. 29–35.

4 Instead of cancelling the title, the decision was taken to merge it with another failing IPC comic, *Star Lord* (see also p. 58), which happened in 1978. This proved to be an important element in *2000AD*'s eventual revival both because it pulled in a much-needed secondary readership, and because it brought together the best characters from both comics (those from *Star Lord* included 'Strontium Dog' and 'Ro-Busters'). As Steve MacManus, who joined the *2000AD* editorial team in 1978 (and who later became editor), later recalled: 'It seemed that with the merger there was now a range of heroes who clicked together: the comic suddenly had an identity that it did not have before' (interview with Steve MacManus 7 April 1992).

5 Other *2000AD* creators who had over the years contributed to either the underground or the 'ground levels' (see pp. 72–3 for a definition) included Steve Parkhouse, Grant Morrison, John Higgins, Brett Ewins, Brendan McCarthy, David Hine, Ian Gibson, Gary Leach, Jim Baikie, Steve Dillon and Graham Higgins (who contributed to an Arts Lab Comix under the pseudonym 'Pokketts').

6 Dave Gibbons and Brian Bolland had worked on *Powerman* (Pickin Publications 1975), a comic for sale only in Africa, while Kevin O'Neill had previously worked at IPC on children's titles.

7　Alan Moore, quoted in *Ten Years of 2000AD*, op. cit.

8　Interview with Alan Grant, 15 May 1992.

9　Interview with Dave Gibbons, 28 January 1990.

10　It should be noted that the music papers themselves carried strips. Comics creators who were employed in this capacity at one time or another included Alan Moore, Savage Pencil, Eddie Campbell, Brendan McCarthy, Bryan Talbot, Mark Beyer and Lynda Barry.

11　*2000AD* is often characterised by commentators as a 'punk' comic. However, this assertion seems to be based mainly on the twin facts that the comic was founded in 1977, the year punk took off in Britain, and that it was markedly more violent than other comics. The date was clearly a coincidence, while the violence can be seen as both a hangover from *Action*, and an expression of the more liberated artistic sensibility of ex-underground creators.

　　　　Punk's influence on comics is best seen elsewhere. Martin Barker has identified a correlation with *Action* and its anti-authoritarianism (*Action*, p. 12). I see it more in the late 1970s underground (which had a degree of crossover with the punk fanzine boom), the early 1980s small press and in *Viz*, which as an expression of alternative comedy exhibited a punk sensibility. (See also chapter 8, n. 3.)

12　Interview with Pat Mills, 29 September 1988.

13　This was exacerbated by the fact that by now reprint albums of strips were appearing, published by Titan Books, for which the creators saw virtually no return (a 1 per cent royalty for the artist and 1 per cent for the writer for producing new covers and introductions to the volumes). Especially hard done by in this respect were the creators of Dredd, who saw virtually no financial return when the character became a world-wide hit and rights to it licensed internationally. It should be said, however, that if the Dredd movie ever does get made they will be reimbursed accordingly: Alan Grant and John Wagner are currently in the process of preparing a manuscript for consideration.)

14　Interview with Steve MacManus, 7 April 1992.

5　Fandom and direct sales

1　Interview with Derek ('Dez') Skinn, 13 February 1991.

2　Kirby and Ditko are the obvious fan favourites to mention, but there were many more down the years – among them, Gil Kane, Neal Adams, Berni Wrightson and Jim Steranko (later, as we shall see, this list would include Howard Chaykin, Frank Miller, Alan Moore, Bill Sienkiewicz, Dave McKean and others).

3　Though there had been precedents of publishers encouraging fan groups in the past – notably EC in the early 1950s and DC in the late 1950s (especially under editor Julius Schwartz, who introduced full names and addresses in letters pages), it was not until the Marvel boom of the early to mid 1960s that the idea caught fire. In particular, Stan Lee was responsible for a number of innovations. He instituted the first really successful comics fan club, the 'Merry Marvel Marching Society', and created the idea of loyalty to the company *per se* rather then to individual characters. To this end, in the comics themselves, he introduced guest appearances by characters in other characters' comics, so that fans of one would then become fans of all the others. This led to the evolution of what became known as the 'Marvel Universe', a richly imagined world of superheroes based in New York, where the plotting and settings in one title would be consistent with that in every other. Collecting was thus encouraged across the entire line.

4   All three men became central figures in fandom, Frank Dobson, sometimes called 'the father of British fandom', edited *Fantasy Advertiser* between 1965 and 1970; he went on to found the less successful EC fanzine *Fant-EC Advertiser*, and in 1992 was running a mail-order business entitled Weird Fantasy. Dez Skinn edited *Fantasy Advertiser* from 1970 to 1975, opened two comics shops and went on to have a varied career in professional comics, including a period as editor at Marvel UK, where he was responsible for launching numerous titles, and a stint publishing and editing the highly-regarded *Warrior* (see pp. 59–60). In 1992 he was publisher and editor of trade magazine-cum-fanzine *Comics International*. Phillip Clarke, as well as organising early conventions (see p. 64), produced the early fanzine *Heroes Unlimited*, and opened one of the first shops (Nostalgia and Comics). He has co-written a book about American comics imported into Britain before 1959, *Nostalgia About Comics* (Birmingham: Pegasus Publishing 1991).

5   Interview with Phillip Clarke, 4 April 1990. (Among the seventy attendees were future comics luminaries Paul Neary, Jim Baikie and Mike Lake.)

6   There was one exception to this rule of taking all hot-off-the-press comics: Derek Stokes, proprietor of Dark They Were, came from a hippie background and refused on principle to handle war comics. (Derek Stokes, interviewed by Martin Barker, 26 February 1992, unpublished, used with kind permission.) See also note 13.

7   *Comic Media News*, 39, (May–June 1979), p. 25.

8   Creators' rights was, and is, an issue that understandably preoccupies modern comics publishing. Despite the history of exploitation of creators (see pp. 33–4), the issue is far from clear-cut, not least because comics are a collaborative medium. The various arguments around the subject are explored in two excellent articles: Gary Groth, 'The Next Panacea?', *Comics Journal*, 87 (December 1983), p. 3; and Paul Dawson 'Creators Rights', *FA* 103 (June 1988), p. 26. It should also be noted that it was in the atmosphere of the reconsideration of creators' rights in the 1980s that artists and writers from the past began to press for recompense (see p. 34).

9   Improvements in technology were a key factor in making fully-painted comics possible. In particular, 'blue lining', a technique involving photography combined with traditional colour separation, made high-quality reproduction feasible.

10   A 'mutant' in comics-language is a superhero with powers that are inherited, carried in the genes, rather than bestowed by outside agencies.

11   Nick Landau and Mike Lake were also central figures in British fandom. As partners in the Titan empire, Landau became more associated with Titan Books, while Lake took responsibility for Titan Distributors. The Forbidden Planet shop, and later chain, was an outgrowth of the business, and eventually became its most profitable arm. Landau was also responsible for the institution of regular London marts in the late 1970s, and for a brief period combined his duties at Titan with a stint as an editor at *2000AD* (between 1977 and 1978).

12   Titan did not in fact start originating comics until 1987. For a critical perspective on their policy before this date, see Frank Plowright, 'And as ye Reap Shall ye Sow', *Comics Journal*, 122 (June 1988), p. 11.

13   Indeed, the underground culture and the new fan culture were not as distinct as some commentators have suggested. As well as the fact that the headshops had provided an important blueprint for the specialist shops, it was also true that hippies had been involved in a more direct sense in getting the new fan scene up and running. Some fans of the original comix also interested themselves in American comics, and became known in hippie parlance as 'comics heads' ('head' being generally synonymous with 'fan'). *Cyclops*, for example, the first British underground, even attempted to set up a fan network: in the words of the editorial to issue 1 (July 1970), 'We would like to link up comic heads with their local turn-on all over the country so if you have news of shops with a special interest in comics [or] local heads turning out their own product, please let us know.' (*Cyclops* was also notable for running the classic American 1930s strip 'Flash Gordon' among its regular fare.) It should come as no surprise, therefore, that the first comics shop, Dark They Were, was set up by a hippie entrepreneur (Derek Stokes), and retained the atmosphere of a headshop.

By the same token, as fandom developed, so some fanzines featured strips by creators associated with the underground – among them, Dave Gibbons, Kevin O'Neill and Bryan Talbot. The ability of these creators to switch from traditional underground fare to subject-matter involving science fiction or superheroes was undoubtedly the chief factor in their popularity.

14   The genesis of *2000AD* and *Warrior* should also be seen in the light of these developments in SF.

15   Because it was the artwork fans were generally interested in, the fact that the comic was in a foreign language did not particularly matter. It is also significant that perhaps the most popular story, the classic 'Arzach' by Moebius, was virtually wordless.

16   'Airbrushing' is an art technique whereby paint is sprayed thinly and selectively, by a mechanical tool, to give a smooth finish.

17   *Heavy Metal*, like many long-running comics, has changed its 'personality' many times since its inception. Although nothing to do with rock music at the start, under the editorship of Ted White (1979–81), strips were commissioned on various aspects of rock culture. The movie *Heavy Metal* (1981) consolidated this trend by featuring a rock soundtrack (although not all the music in the film was heavy metal by any means (see p. 215)). More recently, under the editorship of Julie Simmons-Lynch (1984–), the comic changed tack once again, and began to feature more avant-garde European and American material (including work by Joost Swarte, Daniel Torres and Charles Burns – the sort of creators one might have expected to find in *Raw* or *Escape*). However, the magazine still regularly features semi-naked women on the cover in order to appeal to its traditional readership.

18   The history of 'Luther Arkwright' is a convoluted one. The character first appeared in a prototype story ('The Papist Affair') in the underground comic *Mixed Bunch* (from the *Brainstorm* stable) in 1977. A longer and modified version began to be serialised in *Near Myths* in 1978. This extended story was reprised and continued in *Pssst!* in 1982, and the first collected volume

appeared later in that year (published by Never Ltd). Finally, Talbot finished the story in 1988 and it was published as a nine-issue comic book series by Valkyrie Press. The second collected volume was published by Valkyrie, and the third by Proutt (who also reprinted volume 1). In 1991, Dark Horse Comics reprinted the Valkyrie nine-issue series with new covers by Talbot.

19   To be exact, the term 'ground level' was invented in 1974 by publisher Mike Friedrich to describe *Star*Reach* no. 1. Originally, it was intended to denote overground genres being explored with an underground sensibility. But since the vast majority of such comics tended to be SF, the term evolved to mean 'SF produced in an underground fashion'. In the 1990s, it seems the term is rapidly becoming obsolete (when I asked a random selection of ten long-time dealers at a mart for their definition, four gave the latter, one Friedrich's original version, while five had no idea what I was talking about).

20   Indeed, *Teenage Mutant Ninja Turtles* set in motion a boom in black and white comics, with parodies of parodies appearing like *Adolescent Radioactive Black-belt Hamsters* and *Naive Inter-dimensional Commando Koalas*, which flooded the market and led to an eventual slump. As for *TMNT*, after the idea had been commercialised for children, the story came full circle in 1990–1 when co-creator Kevin Eastman used a proportion of the profits to finance the independent companies Tundra and Tundra UK, both of which specialise in adult comics.

21   Robert Fiore commenting on *Swamp Thing*, in 'A selected Bibliography: Comics, Comics Everywhere', *Print* magazine (Nov.–Dec. 1988), p. 181.

22   *Swamp Thing* is also notable as the first comic to be published by DC without Code approval, Marvel had taken this step long before (see p. 165).

23   Interview with Art Spiegelman, 1 November 1989.

24   Paul Gravett occupies a special place in the history of adult comics in Britain as a behind-the-scenes motivator. He was responsible for founding *Fast Fiction*, then moved on to work for *Pssst!* before establishing *Escape*. Later, he curated several major exhibitions (notably the touring 'Strip Search' in Britain and 'God Save the Comics!' in Europe), and became a consultant to Penguin on their graphic novel line. He has written widely on comics in the national press, and frequently lectures on the subject at book fairs and conventions. In 1992 he was New Projects Director at the Cartoon Art Trust, and is currently writing *The New Penguin Book of Comics* (scheduled for release in 1993).

25   In America it was even true that some of the new specialist shops refused to stock undergrounds for fear of prosecution. However, I have found no evidence for this in Britain.

26   The details of the Knockabout case are complex. The company's premises were raided in 1982 and a number of comics seized, including some relating explicitly to drugs – notably *Cocaine Comix* and *Dope Comix*. (*Knockabout* itself was not taken.) Tony Bennett elected to go to trial, and proceedings began in 1983. The trial focused on the twin issues of whether the comics encouraged people to take drugs, and whether the taking of drugs was itself a 'depraving and cor-rupting' act. The case therefore became quite openly an attempt to extend British obscenity laws to drug-related material, and thus became an important test case in this regard. As in the instance of the *Nasty Tales* trial, in other words, there was an underlying agenda. Though Knockabout were found 'not

guilty', the confiscated comics were then passed on to the magistrates court, where they were found 'guilty' and destroyed.

27 Prophetically, in 1979, the *Comics Journal* ran a series of pieces bemoaning the poor quality of comics criticism, and the sycophancy of the comics press: Paul Levitz, 'A Call for Higher Criticism', *Comics Journal*, 50 (October 1979); 'Eleven Critics Respond to Paul Levitz's Call For Higher Criticism', *Comics Journal*, 51 (November 1979). Within a few years, the changes wrought by direct sales had made a rise in standards possible.

6 'Comics grow up!': dawn of the graphic novel

1 Interview with Igor Goldkind, 6 October 1989.

2 Frank Miller, interviewed by Christopher Sharrett, 'Batman and the Twilight of the Idols: An Interview with Frank Miller', in R. Pearson and W. Uricchio (eds), *The Many Lives of the Batman* (London: BFI Publishing/Routledge 1991), p. 136.

3 Although not a 'revision' in the same sense as *Dark Knight*, *Watchmen* also originated in a reworking of already-existing characters. These were the 'Charlton superheroes', a group of costumed characters once owned by publishers Charlton, but since bought by DC. The Watchmen as they eventually appeared, however, bore very little resemblance, due mainly to the insistence of an editor who objected to Moore's original proposal, which involved the killing off of several of what were now DC properties (see '"A Portal to Another Dimension": Alan Moore and Dave Gibbons discuss the inspiration and details behind *Watchmen*', panel discussion, UKCAC (21 September 1986), reprinted in *Comics Journal*, 116 (July 1987), p. 80).

4 The Rorschach character especially is a complex one. As well as the obvious reference to the Rorschach ink-blot test used in psychological profiling, he also refers back to two heroes created by Steve Ditko: the Charlton superhero 'The Question', and the self-published 'Mr A'. Both were politically extremely right-wing creations, and owed much to the philosophy of Ayn Rand. In using them as a reference point, Moore and Gibbons were attempting to highlight the inherent contradictions of such a political position, and thus intended Rorshach to be, in Moore's words 'a tragic figure, a loser and a fool, who evoked the paranoid world of Steve Ditko, and took vigilantism as far as it could go' (interview with Alan Moore, 4 April 1992). Ironically, however, sections of the fan community read the character in completely the opposite fashion, and instead of reacting against or pitying him, singled him out as a hero – much to Moore's disgust.

5 Interview with Alan Moore, 17 January 1989.

6 *Maus* first appeared in prototype form in 1972 in the underground comic *Funny Aminals* (*sic*).

7 Interview with Art Spiegelman, 1 November 1989. Some critics did not agree with Spiegelman, however, and have attacked this device for its tendency to stereotype. Specifically, it has been argued that, with all Germans depicted as predatory cats, all Poles as collaborating pigs and so on, there is little room for positive images of those nationals sympathetic to the Jewish plight – stereotyping analogous to the kind the Nazis themselves were guilty of. See, for example, Richard Haynes, 'Caught in the Maus Trap', the *Guardian* (29 August 1987) p. 12 and H. Pekar 'Where Maus Fails', *Comics Journal* (July

1986), p. 14. Spiegelman later defended himself thus: 'it's my view that comics have a natural tendency to abstraction. In everyday life, your brain simplifies and abstracts images all the time. To do the story totally straight would have been very corny' (interview with Spiegelman, *op. cit*). ✔

8   In retrospect, *Maus* can be seen as a part of a trend in the arts for re-evaluating the holocaust from fresh perspectives. Other examples might include Claude Lanzmann's six-hour documentary *Shoah* (France: 1988) which purposely eschewed the use of archive footage, and Martin Amis's novel *Time's Arrow* (London: Jonathan Cape 1991) which used the stylistic device of reversing time to explore the morality of life in a concentration camp. ✓

9   The so-called 'style magazines' emerged at the beginning of the 1980s, essentially as an extension of the music press (the archetype was the *Face*, later joined by *iD*, the *Cut* and numerous others). They cover fashion, music, film and youth culture generally. In their relationship with comics, they can be seen to be continuing the connection started by the alternative press in the 1960s, and carried on by the music press in the 1970s.

10 This 'breaking down of the boundaries' between high and low culture can be exaggerated. Yet, a quick scan of the quality newspapers from the early 1980s to the end of that decade reveals dramatic changes on the arts pages, with the appearance of many more rock reviews and articles, regular TV columns and so on. Indeed, it is obvious that these years saw the co-option of not just ideas from the style and rock press, but also the journalists themselves: for example, work has appeared by Jon Savage (*Sounds*) in the *Observer*, Charles Shaar Murray (*Oz, NME*) in the *Observer* and *Daily Telegraph*, and Julie Burchill (*NME*) in the *Sunday Times*.

11 This was certainly not the first time that a new term had been used to distance comics from their childish associations. To cite a few other examples: in the 1940s, some American crime comics were published under the label 'illustories': in the 1960s, the underground used the word 'comix'; in the 1980s, *Escape* coined the term 'UKBD' to describe its contents; while Art Spiegelman, in *Raw*, used the term 'Commix' to indicate the titles' "co-mix" of styles and influences.

12 As historian/publisher Paul Gravett has pointed out, this marketing strategy also contained an element of appealing to the prevailing 1980s 'style culture': at a time when vinyl records were being superseded by CDs, diaries by filofaxes and so on, the graphic novel could be marketed as the designer version of the comic. (See 'Do the Panel Think?' in the catalogue for the 'Strip Search' exhibition, London: Camden Arts 1990.)

13 The phrase 'literature for the post-literate generation' was one which was used frequently by some creators as well as by industry PR. Alan Moore spoke of it on *Signals*, Channel 4 (18 January 1989), while Art Spiegelman used the self-mocking subheading 'Required Reading for the Post-Literate' in *Raw*, 2 no. 2 (August 1990).

14 The idea of 'the death of the novel' is especially vulnerable. In fact, it can be argued that rather than going into a decline the novel is in fact thriving. Most adherents of the negative argument begin with a notion of the novel as meaning a canon of 'classic' works by 'classic' authors. But although this kind of writing

is much rarer today, 'blockbuster' novels, such as those by Jackie Collins, sell in far greater numbers than the classic texts ever did.

15   Interview with Paul Hudson, proprietor of Comics Showcase, 8 February 1990.

16   There had been minor exceptions to the rule. For example, both Knockabout and Titan had previously had some success in getting square-bound volumes into certain bookshops. Also, *Tintin* and *Asterix* albums were frequently stocked in the childrens sections.

17   Interview with Igor Goldkind, 16 October 1989.

18   All figures are approximate, and should be treated with caution. The *Dark Knight* and *Watchmen* figures do not include imports of the original DC imprints (which were considerable owing to fans' desire to obtain the 'original'), and the *Maus* figures do not include Pantheon imports or André Deutsch hardback figures.

7   From boom to bust

1   Dick Hansom, *Speakeasy* 102, (September 1989), p. 3.

2   To be exact, the 'Dow-Jones Top 100 Movable Commodity Index' (June 1988) listed comics in fourth place, behind industrial diamonds, fine art and furniture. It was even true that in the wake of the stock market crash of 1987, there was a rush to invest in comics.

3   Although Marvel was always the bigger of the two in direct sales, it was DC that capitalised on the adult readership in this period (having published *Watchmen* and *Dark Knight*). According to a market report, nearly half of DC's readership were 25 or older in 1990 (*A Survey of Young Upwardly Mobile Men*, conducted for DC Comics by Mediamark Research Inc., 1990). To follow this through, they went on to set up a creator-owned imprint in the style of Marvel's Epic, called Piranha Press, in 1989.

4   Also worthy of note in the context of the 'Bat-wave' was Frank Miller's *Batman: Year 1* (with artwork by Dave Mazzuchelli), which re-told the character's origin-story, and appeared as a graphic novel in 1988. Chronologically speaking, however, Miller had completed this story pre-*Dark Knight*, as a four-part stint on the continuing *Batman* comic.

5   Interview with Alan Moore, 17 January 1989.

6   There had been other adult horror comics before this date. The underground had produced *Skull, Snarf, Bogeyman* and *Slow Death* among others, while some independents had experimented with adult horror pre-1986 (notably Eclipse with *Twisted Tales*). Also it should be noted that in America, some previous news-stand horror comics had garnered adult followings – notably the EC titles *Vault of Horror, Tale From the Crypt* and *Haunt of Fear* in the 1950s and the Warren magazines *Creepy, Eerie* and *Vampirella* in the 1960s (see also chapters 11 and 13).

7   Both *Hellblazer* and *Sandman* were DC comics, and were reworkings of already-existing characters (John Constantine, star of *Hellblazer*, had been a minor character in *Swamp Thing*; the Sandman was a minor Golden Age superhero – though the Gaiman version was reinvented specifically as a horror story rather than a revisionist superhero tale).

8   David Britton, quoted in *Speakeasy* 103 (October, 1989), p. 5.

9   It should be noted that these were not the first adult war comics. The under-

ground had produced a number of anti-war titles involving Vietnam, notably *The Legion of Charlies* (Last Gasp 1972). In America, several news-stand titles had garnered sizeable adult followings, notably the EC comics *Frontline Combat* and *Two Fisted Tales* in the 1950s, and the Warren magazine *Blazing Combat* in the 1960s (see also chapters 11 and 13).

10 The Gulf War comics were, to the best of my knowledge, the first fictional response to the conflict. The comics medium had also been the first to respond to the Vietnam War in the 1960s.

11 Interview with Ravi Mirchandani, 6 July 1989.

12 'Strip Search', London: Swiss Cottage Library (10 Feb.–17 May 1990).

13 *Crisis* garnered more media attention than any other comic following the Big 3; the Amnesty issue was even covered on Channel 4's 7 o'clock news. This may have had something to do with the fact that the person responsible for its promotion was Igor Goldkind, who had moved to Fleetway from Titan in 1988. (Goldkind went on actually to write comic strips, first for *Crisis*, and later for DC, among others.)

14 'The Day Comics Grew up!', *Signals*, Channel 4 (8 January 1989). (There had been a London Weekend Television documentary on comics in their *South of Watford* series in 1988, but this was the first national programme.)

15 Both writers also had careers outside comics. Morrison won the Independent Edinburgh Fringe Award with his play *Red King Rising* in 1989, while Gaiman is also known for his SF short stories, and his co-authorship (with Terry Pratchett) of the best seller, *Good Omens* (Gollancz, 1989).

16. Some idea of the level of Moore's popularity in fan circles can be gauged from a readers' poll in *FA* magazine, in which he came top of every category he could be entered for (including 'All Time Favourite Comic Writer') (*FA* 105 (August 1988), pp. 26–7). He eventually retreated from fandom altogether after being mobbed at conventions and pestered by fans telephoning him.

17 The individual strips in the style magazines were: 'Ginsberg, Stipe, and Kerouac', by Jamie Hewlett and Alan Martin, in *iD*, 'Signal to Noise', by Neil Gaiman and Dave McKean in the *Face* (published as a graphic novel by Gollancz in 1992) and 'The New Adventures of Hitler', by Grant Morrison and Steve Yeowell in the *Cut* (a strip considered so controversial by some of the *Cut* staff that they resigned).

18 Pop Will Eat Itself, *Defcon 1* (RCA Records, 1989).

19 Interview with Dez Skinn, 13 February 1991.

20 Some commentators have interpreted the aggressiveness of Marvel and DC (Marvel especially) as at least in part an attempt to force the independents out of business. In the words of Catherine Yronwode, editor-in-chief at Eclipse Comics: 'the managers at Marvel and DC come from a philosophical school where winning isn't enough – you have to have *all* the marbles' (interview with Catherine Yronwode, 16 April 1992).

It is also argued that in future this trend will be intensified. In the case of Marvel, the 1990 *Spider-Man* re-launch is said to be just the beginning of a campaign to maximise profits, spurred by the publisher's post-1988 status as a public limited company. According to an editorial by Thomas Harrington in *Amazing Heroes*, 197 (December 1991):

Marvel has become the property of junk bond king Ron Perelman . . .

[who] purchased Marvel for $84 million, $73.5 million of which was borrowed from banks .... Even though Marvel is pulling its own weight, Perelman still owes about a billion dollars in bank debts from other acquisitions, and that's why he put 30% of Marvel up for sale. In other words, the money you [the reader] spend on Marvel stock will not benefit Marvel in any way .... The reason Marvel went public, the reason why it is raising prices, the reason it is going to greatly increase the number of its titles is because it is now in the business of paying off debts that it is in no way responsible for.

21 The decision in 1991 by MacDonald–Futura not to go ahead with their projected graphic novel list was interpreted by commentators as a particularly heavy blow, and as sending out a negative signal to other book publishers. Certainly, the decision was at least in part due to fears about having product shelved next to adolescent titles like *X-Men* (interview with the graphic novel consultant to MacDonald-Futura, Dave Thorpe, 31 August 1991).

22 A number of planned newsagent titles were also scrapped. Notably, this included a line from John Brown Publishing (including *Heartbeat*, which was to have featured reprint strips from *Love and Rockets*), and a glossy monthly from Fleetway, entitled *X-Presso*, which was intended to reprint 'the best of international comics', but which only got as far as the appearance of two taster 'specials'.

23 Roger Williams, 'Raw: Open Wounds from the Cutting Edge of Comics' (review of *Raw* vol. 2, no. 1), *Sunday Times* (24 October 1989). (It should be noted that the review was not typical because the journalist was clearly not familiar with what was happening in comics. It is interesting, of course, for this very reason.)

24 Julie Burchill, 'Grin and Bear It', *20/20* magazine (September 1989), p. 20.

25 David Lister 'Traditional Novel In Danger as Teenagers turn to Comics', *The Independent* (9 September 1989). The most sustained attacks came from the right-wing newspapers, and especially the *Sunday Telegraph*. See, for example, Nicholas Farrell and Valerie Elliott, 'Police Powerless to Halt Sex Comics', *Sunday Telegraph* (21 October 1990); Nicholas Farell, 'Slagging off the Wimmin', *Sunday Telegraph* (10 March 1991).

26 This 'return to standards' movement should not be over-exaggerated, but it does exist. It encompasses two distinct arguments. The first is the conservative view that simply seeks to re-establish old notions of high culture. The second is the liberal stance (eloquently argued by playwright David Hare in the pages of the *Guardian* at various times in 1991), which has as its primary concern the perceived lack of criticism that the blurring of high and low culture implies (a position which takes as self-evident that 'John Keats was a better poet than Bob Dylan' – but with the caveat that both are worth giving serious critical attention).

27 'Skin' was taken to several other publishers after Fleetway, none of which were inclined to touch it. It is now to be published as a graphic novel by Tundra UK.

28 The fan market eventually proved not to be recession proof. By 1992, growth had effectively stalled, and shops were beginning to close. Titan Distributors, who had borne the brunt of bad debts on several occasions, responded by holding crisis meetings on the situation.

8 *Viz*: 'More fun than a jammy bun!'

1   Auberon Waugh, interviewed by Philip Branston for *Viz: The Documentary*, Channel 4 (4 May 1990).

2   Dating the origins of 'alternative comedy' is not easy. It is no coincidence that the legendary 'Comedy Store' club, which featured names such as Alexei Sayle, Ade Edmondson, Rik Mayall, Dawn French and Jennifer Saunders opened in London in 1979 (the same year that *Viz* began). Yet acts in a broadly similar vein can be traced to several years before: for example, the 'adult cabaret' troupe The Greatest Show on Legs, 'punk poet' John Cooper Clarke and comedian Johnny Rubbish were certainly performing contemporaneously with the height of punk (often on the same bill as bands).

3   Although *Viz* was clearly influenced by punk, there were very few identifiable 'punk comics' as such. The main reason for this was undoubtedly that alternative comics were still very much associated with the underground, and hence with the hippie movement. Thus, any punk comics that did emerge were an alternative to the alternative, and hence very marginalised. However, some creators did attempt a more spontaneous 'punk' approach to their strips, and this work can generally be located in the more progressive undergrounds, the avant-garde or in the small press. They included Andy 'Dog' Johnson (*Brainstorm*, *Art Attack*, *Black Meat*, *Nyak! Nyak!*), and Edwin 'Savage Pencil' Pouncey (*Knockabout*, *Escape*, *Nyak! Nyak!*, *Corpsemeat*). Savage Pencil additionally produced what is perhaps the most memorable graphic expression of punk in his strip 'Rock n' Roll Zoo', which appeared in *Sounds* between 1977 and 1979. In America, punk-influenced creators were a much more clearly-defined group (see p. 176).

4   There was one other important contributor in the early days—Jim Brownlow, a friend of Chris Donald's, who created 'Paul Whicker, the Tall Vicar'.

5   Simon Donald, quoted in Steve Dodd, 'The Viz Vision', the *Guardian* (29 November 1988).

6   Interview with Chris Donald, 3 November 1988.

7   This rehabilitation of *Carry On* humour was selective. Arguably, alternative comedy marked as much a 'year zero' in comedy as punk had in music. Political correctness was a keynote: the ideal was for comedy henceforward to be non-racist, non-sexist and non-heterosexist. Thus (supposedly) certain comedians were 'out' (Benny Hill, Bernard Manning), while others could be co-opted (Frankie Howerd). This echoed the way punk had 'rejected' certain bands (Genesis, Pink Floyd) and co-opted others (The Stooges, New York Dolls). In this context, the *Carry Ons* were only semi-acceptable, and hence the more ideologically unsound aspects of the original movies (notably their pervasive racism) were conveniently forgotten as their toilet humour and sense of camp were revived. An essential part of the process was the element of laughing as much at the humour as with it; it is always as much 'the idea' that a *double entendre* might be funny as the *double entendre* itself.

8   Interview with John Brown, 6 July 1989.

9   How far the years of Mrs Thatcher's government produced a 'cultural revolution' in the sense that Conservative free market ideology engendered a major change in values (usually characterised as meaning a spirit of ruthlessness,

brutality and philistinism) is discussed in Robert Skidelsky (ed.), *Thatcherism* (London: Chatto & Windus 1988).

10 The feminist response to these characters, and to *Viz* generally, has not been unified. Most commentators reject the comic as 'misogynist', yet 'The Fat Slags' have been hailed as 'assertive women with healthy sexual appetites' and embraced (along with Millie Tant) as positive symbols by some feminist groups, appearing regularly on banners at marches. Even the 'Women's Page' of the *Guardian*, often perceived as a barometer of feminist thought, has been complimentary (see, for example, Helen Oldfield, 'Comic Strippers', the *Guardian* (7 November 1989).

11 *Viz* reached a nadir in 1990 with the racist strip 'Those Thieving Gypsy Bastards', for which the editors had to apologise in a subsequent issue (*Viz*, 44 (October 1990)).

12 The only real parallel to *Viz*'s phenomenal rise in adult comics history in terms of sales is the story of *Mad* in America in the 1950s (see pp. 154–5, 166).

13 With the profits made from *Viz*, John Brown Publishing went on to put out several other adult comics (notably *Blast!*, *Point Blank* and the graphic novel *Russell: the Saga of a Peaceful Man*). After they failed, Brown withdrew completely from comics publishing apart from *Viz*, and has vowed never to return. The episode served to reinforce the fact that the public were not interested in 'adult comics': they were interested in *Viz* (interview with John Brown, 15 January 1992).

14 *Viz* had a significant impact on one other area of small-scale publishing – football fanzines. The 'soccer-zine' explosion occurred contemporaneously with *Viz*'s peak period, and many included strips inspired by it.

9 The future

1 Interview with Dominic Wells, editor, *Time Out* magazine, 8 May 1992.
2 Interview with Art Spiegelman, 1 November 1989.
3 Stuart Green, editorial, *Blast!*, 7 (December 1991).

10 Strips and proto-comics

1 Although there is no doubt that immigrant populations were a target readership, whether proficiency in English was a prerequisite to understanding the strips is a debatable point. Certainly, many strips could be understood with little reference to the text; others, however, relied on a subtle play on words to make their point. (Indeed, many of the earliest strips actually used 'immigrant dialects' as a source of humour – examples include the Irish 'street-speak' of the 'Yellow Kid' and the mock German of 'The Katzenjammer Kids'.)

2 The fact that 'The Katzenjammer Kids' was a version of an earlier German strip entitled 'Max und Moritz' by Wilhelm Busch, is perhaps the most compelling evidence that claims made by some historians for the medium as an 'American invention' should be treated with a degree of caution.

3 It should be noted that Britain did not get newspaper strips until 1915 – and then only in black and white and three or four panels long.

4 Winsor McCay, newspaper interview, 1907, quoted in the introduction to idem, *Dreams of the Rarebit Fiend* (New York: Dover Publications 1973).

5 It is not without relevance, for example, that both strips have been reprinted in *Raw*.

6　Les Daniels, *Comix: A History of Comic Books in America* (New York: Bonanza Books 1971) p. 4.

7　See William H. Young Jr, 'The Serious Funnies: Adventure Comics During the Depression, 1929–38', *Journal of Popular Culture*, 3 no. 3 (Winter 1969), pp. 404–27.

8　As with British comics, defining a 'first' is inevitably contentious. Denis Gifford cites *Stuff and Nonsense* (1884) in his *The American Comic Book Catalogue: The Evolutionary Era, 1884–1939* (London: Mansell 1990).

9　Indeed, it has been suggested that some creators of the original characters moonlighted on the 'Dirty Comics' to make some extra money. This seems highly unlikely, however, bearing in mind the generally amateurish nature of the artwork.

10　Les Daniels, op. cit., p. 66.

11　Comic books for everyone

1　Al Feldstein, interviewed in the video *Comic Book Confidential* (Canada: Castle Hendring 1989).

2　It is interesting to note that throughout this entire period, no British comic made an impact in America, in contrast to significant (if restricted) reverse traffic. Obviously, the American industry was much more powerful, but this does indicate a level of cultural resistance.

3　Indeed it is true that the evolution of the comic from anthologies to genre titles mirrored that of the pulps, in the 1920s.

4　Umberto Eco has argued that the stripping of a comic of its political elements is an inevitable process under advanced capitalism – see 'The Myth of Superman', in idem, *The Role of the Reader* (London: Hutchinson 1981), pp. 107–25.

5　Children's Book Committee of the Child Study Association, 1943, quoted in M. Benton, *Horror Comics* (Dallas, Texas: Taylor Publishing 1991), p. 39.

6　*Senate Committee Report on the Effect of Crime Comic Books Upon Juvenile Deliquency*, 1950, quoted in ibid., p. 48.

7　In this period, the American army used the comics medium for instruction manuals distributed to the troops. They realised that it was an effective means of getting detailed information across in a comprehensible fashion (see p. 8). One creator particularly associated with this kind of work was Will Eisner.

8　Figures from Bernard Rosenberg and David Manning White (eds), *Mass Culture: The Popular Arts in America* (Glencoe, Ill.: The Free Press 1957), p. 187. Quoted in Patrick Parsons, 'Batman and his Audience', in R. Pearson and W. Uricchio (eds), *The Many Lives of the Batman* (London: BFI Publishing/ Routledge 1991), p. 69. There was also a significant demand among servicemen for the 'Dirty Comics' of the 1930s, which were reprinted in large numbers in this period.

9　Interview with Will Eisner, 26 May 1989.

10　Tangentially connected to the crime comics were westerns, which boomed at around the same time. They, too, were very violent and often dealt with similar subject-matter (who was Jesse James if not a criminal from another era?). Although there was some crossover of readership, they generally attracted a younger age-range, which is why they are not discussed here. For a general discussion see M. Benton, *The Comic Book in America* (Dallas, Texas: Taylor Publishing 1989), pp. 188–9.

11 The influence of Wertham on women's groups in particular is discussed in Les Daniels, *Comix: A History of Comic Books in America* (New York: Bonanza 1971), pp. 87–9.

12 Indeed, there was an early attempt by publishers to set up 'standards of decency' in comics. In 1948, Bill Gaines (EC), Leverett Gleason (Lev Gleason), Harold Moore (Famous Funnies) and Rae Herman (Orbit), along with a number of distributors, formed the Association of Comics Magazine Publishers (ACMP), and attempted to impose a code of ethics. However, the system failed because other publishers simply boycotted it. Nevertheless, the ACMP remains an important historical precursor to the 1954 Comics Code Authority.

13 Joe Simon (n.d.), quoted in Benton, *Comic Book*, op. cit., p. 43.

14 Figures from ibid., p. 43.

15 One group did complain about the war comics – the American Communist Party. The Communist *Daily Worker* (n.d.) accused them of 'providing cannon-fodder for Korea'. Reported in Dwight R. Decker, 'Doc's Bookshelf: Bill Gaines was Right!', *Amazing Heroes*, 153 (November 1988), p. 55.

16 William Savage, *Comic Books and America 1945–1954* (Oklahoma: University of Oklahoma Press 1990), p. 81.

17 In the same way that westerns were connected with crime comics, so too science fiction titles were associated with horror. However, they were never as commercially successful as horror, and generally appealed to a younger age-range (which is why they are not explored here). The exception to this was the EC SF line, headed by *Weird Science* and *Weird Fantasy*, which did contain adult elements, and which were notable for adapting stories by SF author Ray Bradbury. On SF comics generally, see Benton, *Comic Book*, op. cit., pp. 171–4. On the EC line, see Thomas Inge, *Comics as Culture* (Jackson, Mississippi: University of Mississippi Press 1990), chapter 10, 'The EC Comic Books and Science Fiction', pp. 117–30.

18 *Mad*'s humour tended to be very parochial, and therefore the British versions were heavily Anglicised. (Indeed, it could be argued that the humour was not just particular to America but to New York, and in some cases even to Madison Avenue.)

19 The one character that it was perhaps not wise for *Mad* to attack was Archie (who they parodied as 'Starchie'). This was because the publisher of *Archie*, John Goldwater, would later become the head of the Comics Code Authority.

20 Technically speaking, the 'fetish comics' were not illegal. This was because, unlike the 'Dirty Comics' of the 1930s, the characters appeared clothed – albeit often in leather or rubber – and therefore the comics could not be classified as obscene. However, because of their nature, they were rarely sold 'above the counter'.

21 How far the fetish comics had an influence on the mainstream is debatable. Certainly some mainstream comics were incorporating fetishistic elements long before they came into vogue. Recent critiques of *Wonderwoman*, for example, have highlighted stories involving bondage, fights between women and the symbolic significance of the character's lassoo.

12   1954 – seduction of the experienced?

1   Fredric Wertham, *Seduction of the Innocent* (New York: Rinehart 1954; London: Museum Press 1955), pp. 212–14.

2   Will Gaines, quoted from an un-named early 1950s fanzine in M. Benton, *Horror Comics* (Dallas, Texas: Taylor Publishing 1991), p. 36.

3   William Savage, *Comic Books and America 1945–1954* (Oklahoma: University of Oklahoma Press 1990), pp. 102–3.

4   It was true that some of the psychiatrists who opposed Wertham had acted on occasion as paid advisers to comics publishers. Whether this compromised their position is debatable.

5   Wertham, op. cit., p. 348.

6   Contrary to common belief Wertham's political orientation was in fact liberal. He is often painted as a puritan, even a fascist, but in his earlier life he had campaigned against the abortion laws and for freedom of speech. He was a supporter of Civil Rights and opened the first psychiatric clinic in Harlem (charging less than the going rate because the locals were poor). Thus, in one sense, his opposition to blanket censorship was in keeping with his overall political philosophy.

7   *Hearings Before the Subcommittee to Investigate Juvenile Delinquency of the Committee on the Judiciary, US Senate, 83rd Congress, 2nd Session, 1954* (Washington, US Govt Printing Office 1954) p. 290.

8   This last story, entitled 'The Orphan', has been shown by historian Martin Barker to have been the most rigorously attacked strip in the whole hearings: yet, once again, it contained no overt violence at all (see M. Barker, *A Haunt of Fears: The Strange History of the British Horror Comics Campaign* (London: Pluto Press 1984), pp. 91–111). Note: in Britain, the strip appeared as a reprint in *Haunt of Fear*, no. 1 (Arnold Book Company 1954).

9   The government threat was not explicit, but the fact that Wertham had been summoned, and the general publicity around the campaign, convinced publishers that legislation was on the way. Indeed, some states and town councils had already enacted laws (see p. 154). Senator Hendrickson closed proceedings with the words 'any action on the parts of distributors, wholesalers or dealers with reference to these materials which will tend to eliminate [them] from production and sale shall receive the acclaim of myself and my colleagues. A competent job of self-policing will achieve much'. *Hearings*, op. cit., p. 310.

10   It was no coincidence that the words 'horror', 'terror' and 'weird' were banned by the Code from appearing on comics – 'All the words that appeared on the cover of my comics, in fact', as Gaines later reminisced. (Interviewed in the video, *Comic Book Confidential* (Canada: Castle Hendring 1989).)

11   Les Daniels, *Comix: A History of Comic Books in America* (New York: Bonanza Books 1971), p. 84.

13   The years of collapse: survivors and adaptors

1   Interview with Archie Goodwin, 8 September 1989.

2   The story of EC in the immediate post-Code period is convoluted. The company tried to rally with comics that were as sophisticated as before but which conformed to the Code. Their new line, dubbed the 'New Direction', included titles such as *Aces High* and *Impact* (which contained the celebrated strip by Bernard

Krigstein 'The Master Race'). However, they failed to garner the same popularity as their predecessors, and were quickly axed. EC also tried illustrated text magazines, which they called 'Picto-Fiction' – *Shock Illustrated*, *Crime Illustrated*, etc. These also failed. Eventually the company was reduced to one magazine, which, thankfully, was a success – *Mad*.

3   Figures from Patrick Parsons, 'Batman and his Audience', in R. Pearson and W. Uricchio (eds), *The Many Lives of the Batman* (London: BFI Publishing/ Routledge 1991), p. 72.

4   David Kunzle, introduction to the 1991 edition of A. Dorfman and A. Mattelart, *How to Read Donald Duck* (New York: International General).

5   TV tie-ins and film tie-ins peaked between the years 1953–69. In the 1960s, this trend encompassed programmes like *Mission Impossible* and *Man From Uncle*, plus movies like *Those Magnificent Men in Their Flying Machines* and *Zulu*.

6   In one sense it was certainly true that Stan Lee was 'doing his own thing', and stepping aside from the constant treadmill of copying other publishing initiatives. On the other hand, DC had just released *The Justice League of America*, and there can be little doubt that Lee was also influenced by this.

7   In 1965, *Esquire* magazine ran an article entitled 'Spider-Man on Campus', which claimed the character was as popular among student radicals as Che Guevara (reported in Les Daniels, *Comix: A History of Comic Books in America* (New York: Bonanza 1971), p. 139).

8   See Donald Palumbo, 'The Marvel Comic Group's Spider-Man as an Existentialist Superhero; or "Life has no Meaning Without my Latest Marvels"', *Journal of Popular Culture*, 17 no. 2 (Autumn 1983).

9   M. Benton, *Horror Comics* (Dallas, Texas: Taylor Publishing 1991), p. 123.

10 Kurtzman has stated that the *Mad* offices received a 'threatening letter' from Washington at the time of the controversy (quoted in William F. Ryan, 'H. Kurtz: Still Laughing in the Jungle', *Amazing Heroes*, 178 (April 1990), p. 41. Unfortunately, it has not been possible to obtain further information about this.

11 Harvey Kurtzman, interviewed in G. Groth and R. Fiore (eds), *The New Comics* (New York: Berkley Books 1988), p. 36.

12 Kurtzman continued in the vein of producing strips for an adult readership with his 'Little Annie Fanny' (a pun on Little Orphan Annie) co-created by Will Elder, about a big-busted *ingénue* forever losing her clothes, which appeared in *Playboy* from 1962 to 1985.

13 Interview with Archie Goodwin, 3 April 1992.

14 Whether *Blazing Combat* was actually 'killed' by the distributors is debatable. According to Archie Goodwin, it was only banned on army bases, and publisher James Warren would have axed it regardless due to unimpressive sales (interview with Archie Goodwin, 3 April 1992).

14   The modern era

1   Tom De Falco, quoted in Les Daniels, *Marvel: Five Fabulous Decades of the World's Greatest Comics* (London: Virgin 1991), p. 59.

2   Gary Groth, 'Creator's Rights: The Latest Panacea', the *Comics Journal*, 87 (December 1983), p. 8.

3   This terminology was officially taken up in 1967 when the Underground Press

Syndicate (UPS) was founded, of which comic strips were considered an integral part.

4   Mark Estren, *A History of Underground Comics* (San Francisco, Calif.: Straight Arrow, rev. edn 1987), p. 7.

5   Bill Griffith, interviewed in *Cascade Comix Monthly*, 5 (July 1978).

6   On the various court cases, see Estren, op. cit., chapter 10, 'Suppression', pp. 230–41.

7   The small press is sometimes referred to in America as 'mini-comics' (so-called because they are of a size to fit into envelopes for postal sale) or, more rarely, as 'new wave comics'. Historians disagree about when to date their origin: Jay Kennedy, in *The Official Underground and Newave Comix Price Guide* (Cambridge, Mass.: Boatner Norton Press 1982), pp. 14–15, claims they emerged before the ground levels.

8   Mikal Gilmore, 'Daredevil Authors: Today's Real Superheroes', *Rolling Stone* (17 May 1990), p. 62.

9   Interview with Alan Grant, 15 May 1992.

10 Jon Savage in *England's Dreaming* (London: Faber 1991), identifies the origins of the term punk in an American fanzine, *Punk*, put out by cartoonist John Holstrom. Holstrom later joined with Peter Bagge and others to produce *Comical Funnies* – a notable early punk comic. It might also be noted that Gary Panter's strip 'Jimbo' first appeared in the punk fanzine *Slash*.

11 Peter Bagge, interviewed by Martin Skidmore, *FA*, 110 (March 1989), p. 33. (Certain members of the old underground including S. Clay Wilson even went so far as to produce a comic satirising the work of Gary Panter.)

12 Harvey Pekar, quoted in Judith O'Sullivan, *The Great American Comic Strip* (Boston, Mass.: Bulfinch Press 1990), p. 182.

13 There is even evidence that in some cases Marvel and DC have been prepared to keep product in the bookshops even if it makes a loss. This is because it is good 'advertising' for their other licensed products. The independent companies are invariably unable to do this, and so have been more prone to disengage from the bookshop market: Eclipse, for example, have recently withdrawn from Waldenbooks.

14 DC have denied that the labelling policy was a result of right-wing pressure; however, the timing of the decision certainly suggests otherwise. For their side of the story, see Dick Giordano interviewed by Gary Groth, 'Newswatch', *Comics Journal*, 117 (September 1987), pp. 11–12. The ratings system is still fairly arbitrary. Marvel, DC and most independents use it for sexual themes, religious themes and certain kinds of violence, and also if the content is thought to 'go over the head of' a child. For higher-priced albums, the rating is sometimes left off altogether because the price is deemed to be enough to put a child off. Other publishers use an 'Adults Only' label for explicit sex and violence.

15   Worldcomics

1   Paul Gravett, speaking at a press briefing for the Angoulême Festival 1990 (London, 7 December 1989).

2   This relationship with first world comics does not conform to what we might expect from the origins of the term 'worldcomics', which has an antecedent in

the phrase 'world music', used to describe contemporary music primarily from developing countries.

3   Hergé's alleged fascist allegiances are a hotly debated point. His defenders point to the fact that Casterman were a Catholic publisher which leant politically to the right, and say he was no more or less right-wing than any of his colleagues and was consequently 'just doing his job'. They also point to what is seen as the over-eagerness of the Belgian Resistance after the war to persecute anybody they suspected of collaboration. Hergé's attackers point to the fact that many of his colleagues in fact resigned on principle when the Germans arrived, and that he produced not just one but several stories that indicate that he was more ideologically sympathetic to fascism than simply following the easiest path (including the aforementioned *Land of the Soviets*, plus the very racist *Tintin in the Congo* and *The Shooting Star*, in which the villain was Jewish). The controversy shows no sign of abating: Hergé's estate are currently in the process of suing a Belgian magazine for defamation (as reported in the *Comics Journal*, 148 (February 1992), p. 25).

4   An interesting aside to this point is that in Belgium, because *Tintin* was published by a Catholic publisher, there was felt to be a moral obligation to be scrupulous about creators' rights. Casterman thus set the tone in this regard, which other publishers then followed.

5   It should be noted that, in Britain, *Tintin* has never made a similar crossover to an adult readership. Although the character has a cult adult following (there is a Tintin shop selling memorabilia in London's Covent Garden), he is generally considered to be for children, and albums tend to be stocked in the children's sections of bookshops and libraries. (The same might equally be said of *Asterix*.) The only time Tintin has appeared in an adult comic in Britain was in 1988 in a 'bootleg' graphic novel produced by an anarchist group which recast him as a syndicalist revolutionary: the character's political reorientation was doubly amusing bearing in mind Hergé's (alleged) right-wing politics.

6   To a degree this trend had already begun during the war years due to the German occupation and consequent banning of imports from America. Nevertheless, American comics flooded back in from 1944 onwards. After 1949, this isolationism from American material was not necessarily duplicated in other parts of Europe. In Germany, for example, American comics were common, with original material often entering the country post-1945 via the military bases there. (For this reason, the horror comics scare in the 1950s was felt more keenly in some areas of Europe than in others.)

7   The film was also a box-office hit in Britain and the USA, and thus introduced audiences there to the character, the strip not being well-known.

8   Although sexual permissiveness was more advanced in comics in Europe, it is arguable that in terms of pictorial narrative as a whole things were more liberal. Indeed, in Britain, newspaper strips had a long history of being relatively far more explicit ('Jane' in the *Daily Mirror* being a prime example).

9   For more on this swathe of new 'erotic' characters, see Maurice Horn, *Sex in the Comics* (New York: Chelsea House 1985), pp. 94–209.

10   Indeed, underground creators had an enduring appeal in Europe, while they went out of fashion in Britain and the USA. It is no coincidence, for example,

that in recent years both Gilbert Shelton and Robert Crumb have emigrated to France.

11 *Pilote* itself went through a period of mutation after 1968. We have seen how more adult strips, like 'Cellulite', were added as time went on. This trend was consolidated in 1973 by the appearance of 'The Detour', a revolutionary strip by Moebius that was heavily drug-influenced. Eventually, the stresses of trying to cater to different audiences, and of attempting to be radical but at the same time mainstream, expressed themselves in an ugly dispute between creators and management. This resulted in several resignations, and the subsequent founding of *L'Écho des savanes* and *Métal Hurlant* (see pp. 191–2).

12 It is often assumed that Giraud took the 'Moebius' pseudonym specifically for his work in *Métal Hurlant*. In fact, he first used it in 1973 in *Pilote*, for the strip 'The Detour' (he also used the name for his work in *Hara Kiri*). Although Giraud himself has spoken of the name as being symbolic of his *alter ego* when creating SF (his drawing style is quite different to that used for 'Blueberry'), he has therefore used it for other kinds of subject-matter. It would also be wrong to see it as simply a way of denoting when he both writes and draws a strip: after the death of Jean Michel Charlier in 1990, Giraud continued with 'Blueberry' on his own, continuing to sign his work 'Gir'.

13 Which is not to say there was no underground in Europe. Perhaps the best-known groups were Valvoline in Italy and Bazooka in France. The Valvoline group included Igort, Mattotti, Daniel Broli, Giogio Carpenteri and, for a while, the American, Charles Burns. In the early 1980s, it produced autonomous sections in anthology comics and magazines, which would be edited by the group. Their work appeared in, among others, *Alter Alter* and *Frigidaire*, and they were eventually given their own magazine *Dolce Vita*. The Bazooka group was a gathering of ex-fine art students, based in Paris in the mid-1970s. They sold their work to various comics magazines, and also to the newspaper *Libération*, which published a supplement by them. The best-known Bazooka creators went by the pseudonyms 'Kiki Picasso' and 'Lulu Picasso'. This French tradition has been taken up in the 1990s by the comic *Psykopat*.

14 Interview with Jean Giraud, 15 May 1989.

15 ibid.

16 Gary Groth, editorial, 'Paradise Lost', the *Comics Journal*, 96 (March 1985), p. 6. This is a personal view of European comics, and contains many insightful points.

17 Principally because Angoulême did become such an adult-orientated event, a new annual convention was established in Grenoble in 1990 with the aim of catering more for children.

18 Jack Lang, French Minister of Culture, speaking at the opening of the CNBDI, 23 January 1990.

19 The issue of whether the French adult comics industry is in decline is a complex one. Certainly the magazine-type anthologies have been seeing increasingly hard times. Indeed, many of the pioneering titles have recently closed down – including *Pilote* and *Métal Hurlant*. (*L'Écho des savanes* is today more of a soft-porn magazine than a comic.) However, against this, album sales have continued to be strong, with some sections claiming growth (this has been especially true of the new 'pocket-edition' albums, which have proved particularly well

suited to humour strips, and which sell in large quantities in railway kiosks). Indeed, the *Bookseller* reported a Ministry of Culture study to the effect that albums were the fastest-growing category of books sold, with an annual growth rate of 25 per cent in turnover and 29.7 per cent in units sold (Vivienne Merkes, 'Cartoon Growth in France', *Bookseller* (31 March 1989)).

20   In Spain a tiny number of adult comics existed before this date, though they were 'underground' in the true sense, and creators could be imprisoned for subversive comment. Also it should be noted that some creators in mainstream comics attempted to incorporate anti-establishment views in their work (see Horn, op. cit., pp. 83–9).

21   As reported in the *Comics Journal*, 125 (October 1988), p. 31. In the end, in the face of such hostility, Glenat did not go through with their plans.

22   Interview with Thierry Groensteen, 28 January 1989.

23   The word 'manga' is believed to have been coined by woodblock artist Hokusai Katsushika in 1814 to describe his 'irresponsible pictures' – topical prints that were often erotic and humorous in tone.

24   Frederik Schodt, *Manga! Manga!: The World of Japanese Comics* (New York: Kodansha International, rev. edn 1988), p. 87.

25   *Lone Wolf and Cub* has undoubtedly been the most influential Japanese comic in the west. In comics, Frank Miller paid homage in his *Ronin*, while in the world of film, directors John Milius and John Carpenter have cited it as an influence.

26   See, Kenneth A. Skinner, 'Salaryman Comics in Japan–Images of Self-Perception', *Journal of Popular Culture*, 13 no. 1 (summer 1979), pp. 141–60.

27   Shotaro Ishinomori, interviewed in 'The Day Comics Grew Up!', *Signals*, Channel 4 (18 January 1989).

28   Keiji Nakazawa, quoted in the introduction to *Barefoot Gen* (Harmondsworth: Penguin 1989).

29   Animation, or 'anime' as it is known, plays a more important role in film and television in Japan than anywhere else in the world. Like manga, the medium has never been stereotyped as exclusively juvenile. The father of anime was the 'God of Comics' himself Ozamu Tezuka, who always intended that the medium deal with adult concerns (his *Hi No Tori* cycle examines the concept of the soul and individual responsibility). Since Tezuka, the industry has grown to incorporate all the themes of manga from sex to cookery. *Akira* is the best-known feature length movie in the west, but there are countless others: manga creators who have become especially associated with anime include Rumiko Takahashi, Go Nagai and Shiro Masamune.

30   The main legal barrier to this kind of subject-matter is Article 175 of the Penal Code. There is one loophole, however: children's genitals are allowed to be shown. This has led to a thriving industry in child pornography, or 'Lolita comics' as they are known. In the 1990s, a protest lobby has emerged, and there is now a possibility of new laws being passed.

31   A Japanese underground exists that recognises no artistic constraints and is sexually explicit. Indeed, such comics, though marginalised in similar fashion to those in the west, can still sell in excess of 50,000 copies an issue.

32   This reversal of Wertham's hypothesis is debatable. Indeed, in the 1980s and 1990s, crime figures in Japan have risen alarmingly.

33 See, 'Censorship Update – Crackdown in Japan', *Comics Journal*, 143 (April 1991), p. 15.

34 Yoshiya Soeda, quoted in Darnan Darling, 'Grown Men in Japan Still Read Comics and Have Fantasies', *Wall Street Journal* (21 July 1987), p. 1.

35 Of course not every creator reaches such heights. In Tokyo alone there are estimated to be thousands who work ludicrously long hours on obscure titles. The pay is usually satisfactory, but the pressure is not, and the suicide rate is high.

36 The 'Japan Festival 1991', a multi-million pound arts exposition intended to give the British public an idea of the breadth of Japanese culture, astonishingly did not include an exhibition of manga because funding could not be found. Instead, the festival featured theatre, cinema and other media which mirrored the interests of the west, and confirmed images of Japan, rather than showing what the Japanese public were really interested in as cultural consumers. In response, a 'pirate' manga exhibition was successfully staged at the Pomeroy Purdey Gallery in London (Oct.–Nov. 1991), featuring the work of Ozamu Tezuka, Keiko Takemiya, Suehiro Maruo, Mitsuhiko Yoshida and others.

37 Ozamu Tezuka, quoted in Paul Gravett, 'In the Age of Comics as Air', in K. Tsuzuki and A. Birnbaum (eds), *Manga – Comic Strip Books From Japan* (London: Saunders & Williams 1991), p. 8.

16   Adult comics and other media

1 Howard Chaykin, interviewed by Jami Bernard, *New York Post*, quoted in W. Schoell, *Comic Book Heroes of the Screen* (London: Plexus 1991), pp. 209–11.

2 Peter Bailey, 'Ally Sloper's Half Holiday: Comic Art in the 1880s', *History Workshop*, 16 (1983), p. 5.

3 British audiences often became aware of American strip and comics characters through other media – notably on film and TV (examples include Flash Gordon, Dick Tracy and Prince Valiant).

4 The American children's entertainment industry developed in a subtly different manner to its British counterpart. Because American culture was never so strictly demarcated between children and adults, a system of 'dual address' evolved whereby both audiences would be targeted simultaneously. This was especially true in television – classic examples include the cartoons *The Flintstones* and *Bugs Bunny* and the live-action *Batman*, though it was also common in film: Walt Disney, for example, disliked being referred to as a 'children's animator' and made *Fantasia* expressly as dual address.

5 David Kunzle, introduction to A. Dorfman and A. Mattelart, *How to Read Donald Duck* (New York: International General, rev. edn 1991), p. 18.

6 Hunt Emerson was about as prolific in poster art, etc. as he was in comics. However, undoubtedly the greatest British psychedelic poster artist of the period was Martin Sharp, who also produced work for the alternative press and *Cyclops*. He was not primarily considered a comics creator, however.

7 Ralph Bakshi, interviewed by Ed Naha for 'A Comic Book Comes "Alive"', *Comics Scene*, 9 (May 1983), p. 32.

8 This move to copyrighting material is chronicled in Mark Estren, *Underground Comics* (San Francisco, Calif.: Straight Arrow rev. edn 1987). Crumb had not copyrighted 'Fritz the Cat' and could do nothing about it retrospectively. In a

BBC documentary he recalled: 'The movie was really horrible. [Afterwards] I tried to kill off the character by having his jilted girlfriend stab him with an icepick. Then they made *The Nine Lives of Fritz the Cat* . . . . Sometimes you can't win.' (*Arena* BBC 2 (June 1987).)

9   Interview with Denis Kitchen, 28 May 1992. (In 1971 Kitchen had been one of the founder members, along with Crumb, Spain, Spiegelman and others, of one of the best-known of these 'unions', the 'United Cartoon Workers of America'.)

10   Interview with Dez Skinn, 13 February 1991.

11   The first stage in the production of any live-action movie is the construction of a 'storyboard', showing in sequential panel illustrations the progress of the plot. (The storyboard is not a 'comic strip', however, because the two forms have different functions; and the former does not require the merging of text and image to be a priority.)

12   *Blade Runner* and *The Empire Strikes Back* used Moebius' work in an 'unofficial' capacity (and are considered to be 'homages' by Moebius's publisher). *Heavy Metal*, on the other hand, directly adapted Moebius's stories without permission. Moebius has continued to be very in demand for movies, and has recently worked on *Willow* and *The Abyss*.

13   The movie was followed by *Return of Swamp Thing* (1990), which was closer to the Moore version, and in America by a cable TV series.

14   Howard Chaykin, quoted in Schoell, op. cit.

15   One reason graphics became important to the new dance culture was because 'raves' were often organised at short notice at illegal venues (typically derelict warehouses). Thus, in order for the organisers to have any chance of making a profit, the event had to be publicised as efficiently and in as eye-catching a manner as possible. Therefore, the illustrated 'flyer' became ubiquitous as a means of communication.

16   How far the *Batman* movie was derived from *Dark Knight* is debatable. Certainly, the timing of the film was indicative of its intention to cash in on *Dark Knight*, and its generally grim tone was confirmation of this. However, elements in the film drew from other sources. The Joker origin story, for instance, owes much to the Alan Moore–Brian Bolland graphic novel *The Killing Joke*, which in turn drew from *Detective Comics* 168 (1951). Further, the official advisor on the movie was not Frank Miller, but Bob Kane, the character's original creator. It should be noted that in modifying the Miller version, Warners incurred the wrath of comics fans: in particular, the hiring of Tim Burton and Michael Keaton, both previously associated with comedy films, was met with sacks of hate mail.

17   *Comics Scene*, 25 (April 1992), pp. 68–9.

18   In the west, animation is considered a children's medium: in Japan, no such distinction has ever been made. See note 29, p. 285.

19   *The Simpsons* was screened in Britain on Rupert Murdoch's Sky TV satellite channel, and therefore was only seen by a tiny percentage of the population (at the time, only approximately one in eighteen homes had Sky satellite dishes). However, *The Simpsons* fame was established through video sales, merchandising, advertising and hit pop singles ('Do the Bartman' made number one in the charts in July 1990).

20   In a more avant-garde vein, *Liquid Television* (1991), originally commissioned

for MTV, mixed cartooning, puppetry and live-action. It included adaptations of work by Mark Beyer, Charles Burns and Richard Sala, among others.

21 A notable example of licensing in reverse occurred when Dark Horse Comics struck several deals with Hollywood movie companies (notably 20th Century Fox) to turn top films, such as *The Terminator*, *Predator* and *Aliens*, into ongoing comics. 'We wanted characters people don't get enough of', Dark Horse founder Mike Richardson told *Premiere* magazine, adding: 'we write our movie comics as if they're sequels – we don't live off what's already there' (*Premiere* (June 1992), p. 57). What is so clever about this arrangement is that it allows for the possibility that plots generated in the comics might then be used in future films.

22 One side-effect of this kind of tight control is a greater level of censorship. A good example is the Grant Morrison–Dave McKean Batman graphic novel *Arkham Asylum*, which was due for release just before the 1989 movie, but which because of its 'unsympathetic content' (it cast aspersions on Batman's sexuality, which was definitely not in keeping with the macho image of the film), had to be significantly modified.

17   Women and adult comics

1 Interview with Carol Bennett, 29 May 1990.

2 Interview with Trina Robbins, 19 March 1992.

3 This trend towards courting a female readership was prefigured in the Victorian satirical magazines – for example, *Judy* was designed as the 'female counterpart' to *Punch*.

4 See Martin Barker, *Comics: Ideology, Power and the Critics* (Manchester: Manchester University Press 1989), chapter 5, 'The Vicissitudes of Identification', where it is persuasively argued that in the case of the *Beano* and its ilk, girls identify with characters not as males or females, but as people.

5 This had a tradition going back to boys' papers and similar 'improving literature' of the Victorian and Edwardian ages.

6 Indeed, it seems that the comics industry was seen as such a 'closed shop' that women wishing to become involved in this kind of work tended instead to drift into book illustration (especially children's book illustration).

7 It should be noted that the history of women and comics in America is, as they say, another story. It involves the legacy of women and the pulps, and women in early newspaper strips, plus comic genres such as the 'working girl' titles of the 1940s. All these aspects are covered in Trina Robbins and Catherine Yronwode, *Women and the Comics* (Forestville, Calif.: Eclipse Books 1985).

8 See Carl Macek, 'Good Girl Art – An Introduction. Why It Was and What It Is', in Robert M. Overstreet, *The Comic Book Price Guide 1976–77* (Cleveland, TN: Overstreet Publications 1976). In some collecting circles, 'Good Girl Art' is particularly prized. Some collectors' price guides, for example, add to entries on comics the codes 'GGA' for 'Good Girl Art' and 'GGAB' for 'Good Girl Art with Bondage'.

9 See Robbins and Yronwode, op. cit., pp. 47–67.

10 Of central importance to this reassessment was Barker, op. cit., especially chapters 7–11.

11 Melinda Gebbie, speaking at the ICA (Institute for Contemporary Arts), London (9 December 1989).

12 Of these three, Crumb tended to be criticised the most because he was the most influential figure. Indeed, it has been argued that by example he set in motion a vogue for misogynist comix featuring violence against women. For his part, Crumb has said that his work became more extreme (in every sense) since he met S. Clay Wilson in San Francisco in 1968. Certainly, there is a marked change in his depiction of women from that date. Crumb also reacted indignantly to being labelled sexist, and in *Zap* 4 produced a notorious strip, 'A Note to You Feminist Women', in which he protested that it was every artist's right to express his or her true feelings on any subject, and that the feminist stance was analogous to fascism. Though his position has mellowed over the years, it is a dialogue that still persists. For a critical feminist view of Crumb's work see Trina Robbins, 'Comments on Crumb', *Blab!*, 3 (September 1988) (Kitchen Sink).

13 Which is not to say there was no overlap of goals. On the confused relationship between the underground press and feminism, see Elizabeth Nelson, *The British Counter-Culture 1966–73* (London: Macmillan 1989), pp. 138–9.

14 'Introduction', *Wimmins Comix*, no. 3 (1973) (Last Gasp).

15 Lynn Chively and Joyce Farmer, founders/editors of *Tits 'n' Clits*, in Jay Kennedy, *The Official Underground and Newave Comix Price Guide* (Cambridge, Mass.: Boatner Norton Press 1982), p. 28.

16 So far as the British authorities generally were concerned, men dealing with sex in comics was bad enough: women dealing with sex was beyond the pale. The worst example of censorship occurred in 1985, when Melinda Gebbie's solo comic *Frezca Zisis* was declared obscene by the courts and destroyed.

17 See Lynn Chively and Joyce Farmer, in Kennedy, op. cit. p. 29, where it is pointed out that the more extreme anti-male material can be traced to particular issues of specific comics, for example *Wimmins Comix*, no. 7, which had as its theme 'violence' (and featured a cover depicting a dead man surrounded by armed women).

18 Gebbie was particularly interesting for the way in which she reversed taboos and illustrated scenes of women inflicting violence upon men (she was responsible for the cover mentioned in note 17). She became known as 'the female S. Clay Wilson' – and perhaps the fact that the two were partners for a while has something to do with the similarities. However, it can be strongly argued that because the power relations in Gebbie's work are inverted, the two creators are not strictly comparable.

19 Interview with Suzy Varty, 1 March 1992.

20 Perhaps the two most well-known Halo Jones spin-offs were the theatre production *Halo Jones*, a surprise hit at the Edinburgh Fringe Festival in 1989 and the pop song 'Hanging Out with Halo Jones' by Transvision Vamp (on the album *Pop Art* (MCA 1988)).

21 A major attraction of fandom for many men was – and is – undoubtedly the fact that it offers the opportunity for an 'extended adolescence', whereby comics (especially superhero titles) can be enjoyed at an age far in excess of their intended target age-range. However, for women this kind of behaviour has never been as culturally acceptable. Instead the common pattern for women is to stop reading comics at around the age of 13, and then to move on to either

'teen' magazines or women's magazines. In other words, it could be argued that women are expected to 'grow up' much faster than men.

22 Interview with Trina Robbins, 19 March 1992.

23 Jaime Hernandez, interviewed in *Speakeasy* 84 (March 1988), p. 15.

24 Interview with Catherine Yronwode, 16 May 1990.

25 Interview with Myra Hancock, 7 November 1989.

26 For Pat Mills, 'Eve' was a conscious attempt to reach a female audience. As he explained at the time:

> 'I enjoy writing female characters, and for a female readership. To my mind, women do not see force as the answer to everything, and expect a little bit more from a comics plot-line. It makes you work harder, but in the end it's more rewarding'.
>
> (Interview, 29 September 1988)

27 Numerically speaking, by far the most popular comic among women in this period was *Viz* (see p. 121).

28 Interview with Frank Plowright, 10 September 1989.

29 Heather Kirby, 'Cult Comic Heroines Show Who's the Boss', *Sunday Express* (19 November 1989).

30 Two editors have told me, off the record, that PR was the priority in hiring women creators. In their opinions, this practice was repeated widely in the industry.

31 Howard Stangroom, '"Rape Chic" Comics' New Sexual Revolution' *FA*, 100 (March 1988), p. 30.

32 Knockabout reinforced their commitment to women's comics by co-staging an exhibition of artwork from *Seven Ages of Woman* at the Basement Gallery in London, and by creating an index of women creators – the 'Fanny File'.

33 Interview with Carol Bennett, 29 May 1990.

18 The graphic novel in context

1 Interview with Will Eisner, 26 May 1989.

2 Art Spiegelman 'Commix: An Idiosyncratic Historical and Aesthetic Overview', *Print* Magazine (New York: Nov.–Dec. 1988), p. 196.

3 Interview with Art Spiegelman, 1 November 1989.

4 A property of some graphic novels is therefore that they are best understood as part of a longer continuity. This gives them a greater sense of context, and enriches the reader's understanding of the individual parts.   ✓

5 There has been some debate over what length of narrative should constitute a graphic novel. Some commentators, for example, dislike using the term for forty-eight-page albums on the European model; this is no comparison, they say, to a 'proper novel' (or for that matter to something like the 200-page volumes in the *Cerebus* series). But this argument raises two questions. First, what is a 'novelistic length'? The short novel is an established literary form, and, historically, novels of less than 100 pages have been common. Second, there is the issue of pacing. For instance, a forty-eight page work might be very dense, and make considerable demands on the reader; on the other hand, a 1,000-page manga might be designed to be speed-read in a few minutes.

6 Outside the comics industry, there were other precedents. In a fine art context,

long graphic narratives in book form have existed since the 1920s, and can be traced to the revival of woodcut art in Europe. The pioneer of woodcut-storytelling, the Belgian Franz Masereel, produced several large-scale wordless novels ('romans in beelden'), including *Passionate Journey* (1922), *The Idea* (1924) and his acclaimed masterpiece *The City* (1925), about the soul-destroying effects of alienation in a European metropolis. Intended for an adult audience, they were expressionist and highly political, dealing with themes of alienation and urban chaos, typically with heroes who by force of will transcend their environment.

There were several other European artists working in the medium in the same period, but Masereel was the undisputed king. His work was known all over the continent, and his fans included Stefan Zweig, Hermann Hesse and Thomas Mann. When his reputation spread to America, it inspired a similar woodcut boom there. The best-known American creator was Lynd Ward, who produced more linear narratives than the Europeans, again for an adult audience. His acclaimed *God's Man* (1935), subtitled 'a novel in woodcuts', concerned an impoverished artist's Faustian deal with the Devil. (Will Eisner was later to acknowledge his debt to Ward, and to this work in particular.)

Whether any of these early fine art publications can strictly be called 'comics' is a subject for debate. Certainly they did not originate from the same creative source as most comics, and were not intended for a mass-market. Yet, when they have been republished, they are invariably treated as comics, and reviewed as such, by the fan press.

7   Names that might also have been added to this list, but for space, include: Eddie Campbell (*Deadface*, *Alec*); Jack Jackson (*Comanche Moon*, *Los Tejanos*); Wendy Pini (*Elfquest*); Gilbert Hernandez (*Heartbreak Soup*, *Human Diastrophism*) and Jamie Hernandez (*Mechanics*, *Ape Sex*).

8   In America, *Contract* was distributed to mainstream bookshops; in Britain distribution was more patchy, and it tended to be sold from specialist outlets.

9   Interview with Will Eisner, 26 May 1989.

10   Interview with Dave Sim, 3 April 1992.

11   Interview with Bryan Talbot, 13 September 1990.

12   Interview with Art Spiegelman, 1 November 1989.

13   In fact the first mini-series was introduced by DC in 1979, entitled *World of Krypton*.

14   Michael Moorcock, introduction to Howard Chaykin, *American Flagg! Hard Times* (Illinois: First 1985).

15   Although Howard Chaykin's *Empire* (Byron Preiss, 1978) was an important early graphic novel (and was distributed both to fan shops and some mainstream bookshops), the first graphic novel to be published specifically for direct sales is generally agreed to have been *Sabre* by Don McGregor and Paul Gulacy (Eclipse, 1978). The first British-originated graphic novel also appeared in 1978, *The Jewel in the Skull*, an adaptation of a Michael Moorcock story published by Savoy. Significantly, all three titles emerged out of the vogue for adult SF comics that followed in the wake of the underground (see pp. 70–74).

16   Robet Fiore, 'Comics for Beginners', in Gary Groth and Robert Fiore (eds), *The New Comics* (New York: Berkley Books 1988), p. 5.

17 Chris McCubbin and Thomas Power, 'Graphic Novel Explosion in '88', *Comics Journal* 121 (April 1985), p. 6.

18 Naturally, different academic courses approach graphic novels in different ways. They have been adopted as a subject on courses including cultural studies, languages (especially French and Japanese), English literature and media studies. The case for including graphic novels on English literature syllabuses is persuasively argued by Paul Dawson in 'Coming to terms with the Graphic Novel', in the brochure to the 'Strip Search' exhibition (Camden Arts, 1990), pp. 5–7.

19 Dawson, ibid., p. 5.

20 'The Hated 100' *Time Out* (12 November 1991).

Bibliography

It is not surprising, bearing in mind the low cultural status of comics over the years, that there has been very little produced in the way of serious critical comment or of scholarly research. Most of the secondary sources that exist have been produced by fans, and are intended to be celebratory rather than analytical (which is not to say by any means that they are without worth).

Because adult comics have historically been only a small proportion of all comics produced, this lack is even more pronounced. Nevertheless, since the boom of 1986, and particularly due to the growing interest of sections of academia, more serious works are beginning to appear – as the list below shows.

It goes without saying that for the reader who is relatively unfamiliar with comics, further reading should commence with the comics themselves, and particularly with the creators and works mentioned in the text. For the first time this is possible without recourse to primary sources, since most have been reprinted post-1986 in readily available volume form.

For those who do wish to consult primary sources, there are problems owing to the reluctance of most archives to stock comics. The best open access collections are the Rakoff Collection at the Victoria and Albert Museum (mostly American comics – currently being catalogued) and the British Newspaper Library collection at Colindale (exclusively British comics).

So far as the following secondary sources are concerned, it should be noted that some are out of print, and only available from specialist shops or libraries:

English language

Adams, J. P. (1946) *Milton Caniff: Rembrandt of the Comic Strip*, New York: David McKay.
Bails, J. and Ware, J. (1973) *The Who's Who of American Comic Books*, Detroit, Mich.: Simpson.

Baker, S. (1992) *Picturing the Beast*, Manchester: Manchester University Press.

Barker, M. (1984) *A Haunt of Fears: The Strange History of the British Horror Comics Campaign*, London: Pluto Press.

— (1989) *Comics: Ideology, Power and the Critics*, Manchester: Manchester University Press.

— (1990) *Action: The Story of a Violent Comic*, London: Titan Books.

Barrier, M. (1981) *Carl Barks and the Art of the Comic Book*, New York: M. Lilien.

Barrier, M. and Williams, M. (1981) *A Smithsonian Book of Comic-Book Comics*, Washington DC: Smithsonian Institution Press/Harry N. Abrams Inc.

Baxendale, L. (1978) *A Very Funny Business*, London: Duckworth.

— (1989) *On Comedy*, Stroud: Reaper Books.

Becker, S. (1949) *Comic Art in America*, New York: Simon & Schuster.

Bell, J. (ed.) (1986) *Canuck Comics*, Montreal: Matrix Books.

Benton, M. (1989) *The Comic Book in America*, Dallas, Texas: Taylor Publishing.

— (1991a) *Horror Comics*, Dallas, Texas: Taylor Publishing.

— (1991b) *Superhero Comics of the Silver Age*, Dallas, Texas: Taylor Publishing.

— (1992) *Superhero Comics of the Golden Age*, Dallas, Texas: Taylor Publishing.

— (1992) *Science Fiction Comics*, Dallas, Texas: Taylor Publishing.

— (forthcoming 1993) *Crime and Detective Comics*, Dallas: Texas: Taylor Publishing.

Berger, A. A. (1970), *Li'l Abner: A Study in American Satire*, New York: Twayne Publishers.

— (1973a) *The Comic-Stripped American*, New York: Walker & Co.

— (1973b) *Pop Culture*, New York. Pflaum/Standard.

Blackbeard, B. and Williams, M. (1988) *The Smithsonian Collection of Newspaper Comics*, Washington DC: Smithsonian Institute.

Bloom, C. (forthcoming 1993) *Dark Knights*, London: Pluto.

Canemaker, J. (1981) *Winsor McCay*, Berkeley, Calif: University of California Press.

Carlin, J. and Wagstaff, S. (eds) (1983) *The Comic Art Show: Cartoons in Painting and Popular Culture*, New York: Fantagraphics Books.

Carpenter, K. (ed.) (1983) *Penny Dreadfuls and Comics*, London: Victoria and Albert Museum.

Cawelti, J. (1976) *Adventure, Mystery and Romance*, Chicago, Ill.: University of Chicago Press.

Clark, A. and Ashford, D. (1983) *The Comic Art of Roy Wilson*, London: Midas.

— (1986) *The Comic Art of Reg Parlett*, London: Golden Fun.

Clark, A. and Clark, L. (1991) *Comics: an Illustrated History*, London: Greenwood.

Clarke, P. and Higgs, M. (1991) *Nostalgia About Comics*, Birmingham: Pegasus Publishing.

Coad, E. D. (1991) *Javier Mariscal: Designing the New Spain*, London: Fourth Estate.

Couperie, P., Horn, M., Destefanis, P., François, E., Moliterni, C. and Gassiot-Talabot, G. (1968) *A History of the Comic Strip*, New York: Crown.

Craven, T. (1943) *Cartoon Cavalcade*, New York: Simon & Schuster.

Crawford, H. H. (1978) *Encyclopedia of Comic Books*, New York: Simpson.

Crompton, A. (1985) *The Man who Drew Tomorrow: Frank Hampson*, Bournemouth: Who Dares Publishing.

Cutler, D., Plowright, F., Snowdon, A., Whitaker, S. and Yusuf, H. (1981) *Two Decades of Comics: A Review*, London: Slings & Arrows.

Daniels, L. (1971) *Comix: A History of Comic Books in America*, New York: Bonanza Books.

— (1977) *Fear: A History of Horror in the Mass Media*, London: Paladin.

— (1991) *Marvel: Five Fabulous Decades of the World's Greatest Comics*, London: Virgin.

Davidson, S. (1976), *The Penguin Book of Political Comics*, (rev. edn 1982), Harmondsworth: Penguin.

De Laet, D. and Varende, Y. (1979) *Beyond the Seventh Art*, Brussels: Ministry of Foreign Affairs.

Dorfman, A. (1983) *The Emperor's Old Clothes*, London: Pluto Press.

Dorfman, A. and Mattelart, A. (1975) *How to Read Donald Duck* (rev. edn 1991 with introduction by David Kunzle), New York: International General.

Drotner, K. (1988) *English Children and Their Magazines 1751–1945*, New Haven, Con.: Yale University Press.

Eco, U. (1981) *The Role of the Reader*, London: Hutchinson.

Eisner, W. (1985) *Comics and Sequential Art*, Tarmarac, Florida: Poorhouse Press.

Estren, M. (1974) *A History of Underground Comics* (rev. edn 1987), San Francisco, Calif.: Straight Arrow.

Feiffer, J. (1965) *The Great Comic Book Heroes*, New York: Dial Press.

Fleischer, M. L. (1976) *The Encyclopaedia of Comic Books Heroes, Volume I: Batman*, New York: Macmillan.

Freeman, G. (1967) *The Undergrowth of Literature*, London: Thomas Nelson & Sons.

Fry, P. and Poulos, T. (1978) *Steranko: Graphic Narrative*, Winnipeg: Winnipeg Art Gallery.

Fulce, J. (1990) *Seduction of the Innocent Revisited*, New York: Huntington House Publishers.

Galloway, J. T. Jr (1973) *The Gospel According to Superman*, Philadelphia, UK: Lippincott.

Garrick, P. R. (1978) *Masters of Comic Book Art*, New York: Images Graphiques.

Gifford, D. (1971) *Discovering Comics*, London: Shire.

— (1975) *Happy Days: A Century of Comics*, London: Jupiter

— (1976) *Victorian Comics*, London: Allen & Unwin.

— (1984) *The International Book of Comics* (rev. edn 1990), London: W. H. Smith.

— (1987) *Encyclopaedia of Comic Characters*, London: Longman.

Gilbert, J. (1986) *Cycle of Outrage: America's Reaction to the Juvenile Delinquent in the 1950s*, New York: Oxford University Press.

Glubok, S. (1979) *The Art of the Comic Strip*, New York: Macmillan.

Goddin, P. (1988) *Hergé and Tintin, Reporters*, New York: Sundancer.

Goulart, R. (1986) *The Great History of Comic Books,* Chicago, Ill.: Contemporary Books.

— (1975) *The Adventurous Decade*, New Rochelle, NY: Arlington House.

— (1982) *The Great Comic Book Artists*, vols 1 and 2, New York: Publications International.

— (1988) *The Encyclopaedia of American Comics*, New York: Publications International.

— (1991) *Over 50 Years of American Comic Books*, New York: Publications International.

Gravett, P. (forthcoming 1993) *The New Penguin Book of Comics*, Harmondsworth: Penguin.

Groth, G. and Fiore, R. (eds) (1988) *The New Comics*, New York: Berkley Books.

Hardy, C. and Stern, G. F. (eds) (1986) *Ethnic Images in the Comics*, Philadelphia: Balch Institute.

Harris, P. (ed.) (1977) *The DC Thomson Bumper Fun Book*, Edinburgh: Paul Harris Publishing.

Harrison, H. (1987) *The Art of Jack Davis*, New York: Stabur.

Herderg, W. and Pascal, D. (eds) (1972) *The Art of the Comic Strip*, Zurich: Graphis.

Hildick, E. W. (1966) *A Close Look at Comics and Magazines*, London: Faber & Faber.

Horn, M. (1971) *Seventy Five Years of the Comics*, Boston, Mass.: Boston Book & Art.

— (ed.) (1976) *The World Encyclopaedia of Comics* (6 vols), New York: Chelsea House.

— (1977) *Comics of the American West*, New York: Winchester Press.

— (1980) *Women in the Comics*, New York: Chelsea House.

— (1985) *Sex in the Comics*, New York: Chelsea House.

Inge, M. Thomas (1985) *The American Comic Book,* Columbus, Ohio: Ohio State University.

— (1988) *Handbook of American Popular Literature* (2nd edn, rev. and enlarged 1991), New York: Greenwood Press.

— (1990) *Comics as Culture*, Jackson, Mississippi: University Press of Mississippi.

Inglis, F. (1982) *The Promise of Happiness*, Cambridge: Cambridge University Press.

Jacobs, F. (1972) *The Mad World of William Gaines*, New York: Lyle Stuart Inc.

Kane, R. (1989) *Batman and Me*, Forestville, Calif: Eclipse Books.

Kelly, W. (1959) *Ten Ever-Loving Blue-Eyed Years with Pogo*, New York: Simon & Schuster.

Kunzle, D. (1973) *History of the Comic Strip, Vol. 1: The Early Comic Strip*, Berkeley, Calif.: University of California Press.

— (1989) *History of the Comic Strip, Vol. 2: The Nineteenth Century*, Berkeley, Calif: University of California Press.

Kurtzman, H. (1988) *My Life as a Cartoonist*, New York: Simon & Schuster.

— (1991) *From Aargh! to Zap!*, New York: Prentice-Hall.

Lee, S. and Buscema, J. (1986) *How To Draw Comics The Marvel Way*, London: Titan Books.

Legman, G. (1949) *Love and Death*, New York: Breaking Point.

Louvre, A. and Walsh, J. (eds) (1986) *Tell Me Lies About Vietnam*, Oxford: Oxford University Press.

Lowenthal, L. (1961) *Literature, Popular Culture, and Society*, Englewood Cliffs, NY: Prentice-Hall.

Lupoff, D. and Thompson, D. (eds) (1970) *All in Color for a Dime*, New York: Arlington House.

McAlpine, D. (1990) *Kersplat!*, London: Channel 4 Television.

McClelland, G. (1980) *Rick Griffin*, Limpsfield; Calif.: Dragon's World.

McDonnell, J. *et al.*, (1986) *Krazy Kat: The Comic Art of George Herriman*, New York: Abrams.

Marschall, R. (ed.) (1988) *The Fantastic Visions of Winsor McCay*, Westlake, Calif.: Fantagraphics.

— (1989) *America's Great Comic Strip Artists*, New York: Cross River Press.

Mitchell, W. J. T. (1987) *Iconology: Image, Text, Ideology*, Chicago, Ill.: University of Chicago Press.

Murray, C. S. (1991) *Shots From the Hip*, London: Penguin.

Murrell, W. (1933, 1938) *A History of American Graphic Humour* (2 vols), New York: Cooper Square.

O'Sullivan, J. (1971) *The Art of the Comic Strip*, College Park, Maryland: University of Maryland.

— (1990) *The Great American Comic Strip*, Boston, Mass.: Bulfinch Press.

Pearson, R. and Uricchio, W. (eds) (1991) *The Many Lives of the Batman*, London: BFI Publishing/Routledge.

Peeters, B. (1992) *Tintin and the World of Hergé*, Boston: Little, Brown and Co.

Perry, G. and Aldridge, A. (1967) *The Penguin Book of Comics*, (rev. edn 1971), Harmondsworth: Penguin.

Reidelbach, M. (1991) *Completely MAD*, New York: Little, Brown and Co.

Reitberger, R. and Fuchs, W. (1972) *Comics: Anatomy of a Mass Medium*, London: Studio Vista.

Reynolds, R. (1992) *Superheroes: A Modern Mythology*, London: Batsford.

Richler, M. (1978) *The Great Comic Book Heroes and Other Essays*, Toronto: McLelland & Stewart.

Robbins, T. (1992) *A Century of Women Cartoonists*, Princeton, Wisconsin: Kitchen Sink.

Robbins, T. and Yronwode, C. (1985) *Women and the Comics*, Forestville, Calif.: Eclipse Books.

Robinson, J. (1974) *The Comics: An Illustrated History of Comic Strip Art*, New York: G. P. Puttnam's Sons.

Rosenkranz, P., and Van Baren, H. (1974) *Artsy Fartsy Funnies*, Laren, Netherlands: Paranoia.

Ryan, J. (1979) *Panel by Panel*, Sydney: Cassell.

Savage, W. (1990) *Comic Books and America 1945–1954*, Oklahoma: University of Oklahoma Press.

Schodt, F. (1983) *Manga! Manga! The World of Japanese Comics* (rev. edn 1988), New York: Kodansha International.

Schoell, W. (1991) *Comic Book Heroes of the Screen*, London: Plexus Publishing.

Seldes, G. (1957) *The 7 Lively Arts*, New York: Sagamore Press.

Sheridan, M. (1942) *The Comics and Their Creators*, Boston, Mass.: Hale, Cushman & Flint.

Steranko, J. (1970, 1972) *The Steranko History of Comics* (2 vols), Pennsylvania: Supergraphics.

Thomas, J. L. (ed.) (1983) *Cartoons and Comics in the Classroom*, Littleton, USA: Libraries Unlimited.

Thompson, D. and Lupoff, D. (eds) (1973) *The Comic-Book Book*, New York: Arlington House.

Thompson, H. (1991) *Hergé and His Creation*, London: Hodder & Stoughton.

Threaker, D. (1986) *An Introduction to Canadian Comic Books*, Ontario: Aurora.

Tsuzuki, K. and Birnbaum, A. (eds) (1991) *Manga – Comic Strip Books from Japan*, London: Saunders & Williams.

Van Hisen, J. (ed.) (1989) *How To Draw Art For Comic Books*, Las Vegas, Nevada: Pioneer Books.

Vaz, M. C. (1989) *Tales of the Dark Knight*, London: Futura Publications.

Wagstaff, S. (ed.) (1987) *Comic Iconoclasm*, London: Institute of Contemporary Arts.

Waugh, C. (1947) *The Comics*, New York: Macmillan.

Wertham, F. (1954) *Seduction of the Innocent*, New York: Rinehart (1955, London: Museum Press).

White, D. M. and Abel, H. (eds) (1963) *The Funnies: An American Idiom*, New York: Simon & Schuster.

Willette, A. (1964) *Top Cartoonists Tell How They Create . . .*, Fort Lauderdale, Florida: Simmons Press.

Witek, J. (1989) *Comic Books as History: The Narrative Art of Jack Jackson, Art Spiegelman, and Harvey Pekar*, Mississippi: University Press of Mississippi.

Wooley, C. (1986), *Wooley's History of the Comic Book 1899–1936*, Lake Buena Vista, Florida: Charles Wooley.

Yronwode, C. (1982), *The Art of Will Eisner* (rev. edn 1989), Princeton, Wisconsin: Kitchen Sink.

Foreign language

Adhemar *et al.* (1974) *L'adventure et l'image*, Paris: Vaillant/Gallimard.

Alessandrini, M. (1974) *Graffiti: Robert Crumb*, Paris: Albin Michel.

Alessandrini, M. *et al.* (1979) *Encyclopédie des bandes dessinées*, Paris: Albin Michel.

Arrouyé, J. *et al.* (1982) *A la rencontre de . . . J. Tardi*, Marseilles: Bedesup.

— (1983) *A la rencontre de . . . H. Pratt*, Marseilles: Bedesup.

Aziza, Olivieri and Strick (1981) *Dictionnaire des figures et des personages*, Paris: Garnier.

Baetens, J. (1989) *Hergé écrivain*, Paris: Editions Labor.

Baron-Carvais, A. (1985) *La bande dessinée*, Paris: PUF.

Beaumont, C. (1984) *Pour faire de la B.D.*, Paris: PUF.

Benayoun, R. (1968) *Le ballon dans la bande dessinée*, Paris: André Balland.

Bergala, A. (1979) *Initiation à la semiologie du récit en images*, Paris: Ligue de l'enseigne.

Blanchard, G. (1969) *Histoire de la bande dessinée*, Paris: Verviers.

Bourdil, P.-Y. (1985) *Hergé, Tintin au Tibet*, Brussels: Labor.

Bourdil, P.-Y. and Tordeur, B. (1986) *Bob de Moor, 40 ans de bande dessinée, 35 ans aux côtes d'Hergé*, Paris: Editions du Lombard.

Bourgeois, H. (1978) *Erotisme et pornographie dans la BD*, Grenoble: Glenat.

— (1981) *L'ouvre érotique de C. Pichard*, Grenoble: Glenat.

Bourgeois, M. and Filippini, H. (1976) *La bande dessinée en dix leçons*, Paris: Hachette.

Bronson, P. (1986) *Guide de la B.D.*, Grenoble: Glenat.

Brun, P. (1982) *Historie de Spirou*, Grenoble: Glenat.

Cagnin, A. (1975) *Os quadrinhos*, Saõ Paulo, Brazil: Editora Atica.

Carbonnell, C. O. (ed.) (1975) *Le message politique et social de la bande dessinée*, Paris: Privat.

Carontini, E. (1982) *Le comique au cinéma et dans la B.D.*, Louvain: Bedesup.

Chante, A. *et al.* (1985) *A la recontre de ... Jacques Martin*, Marseilles: Bedesup.

Cirne, H. (1972) *Para les os quadrinhos*, Petropolis, Spain: Ediciones Vozes.

Coma, J. (1984) *El Ocaso de los Heroes en los Comics de Autor*, Barcelona: Ediciones 62.

— (1988) *Cuando la innocencia murio*, Madrid: Ediciones Esueve.

Convard, D. and Saint-Michel, S. (1972) *Le Français et la bande dessinée*, Paris: Nathan.

Couperie, P. *et al.* (1967) *Bande dessinée et figuration narrative*, Paris: Musée des Art Decor.

Couperie, P., Filippini, H. and Moliterni, C. (1974, 1975) *Encyclopédie de la BD* (3 vols), Paris: SERG.

De la Croix, A. and Andriat, F. (1992) *Pour lire la bande dessinée*, Brussels and Paris: De Boeck and Duculot.

Eco, U. (1965) *Communicazioni di massa e teoria della cultura di massa*, Milan: Bompiani.

Faur, J.-C. (1983) *A la recontre de la BD*, Marseilles: Bedesup.

Filippini, H. (1975) *Histoire du journal Vaillant*, Grenoble: Glenat.

— (1977) *Histoire du journal Pilote*: Grenoble, Glenat.

— (1977) *Les années cinquante*, Grenoble: Glenat.

Filippini, H., Glenat, J., Sadoul, N. and Varende, Y. (1980) *Histoire de la bande dessinée en France et en Belgique*, Grenoble: Glenat.

Francart, E. (1952) *La B.D. a l'école*, Paris: J. Depuis.

François, E. (1974) *L'age d'or de la bande dessinée*, Paris: SERG.

Franquin, A. and Gillain, J. (1970) *Comment on devient createur des bandes dessinées*, Paris: Marabout.

Fremion, Y. (1974) *Reiser*, Paris: Albin Michel.

— (1982) *Les nouveaux petits Miquets*, Paris: Citron Hallucinogene.

— (1983) *L'ABC de la BD*, Tournai: Casterman.

— (1990) *Le guide de la bédé francophone*, Paris: Editions Syros.

Fremion, Y. and Joubert, B. (1989) *Images interdites*, Paris: Editions Syros.

Fresnault-Derulle, P. (1972a), *La bande dessinée: Essai d'analyse semiotique*, Paris: Hachette.

— (1972) *Dessin et bulles*, Paris: Bordas.

— (1977a) *La chambre à bulles*, Paris: UGE.

— (1977b) *Récits et discours par la bande*, Paris: Hachette.

Garcia, C. (1983) *Los Comics: Dibujar con la Imagen y la Palabra*, Barcelona: Editorial Humanitas.

Gasca, L. and Gubern, R. (1988) *El Discurso del Comic*, Madrid: Ediciones Catedra.

Gauthier, G. (1973) *Les codes de la bande dessinée*, Paris: Ufoleis.

— (1982) *Vingt leçons sur l'image et le sens*, Paris: Edilig.

Gillain, J. (1983) *Jijé vous avez dit B.D.*, Paris: Dupuis.

Goddin, P. (1984) *Corentin et les chemis du merveilleux*, Paris: Editions du Lombard.

Groensteen, T. (1980) *Tardi*, Paris: Editions Magic Strip.

— (1985) *La bande dessinée dupuis 1975*, Paris: MA Editions.

— (1987) *Avec Alix*, Paris: Casterman.

— (1988) *Animaux en cases*, Paris: Casterman.

— (1990) *L'univers des mangas*, Paris: Casterman.

Gubern, R. (1972) *El lenguaie de los comics*, Barcelona: Ediciones Peninsula.

Gubern, R. and Gasca, L. (1988) *El Discurso del comic*, Madrid: Ediciones Catedra.

Guillaume, M.-A. (1987) *Goscinny*, Paris: Seghers.

Hasebe, T. (1976) *Shomin Manga no Gojunen*, Tokyo: Nippon Ioho Senta.

Herman, P. (1972) *La science-fiction et le fantastique dans la bande dessinée*, Grenoble: Glenat.

— (1982) *Epopée et mythes du western dans la bande dessinée*, Grenoble: Glenat.

Ishigami, M. (1977) *Tezuka Ozamu no Kimyo na Sekai*, Tokyo: Kisotengaisha.

Ishiko, J. (1977) *Manga Meisakukan: Sengo Manga no Shujinkotachi*, Tokyo: Tokuma Shoten.

— (1978) *Shin Mangugaku*, Tokyo: Mainichi Shimbunsha.

— (1979) *Nihon Mangashi*, Tokyo, Otsuki Shoten.

Jacobs, E. P. (1982) *Un opéra de papier*, Paris: Gallimard.

— (1986) *Sex im Comic*, Frankfurt: Ullstein.

Kajii, J. (1979) *Sengo no Kashibon Bunka*, Tokyo: Tokosha.

Knigge, A. (1986) *Sex in Comics*, Frankfurt: Ullstein.

— (1988) *Comic Lexicon*, Frankfurt: Ullstein.

— (1989) *Comic Jahrbuch, 1989*, Hamburg: Carlsen.

— (1990) *Comic Jahrbuch, 1990*, Hamburg: Carlsen.

Lacassin, F. (1971) *Tarzan ou le chevalier crispe*, Paris: UGE.

— (1982) *Pour une 9e art: la bande dessinée*, Geneva: Slatkine.

Lecigne, B. (1981) *Avanies et mascarades,* Paris: Futuropolis.

— (1983) *Les héritiers d'Hergé*, Paris: Editions Magic Strip.

Lecigne, B. and Tamine, J.-P. (1983) *Fac-simile*, Paris: Futuropolis.

Leconte, B. *Propositions pour l'analyse d'image*, Paris: Edilig.

Leguebe, W. (1977) *La société des bulles*, Brussels: Vie Ouvrière.

Lerman, A. (1979) *Histoire du journal Tintin*, Grenoble: Glenat.

Llobera, J. and Oltra, R. (1982) *La bande dessinée*, Paris: Eyrolles.

Lob, J., Sternberg, J. and Caen, M. (1967) *Les chefs d'oeuvre de la bande dessinée*, Paris.

Lo Duca, J.-M. (1982) *Manuel des confesseurs*, Paris: D. Leroy.

— (1983) *Luxure de luxe*, Paris: D. Leroy.

McLean, W. (1970) *Iconographie populaire de l'érotisme*, Paris: Maisonneuve et Larose.

Marny, J. (1968) *Le monde étonnant des bandes dessinées*, Paris: Editions du Centurion.

Martin, A. (ed.) (1982) *Carlos Gimenez*, Barcelona: Norma.

Martin, M. (1982) *Semiologie de l'image et pédagogie*, Paris: PUF.

Martinez, R. (ed.) (1982) *Jesus Blasco*, Barcelona: Norma.

Masotta, O. (1982) *La historieta en el mundo moderno*, Barcelona: Ediciones Paidos.

Massart, R., Nicks, T. and Tilleul, S. (1984) *La bande dessinée a l'Université et ailleurs*, Louvain-la-Neuve: Cabay.

Masson, P. (1985) *Lire la bande dessinée*, Lyon: PU de Lyon.

Matsumoto, R. and Hidaka, S. (eds) *Manga Rekishi Dai Hakubutsukan*, Tokyo: Buronzusha.

Moliterni, C. (1972) *Histoire de la bande dessinée d'expression française*, Paris: SERG.

— (ed.) (1980) *Histoire mondiale de la bande dessinée* Paris: Hora.

Mollica, V. and Paganelli, M. (eds.) (1980) *Hugo Pratt*, Montepulci, Spain: Editori del Grifo.

Oltra, P. and Llobera, H. (1968) *La bande dessinée*, Paris: AFHA.

Peeters, B. (1984) *Les bijoux ravis*, Paris: Editions Magic Strip.

— (1991a) *Case, Planche, Récit*, Paris: Casterman.

— (1991b) *Tintin and the World of Hergé*, Paris: Casterman.

Pennacchioni, I. (1982) *La nostalgie en images*, Paris: Libraire des Meridiens.

Perez-Yglesias, M. and Zeledon-Cambronero, M. (1982) *La B.D. critique latino-americaine (Idéologie et intertextualité)*, Louvain-la-Neuve: Cabay.

Pernin, G. (1974) *Un monde étrange, la bande dessinée*, Paris: Cledor.

Pierre, M. (1976) *La bande dessinée*, Paris: Larousse.

Renard, J. (1978) *La bande dessinée*, Paris: Seghers.

— (1986) *Bandes dessinées et croyances du siècle*, Paris: Editions de Minuit.

Rey, A. (1978) *Les spectres de la bande: Essai sur la BD*, Paris: Editions de Minuit.

— (1982) *Spettri di carta: Saggio sul fumetto*, Naples: Liguori Editore.

Riche, D. and Eizykman, B. (1986) *La bande dessinée de science-fiction americaine*, Paris: Albin Michel.

Rivière, F. (1976) *L'école d'Hergé*, Grenoble: Glenat.

Robin, C. (1974) *Travaux diriges et bande dessinée*, Paris: Sudel.

Rosier, J.-M. (1986) *Didier Comes, Silence*, Brussels: Labor.

Roux, A. (1970) *La bande dessinée peut-être educative*, Paris, Editions de l'Ecole.

Sadoul, J. (1968) *L'enfer des bulles*, Paris: Pauvert.

— (1971) *Les filles de papier*, Paris: Pauvert.

— (1976) *Panorama de la bande dessinée*, Paris: J'ai Lu.

— (1989) *93 ans du B.D.*, Paris: J'ai Lu.

Sadoul, N. (1971) *Archétypes et concordances dans la bande dessinée*, Paris: Author.

— (1974) *Gotlib*, Paris: Albin Michel.

— (1976a) *Mister Moebius et Docteur Gir*, Paris: Albin Michel.

— (1976b) *Portraits à la plume et au pinceau*, Grenoble: Glenat.

— (1989) *Entretiens avec Hergé*, Tournai: Casterman.

Santamaria, C. *et al.* (1990) *Els anys '80 en el comic*, Barcelona: Ficomic.

Smolderen, T. (1983) *Les carnets volés du Major*, Paris: Schlirf Books.

Smolderen, T. and Sterxs, P. (1988a) *Hergé ce que Tintin ne savait pas*, Tournai: Casterman.

— (1988b) *Hergé, portrait biographique*, Tournai: Casterman.

Sohet, P. and Mince de Fontbare, G. (n.d.) *Discours social et production culturelle du medium bande dessinée*, Paris: SERG.

Soumois, F. (1987) *Dossier Tintin*, Paris: Jacques Antoine.

Sternberg, J. *et al.* (eds) (1967) *Les chefs-d'oeuvres de la bande dessinée*, Paris: SERG.

Sterxs, P. (1988) *Hergé dessinateur*, Tournai: Casterman.

Stoll, A. (1978) *Astérix, l'epopée burlesque de la France*, Brussels: Complexe.

Sullerot, E. (1966) *Bande dessinée et culture*, Paris: Opéra Mundi.

Sullerot, E., Pascal, P., Metais, E., Gauthier, G. and Lafond, S. (1970) *Les bandes dessinées*, Bordeux: CRDP.

Tezuka, O. (1981) *Tezuka Osamu no Subete*, Tokyo: Daitosha.

Thevenet, J.-M. (1987) *Bilal*, Paris: Seghers.

Tiberi, J.-P. (1981) *La bande dessinée et le cinéma*, Paris: Regards.

Tibi, J. (1983) *Voyage au pays de Tintin*, St-Etienne: Université de St-Etienne.

Tilleul, J.-L. *et al.* (1991) *Lectures de la bande dessinée*, Paris: Editions Academia.

Tisseron, S. (1978) *Histoire de la psychiatrie en bandes dessinée*, Paris: Savelli.

— (1985) *Tintin chez le psychanalyste*, Paris: Aubier-Archimbaud.

— (1987a) *Hergé*, Paris: Seghers.

— (1987b) *Psychanalyse de la bande dessinée*, Paris: PUF.

— (1990a) *La B.D. au pied du mot*, Paris: Aubier.

— (1990b) *Tintin et les secrets de famille*, Paris: Librairie Seguier.

Vendrome, P. (1959) *Le monde de Tintin*, Paris: Gallimard.

Yonezawa, Y. (1980) *Sengo SF Mangashi*, Tokyo: Shimpyosha.

Zimmer, J. (1978) *La bande dessinée*, Paris: SERG.

Price guides and indices

Bell, J. (ed.) (1986) *Canuck Comics,* Ontario: Matrix Books.

Béra, M., Denni, M. and Mellot, P. (annually) *Trésors de la bande dessinée*, Paris: les Editions de l'Amateur.

Burns, M. (1978) *Comix Index*, Brighton: John Noyce.

Fiene, D. M. (1981) *R. Crumb Checklist of Work and Criticism,* Cambridge, Mass: Boatner Norton Press.

Geist, C. *et al.* (1989) *Directory of Popular Culture Collections*, Phoenix, Arizona: Oryx Press.

Gerber, E. and Gerber, M. (1990) *Photo-Journal Guide to Comic Books* (2 vols), Las Vegas, Nevada: Gerber Publishing Co. Inc.

— (1990) *Photo-Journal Guide to Marvel Comics* (2 vols), Las Vegas, Nevada: Gerber Publishing Co. Inc.

Gifford, D, (1975) *The British Comic Catalogue*, London: Mansell.

— (1985) *The Complete Catalogue of British Comics*, London: Webb and Bower.

— (1990) *The American Comic Book Catalogue: The Evolutionary Era, 1884–1939*, London: Mansell.

Kempkes, W. (1971) *The International Bibliography of Comics Literature*, New York: R. R. Bowker and Company.

Kennedy, J. (1982) *The Official Underground and Newave Comix Price Guide*, Cambridge, Mass.: Boatner Norton Press.

Lent, J. A. (1986) *Comic Art: An International Bibliography*, Drexel Hill, Penn.: J. Lent Publishing.

McAlpine, D. (annually) *The Official Comic Book Price Guide for Great Britain*, London: Price Guide Productions.

Overstreet, R. (annually) *The Official Overstreet Comic Book Price Guide*, Cleveland, Tennessee: Overstreet Publications/House of Collectibles.

Scott, R. H. (1988) *Comic Books and Strips: An Information Source-book*, Phoenix, Arizona: Oryx Press.

— (1990) *Comics Librarianship*, Jefferson, N. Carolina: McFarland.

— (forthcoming 1993) *Comic Art Catolog* (*Michigan State University Library Collection Catalog*), Conn.: Greenwood Press.

Weiner, R. (1979) *Illustrated Checklist to Underground Comix*, Cambridge, Mass.: Archival Press.

Fanzines and journals (current)

British

British Comics World, Alan and David Coates, London. Occasional. Articles on British comics.

Comic World, Aceville, Colchester, Essex. Monthly. Intended 'for buyers, sellers and collectors', but includes interviews and reviews.

Comic Cuts/ACE Newsletter. Association of Comics Enthusiasts Newsletter (by subscription to Denis Gifford, 80 Silverdale, Sydenham, London, SE26). Twice yearly. News for Collectors of British comics.

Comic Journal, A. and B. Whitworth, London. Occasional. Articles on vintage British children's comics.

Comics Forum, magazine of the Society for Strip Illustration, London. Quarterly. Reviews, news and criticism of primarily British and American comics.

Comics International, Derek Skinn, London. Monthly. News and reviews of American and British comics, plus coverage of interest to collectors and investors.

Golden Fun, Alan and Laurel Clark, London. Occasional. Articles on vintage British comics.

Zum!, Luke Walsh, Liverpool. Occasional. Small press news and reviews.

American

Comics Arena, Bob Hickey, Florence, Kentucky. Monthly. News and reviews of American comics, mainly superheroes.

Comic Buyers Guide, Krause Publications, Iola, Wisconsin. Weekly. Collector orientated news.

Comics Interview, Fictioneer Books, New York. Monthly. Interviews with creators and publishers.

Comics Journal, Fantagraphics Books, Seattle, Washington. Monthly. Criticism, reviews and news of mainly American adult comics.

Comics Scene, O'Quinn Studios, New York. Bi-monthly. Articles on comics-related media.

Comikaze!, David Linabury, Royal Oak, Michigan. Occasional.

Music and comics fanzine, with emphasis on new wave in both cases.

Journal of Popular Culture, The Popular Press, Bowling Green State University, Bowling Green, Ohio. Quarterly. One of the very few academic journals to include comics.

Mangajin, Mangajin Inc., Atlanta, Georgia. Quarterly. Japanese comics, plus guide to learning Japanese, with detailed explanations of the strip translations.

Wizard, Wizard Press Ltd, San Francisco, Calif. Monthly. Information for collectors.

Foreign language

(Can be ordered from some specialist shops.)

Les cahiers de la bande dessinée, twice a year, Paris: Glénat.
Fumo di China, bi-monthly, Milan: Ned 50.

It is also possible to obtain back issues of some now defunct fanzines in specialist shops: for example, *Speakeasy*, *BEM*, *FA*, *Ark*, *Comic Media News*, *Comic Reader*, *Amazing Heroes*, etc. Back issues of the comics *Escape* and *Blab!* also contain useful articles.

Videos

Alan Moore: Iconoclasm at the ICA (1988) London: Acme Video/CA Productions.

Bill Sienkiewicz and John Bolton (1988) London: Acme Video/CA Productions.

Comic Book Confidential (1989) Canada: Castle Hendring, London (Dir. Ron Mann).

The Comic Book Greats: Todd McFarlane (1991) New York: Excelsior Productions/Stabur Video.

Masters of Comic Book Art (1988) New York: Stabur Video (Dir. Ken Viola).

Raymond Briggs In Conversation (1982) London: ICA In Conversation Series.

Storm Over Jevington: Don Lawrence Profile (1988) London: Photon.

Ten Years of 2000AD – A Video Celebration (1987) London: Acme Video/CA Productions.

Viz: The Documentary (1990) Channel 4 TV: London: Polygram.

Watch the Men – Dave Gibbons and Alan Moore (1988) London: Acme Video/CA Productions.

Will Eisner: A Life in Sequential Art (1988) London: Acme Video/CA Productions.

Word Balloons: *Interviews with Comics Folk* (1991) New York: Stabur Video (interviews by Keith R. Candido).

Index

origins 116–17; 'Paul Whicker, the Tall Vicar' 118, 276; 'Pathetic Sharks, The' 118; 'Roger Mellie, the Man on the Telly' 118; *Roger Mellie* animation 124, 2189; 'Rude Kid' 118; 'Sid the Sexist' 123, 125; success 119–21; 'Those Thieving Gypsy Bastards' 277; as yob comic 124

Vortex (publisher) 98, 100

Votez Rocky 194

Voyeuse 234

W.H. Smith 45, 52, 73, 105, 120, 246, 266

Wacko 166

Wagner, John 55, 57, 60, 108, 267

Waldenbooks (bookshop) 177, 282

war comics 100, 152–3, 169, 268, 279

War Picture-Library 26

War of the Trenches, The 194

Warner Books (publisher) 177

Warner Brothers 219; Warner Communications 97; Warner Looney Tunes 211

Warren, James 281

Warren Publications (publisher) 32, 168, 273

Warrior 59–60, 106, 268, 269

Watchmen 59, 78, 88–9, 94, 95, 97, 110, 176, 199, 216, 218, 230, 233, 244, 245

Watkins, Dudley 23

Waugh, Auberon 121

Way Out Strips 231

'Weary Willie and Tired Tim' 20, 211, 262

Weird Fantasy 268

Weirdo 84, 98, 176, 230, 231

Welch, Chris 43

Weller, Mike 43

Wertham, Dr Fredric 151, 154, 208, 263, 280; *Seduction of the Innocent* 30, 31, 91, 157–61

Wet Satin 225

Wham 24

When the Wind Blows 215–16, 241

White, Ted 269

White Comanche 173

'Whiteman' 37

Wild 154

Wildenberg, Harry 140

Wilderness 102, 246

Williams, Robert 40, 211

Williamson, Al 168

Williamson, Skip 41, 42, 167, 174

'Willie' (pseudonym) 156

Willyprods (publisher) 104

Wilson, S. Clay 40, 41, 176, 288; criticised 224

Wimmins Comix 41, 225, 226, 226–7, 289

Winebibber 125

Wirgman, Charles 200

Wizard 24

Wizards the movie 215

Woman Trap, The 194

'Wonder Warthog' 39

Wonder Woman 223, 279

Wood, Wally 152, 154, 167

work-for-hire system 33, 55, 58

Wrightson, Berni 267

X-Men 60, 68, 76, 78, 97, 275

X-Presso 275

'Yellow Kid' 133–4, 140, 166, 277

Yeowell, Steve 60, 274

Yoshida, Mitsuhiko 286

Young, Chic 138

Young Romance 151–2

Yronwode, Catherine 229, 274

Yummy Fur 98, 175

Zap 37, 39, 40, 42, 174, 176, 226, 264, 288

Zarate, Oscar 105, 244

'Zenith' 60

'Zippy the Pinhead' 172

Zit 125